YOUR OWNER'S MANUAL FOR LIFE

Source Code of Your Soul

Creating You
and Facilitating Your Life

Maureen Marie Damery

Balboa Press books may be ordered through booksellers or by contacting:

Balboa Press
A Division of Hay House
1663 Liberty Drive
Bloomington, IN 47403
www.balboapress.com
1 (877) 407-4847

1 Timothy 6:10 from the New International Version (NIV)

Print information available on the last page.

ISBN: 978-1-5043-6599-4 (sc)
ISBN: 978-1-5043-6598-7 (hc)
ISBN: 978-1-5043-6596-3 (e)

Library of Congress Control Number: 2016914804

Balboa Press rev. date: 10/15/2016

To my Son, Boston

who is not only my inspiration,

but living confirmation

of the infinite possibilities available to us all.

Thanks for being so patient while I worked on this, Bos.

...more than anything! XOXO

My Infinite Gratitude and Love to

Elaine, Karen, Jill and Kristene ~ My Goddess Constellation $\sqrt{G}$
whose beauty, wisdom, support and love
gifted me the roots and wings to birth this book
and more importantly, my true self.

My Parents and Siblings who were, and continue to be, amazing teachers.

Bob for being a wonderful father to Boston, the support and liberty it afforded me.

Joe, my catalyst for embracing forgiveness and unconditional love.

Bill Darche for saving my hard drive and manuscript more than once.

Those who've wounded me. It is through the growth of those experiences that I found my strength.

Those whose inspirational contributions to my evolution, my work and my life are sprinkled throughout this book and beyond.

The participants of *Source Code of Your Soul*. I am honored by the invitation to be a contribution to your journey and your joy.

Foreword

Some books are deeper and more profound than others. They touch us at a deep soul level. This is one of those books. *Your Owner's Manual for Life* epitomizes the Truth that our greatest resource lies within.

Maureen has gathered and shared an honest and beautifully represented guide to appreciating life's experiences as gifts and opportunities ~ a series of choices by which to learn, grow and expand. In addition to profound wisdom, she provides enlightening and empowering exercises to assist us in connecting with the very essence of our authentic selves and those around us by bringing simplicity and clarity to the often complex and illusive issues of our lives. Maureen illustrates that through enlightenment and compassion, we are able to open to more possibilities, heal past wounds, transcend perceived limitations and live our personal best.

This book is rich with insights and proven, practical tools gleaned from experiential practice with some of the worlds' most renowned leaders in self-empowerment and spirituality. *Your Owner's Manual for Life: Source Code of Your Soul* is a personalized, hands-on resource for navigating our subconscious and traversing the programming we're subjected to in our daily lives ~ a compendium of wisdom which we can consult again and again for perspective, guidance, confirmation and empowerment on our life's journey.

I invite you to gift yourself with this wonderful manual, *Source Code of Your Soul,* as a welcome companion of ease and joy in the creation and living of a rich, fulfilling life.

~Jack Canfield
Co-creator, #1 New York Times best-selling series
Chicken Soup for the Soul®
Author, *The Success Principles*
www.jackcanfield.com

Contents

Foreword ix

Prologue xiii

A Note from the Author xv

Introduction xvii

Chapter 1: Anatomy of Software Programming - Hardware/Software and Mind/Body: The Correlation 1

Chapter 2: Hardware ~ Your Brain, Your Body and Your Network 9

- Your Brain: Left, Right, The Waves and Your Mind 9

- Your Body: Network Communication System - Your Spinal Cord and Nervous System 12

- Your Vibrations: Symptoms and Conditions 13

Chapter 3: Are You a Programmer or a Subscriber? 20

Chapter 4: Metaphysics and the Universal Laws of Nature ~ Living Purposefully in Possibility 35

Chapter 5: Happiness Is… 55

Chapter 6: Shiny Things & Addictions ~ The Art of Distraction & Self Sabotage 72

- The Diversion ~ When the Subconscious Goes Cyber Shopping 72

- The Escape ~ Path to Affliction or Portal to Reflection? 87

Chapter 7: Forgiveness ~
The Get Well Bouquet You Gift To Yourself........ 114

Chapter 8: The Healing Response 133

Chapter 9: *Aha* Moments ~ You, Version Now.*Ohhh!*............ 144

Chapter 10: What's Love Got To Do With It?......................... 156

Chapter 11: The Secret Sauce ~
Creating From the Inside Out..............................207

Chapter 12: Moving Forward With Mindful Ease 242

Chapter 13: The Author of My Life 251

Resources 253

Contributors...285

About the Author 287

Maybe the journey isn't so much about becoming anything. Maybe it's about un-becoming everything that isn't really you and being your authentic self.

Prologue

Writing this book has been my calling for several years. Desiring more meaning, fulfillment and joy in my life, I embarked on a quest to actualize that aspiration. *Your Owner's Manual for Life* is the synthesis of everything I've learned, believe and love. Participating in the transformations yielded through implementing the methodologies discussed herein has provided confirmation of the amazing capabilities inherent within us all. These experiences have appreciated my life and purpose, endowing more joy than I could have imagined.

When I was introduced to the holistic field, I stood witness to numerous testimonials of the healing, empowering capacities of energetic modalities and mindful Spirituality. Being a relentless seeker, researcher and avid skeptic, however, I was determined to obtain confirmation for myself - *and I have experienced many.* The factors contributing to the dis-ease in my life were complex and diverse on many levels, yet so simple to transform through sentience, self-actualization and mindfulness. Becoming aware of the Mind/Body connection and implementing the philosophies and tools herein yielded positive, enduring results on many levels. This was more than confirmation for me - It was profound transformation.

The preference for more sovereignty in our lives and frustration with conventional therapy and medicine is evident in the statistics and the people I encounter on an increasing basis. The World Health

Organization estimates that between 65 and 80 percent of the world's population now relies on holistic medicine as their primary form of health care. Research has shown intention to be a powerful force of nature which you can utilize in the creation of your life. By asking open-ended questions, releasing that which does not serve and living mindfully, you can channel this power to not only heal yourself, but purposefully design the life you prefer.

It's often been conveyed by my family, friends and clients that I don't perceive things the way that many of us are inclined to. I view this not only as a compliment, but also an asset because these same people have also commented *"I'll have what you're having."* The truth is that I've come to perceive and appreciate things with more clarity and ease than ever before. Through meditation, living mindfully and working with my clients, I continue to experience and witness profound transformations and exhilarating joy on all levels.

I offer Source Code as an open door to freedom, empowerment, ease and happiness - inviting you to embrace these possibilities for yourself.

"Start with the heart and work outward. Start with the head and work inward." ~Nancy Foley

A Note from the Author

When the need to refer to a manual of any type is apparent, we just want to know which button to push to get the preferred result. To that end, the cross-reference concepts presented herein are brief, effective and humorously illustrated for effortless consideration.

The tools and methods suggested herein are intended as a supplement to, not a substitute for, medical or psychological diagnosis and treatment.

Any references *to 'Goddess/God', 'Divine', 'Faith' 'Blessings', 'Spirituality'* and the like are intended as non-denominational generalizations referring to those of your personal understanding and choice. If you are at all uncomfortable with any of these terms, I invite you to simply consider them as forces of nature and support in your life. The results will be the same. I use the terms *'Goddess/God'* and *'Universe'* interchangeably, referring to our creative power and capacity of free will.

In this reality, power can be perceived as power *'over'* in a detrimental sense. However, when I make reference to your *'power'*, I'm referring to your free will and the capacity to orchestrate yourself and your realitivity (*Yes, you read that word correctly*) to create and enjoy a fulfilling life.

When I speak of our Soul, Spirit and consciousness, I refer to our Soul as our being and awareness of the being of all things which is consciousness with our Spirit being the expression of our Soul.

I make reference to several children's stories and characters herein as there's a lot to be said for the messages woven within them. Lest we forget that they're written by children with experiential wisdom.

"Your mind is like a parachute. It only works when it is open." -Anthony J. D'Angelo

Introduction

The similarities between the workings of our Mind/Body and computer technology are profoundly parallel. Having worked in the computing industry since the early 1990's and the holistic field since 2003, I consistently see the correlation. Intriguingly, information technologies (I/T) are designed in our own likeness. *Source Code* utilizes this paradigm to illustrate and guide you in orchestrating your life in harmony with your Mind/Body in ways that are ideal for *You*.

We are born into this world an open book, arriving with no opinions, judgments or limitations and the belief that anything is possible. Over time, these attributes can become shadowed within the requisites of life. We can be somewhat unaware of the magnitude to which we're psychically, emotionally and spiritually receptive. As we evolve, we're encoded by the stimuli around us - the cultures and the people within them - adopting and adapting to acclimate within the realities created by them. As we subscribe to these influences, they become perceptions, beliefs and behaviors of our own.

We can become frustrated and somewhat disengaged in our living – feeling unfulfilled in our relationships and work, encountering repetitive patterns and limitations. These are symptoms of a disconnection of mind and heart from truth which is born of our experiences and the limiting beliefs built around them. While our persona tends to mirror those of others, we need not be encapsulated by them.

What if there's nothing erroneous about you or your life, with the possible exception of a belief that there is? What if there's a way to fully embrace your personal best, create and live the life you prefer - one that's not only simple, but one that actually works?

There Is, and You Can ~ My dear friends, we have the technology!

Like words written on a page and later edited, we have the capacity to create and re-create ourselves and our lives at will. Although our conscious sense of our capacities can become obscured as we traverse the mires of life, it is never too late to re-member them and choose something different; and there is no time like the present.

If you're willing to be your authentic self, create and enjoy a phenomenal life, this book is for you.

~ Welcome to your Owner's Manual for Life. ~

~ Presence ~

Congratulations on gifting yourself the openness to
receive the wisdom contained within this book.
Before you begin, please allow yourself a moment...

Close your eyes.

Take a deep breath in.
As you exhale, let go of everything that has
gone on in your world to this point.

Take another deep breath in.
As you exhale, let go of everything that
may be forthcoming in the future.

Take another deep breath in.
As you exhale, allow yourself to come fully present.

Allow yourself to be open to fresh perspective and
a blank page on which to begin creating
the first day of the *Best* of your life.

~ Namaste ~

"The function of good software is to make the complex appear to be simple." - Grady Booch

Chapter 1

Anatomy of Software Programming - Hardware/Software and Mind/Body: The Correlation

The Mind/Body Connection is not new, and it's not a matter of connecting your mind and your body. This connection already exists. It's a matter of being aware of this connection and utilizing it to your benefit.

In this chapter, you'll have a brief overview of software development and how it relates to your Mind/Body in rather intriguing and beneficial ways.

Everything we know may all be wrong, or at least incomplete. True wisdom and learning are primarily an increased awareness of how little we actually do know. What we think we know can hold us back and limit us; and it is only in the new awareness of how little we may know and how limited our thinking may be, that true growth and progress can occur.

If there's one thing I learned from software development, it's that there's no such thing as a foolish question. Foolishness lies only in the absence of asking. *"I don't know"* is a good answer – especially when followed by: *"But I'll find someone who does."* The same is true in life.

Computers only do what they're programmed to do. Our Mind/Body is quite similar. Consciousness is hardwired within us. It is the language of the Universe, the source code of all source codes. With this in mind, let's have a brief overview of some basic software development characteristics and visit our Mind/Body counterparts.

Similar to our own learning process, programming is the creation of a set of instructions that computers use to perform specific operations and exhibit certain behaviors. Programs are an ordered series of instructions for altering the state of a computer in a particular sequence. Software is a collection of programs and related data that tells the computer what to do, how to do it and when. Software provides instructions to the hardware (the computer itself) or serves them as input and output - Parallel to the way our Mind/Body and societies operate.

There are two types of software:

- System Software: Non-task specific functions of the computer.
- Application Software: Employed by the users to accomplish specific tasks.

System software functions like the organs in your body. Your heart performs the specific task of pumping your blood while your lungs do the breathing for you. You don't have to think about these functions or perform an action to set them into operation, they simply run on their own.

Application software can be likened to specific tasks you perform with your body such as brushing your teeth, singing a song or playing a sport. You choose to perform these activities and then set about doing so.

Your Mind/Body is an amazingly intricate system comprised of Hardware, Networking and both System and Application

Software - Each component having its own set of instructions for its particular directive. For example, consider the function of your bladder…*This shan't be graphic, I promise.* As you consume nourishment, your body absorbs liquid. The liquid passes through your kidneys, which filter out waste and extra liquid, producing urine which is stored in your bladder. When the bladder is full, it signals the brain, and you set out for the restroom. We'll discuss this type of intrinsic functionality in a bit more detail during Chapter Two.

Now let's have a look at three of the basic types of software programming models. Our purpose in looking at these is to foster an appreciation of how they relate to our own creative capacities.

The first two types of software are considered 'Proprietary' which means they're the exclusive property of their developers and publishers [creators] and cannot be copied or distributed without complying with their licensing agreements. It also means that you do not have access to the source code which runs the software. The third model is where the *Secret Sauce* lies. Before we can fully appreciate the essence of that *Secret Sauce*, let's sample the first two:

Proprietary Software:

- The traditional or procedural model where a program is seen simply as a list of tasks to perform.

This is Binary code…*Dots & Dashes - No Delight -at least in my opinion.*

- The Object Oriented Programming (OOP) model represents concepts as objects having attributes (Properties and Methods). You can equate these attributes to things such as height, weight and skin color (Properties) with the Methods being your thoughts, feelings, emotions and behaviors.

A bit more interesting than Binary, but again, proprietary....*OOP's!*

- Then there's Open Source Software...*Ah, the Secret Sauce!*

Open Source is software for which the source code is freely available. Not only can it be copied and shared liberally, its code can also be accessed and manipulated. *Something we can play with...Now, we're talkin'!*

Programming, regardless of the context within which the word is used, can be perceived in varying ways. One perception is that it's a *Pandora's Box*, the opening of which should be avoided for the unknown potential hazards of releasing its contents. It can also be perceived as the anticipation of a magical toy which lies within a pretty package with your name on it. The pleasure to be experienced in stepping outside of that box is the objective of *Source Code of Your Soul.*

The traditional (procedural) model is one where a program is seen as a set of tasks to perform - A list of instructions having a linear order of execution with occasional branches and loops. A branch is a command that tells the computer to go to some other part of the program. A loop is a sequence of instructions that's continually repeated until a certain condition is reached. *How many licks does it take to get to the center of a Tootsie Pop?*

An *infinite* loop lacks an exit routine, meaning that the loop repeats continually until the operating system terminates the program. A loop can run until the program automatically terminates after a particular amount of time, referred to as 'Timing Out'. You may have encountered this during an internet session displayed as an error such as '*Your session has timed out*'.

Ever make numerous efforts toward something by means of the same approach, only to become frustrated by a similar, disheartening outcome? There's a lot to be said for perseverance; however, expecting something different to come of approaching something with the same mindset and manner is senseless. You cannot solve a problem with the same consciousness that created it. You must shift your perception in order to see the world anew in order to create something different in your life.

Many of us have experienced or are currently living in the procedural model, feeling like a robot going through the motions, stuck in an endless loop on the proverbial hamster wheel. On some level we know that something monumental is missing and wonder why we've been unable to break the patterns in our lives and have something different show up. Yeah...*Dots & Dashes – No Delight.*

With this in mind, ask yourself: *What creation of insanity am I using to function from its limitations that are holding me captive?* It is not necessary to attempt to answer this question. The intention is simply to present it to your subconscious as an open door to possibility. Asking open-ended questions ignites the frontal lobe portion of your brain which rearranges itself to find a new way of answering these questions by examining *what if's.* We'll expand on this more as we progress.

An OOP (Object-Oriented Program) is a collection of interacting objects...as are we. In OOP, each object is capable of receiving messages, processing data and sending messages to other objects. Each can be viewed as an independent machine with a distinct role or responsibility. While these objects carry their own operators, allowing for some individuality, these operators are inherited either directly or indirectly from similar objects or classes within the program. Most of our programming is fundamentally inherited from our ancestors and the societies we develop within – often by osmosis (unconscious assimilation).

These two models typically involve some level of 'obfuscation'. Now *there's* a word! Obfuscation is the practice of hiding the intended meaning of something and willfully making it more difficult to interpret or understand. The formatting of legal documentation comes to mind here *-No offense intended.* In the software world, obfuscation does serve a viable function. Proprietary software utilizes it for privacy, data integrity, security and anti-piracy purposes. Typically there are major restrictions on its use, and its source code is inaccessible. On the other hand, the code of Open Source programs is freely available. They are usually downloadable at no cost, modifiable and can be shared liberally.

Source code is the language a program is written in by a human being which is converted into machine code instructions for a computer. When modifying a program, it's beneficial to find that the original developer has commented their code. Comments are lines of text which are not executed by the computer. Their function is to provide readability to other developers for maintenance and upgrade purposes.

When considering a revision to our own internal code, we often seek input from outside of ourselves – counseling, trusted advice, books, etc. Ultimately, however, the capacity to modify our lives already lies within. A software developer approaching a similar task may employ Reverse Engineering – the process of retrieving the source code and studying how it operates in order to improve or adapt it for other uses. This can be quite a complex task - similar to peeling the layers of a big fat onion. However, onion peeling will not be necessary in our kitchen.

Our approach is some good old fashioned self-awareness. Our objective is to reconnect with what we already know as truth. If you would like to change your life, your mission – *should you choose to accept it* – is to identify your programs, become acquainted with their source code and edit them to your liking. While this may seem a bit ominous at first, rest assured that it's not only simple, it's *Fun.*

There's one more techie term I'd like to mention before we move on, Crippleware. This is a type of software which cannot be fully utilized unless or until certain criteria are met. There are two flavors of crippling: One allows the user to operate some but not all of the features of a program prior to full purchase or registration. The other allows the user to take full advantage of all the features of the program, but only for a limited time. Once that time has expired, the user must purchase and register the full version of the program before it can be run again. Similarly, there are works of wisdom in this world from which you may have derived a sampling of the possibilities in the banquet of life, but not the whole enchilada. We'll take a closer look at the enchilada in Chapter Four.

Your own mind can often be your worst enemy. When understood, appreciated and utilized wisely, however, it becomes your finest ally. You may have tossed aside the seemingly unnecessary *Owner's Manual* to that pretty box with your name on it or perhaps viewed it as erroneously written in a language you were unfamiliar with. Nevertheless, a user-friendly version is now in your hands welcoming your invitation.

What is it that you know that you're denying or forgetting that you know that if you knew would change everything?

For more information, please visit Resources.

Musings…

"You could have a gorgeous computer sitting on your desk;
but if you don't know what to do with it, it's
nothing more than a piece of junk.
If, however, you learn the language of the computer,
miracles can happen". - Louise Hay

Chapter 2

Hardware ~ Your Brain, Your Body and Your Network

In this chapter, you'll become acquainted with your Mind/Body network and communication systems.

Our bodies are amazing entities. They're surprisingly similar to computers and the networks that connect them. Although one could spend a lifetime researching the intricacies of nature's operating system, we'll briefly touch on the basics to derive an understanding of the fundamentals.

Your Brain: Left, Right, The Waves and Your Mind

If the brain is the hardware, the mind is the software; *right*? Is the mind created by the brain or vice-versa? The following is from *Leadership Brain for Dummies* by Marilee B. Sprenger. In a section entitled, *A Mind is What the Brain Does,* Neuroscientist Susan Greenfield theorizes that the mind may be *"the personalization of the brain."*

> According to many researchers, the brain's functions, such as feeling, thoughts, problem-solving and communication, create the mind; but that the mind also constructs the brain. The feelings, thoughts,

experiences and memories which build the personal mind also change the structure and function of the brain. *Yup, it's all in your head….*

It is my assertion that the brain is our mechanical computer for processing information while our consciousness manipulates the brain to create the mind which is ultimately the C.E.O. (Chief Executive Officer) at the helm. *So, what's the matter?* Your brain consists of Grey and White Matter, two components of your Central Nervous System (CNS). White Matter is the inner layer consisting of nerve tissues. These are the data lines that transmit information between your brain's nerve cells and your spinal cord. The Gray Matter is the outer layer consisting of neurons. These are composed of nerve cells and blood vessels having electrical properties similar to those of transistors.

This portion of the brain is responsible for sensing and interpreting input and maintaining cognitive function such as thinking, understanding and perceiving. Your brain interprets signals from your senses, creating images in your mind which is your perception of reality. This is where your programming resides.

What do you see (*perceive*)
in this picture?
A young woman or
an old lady?

Image, My Wife and My Mother-In-Law, is believed to have been created by W.E. Hill, a British cartoonist, in 1915.

"It's not what you look at that matters. It's what you see". -Henry David Thoreau

Each side of the human brain controls different types of thinking. The left is associated with linear and analytical thought - The logical side which seeks organization and structure. The right side is associated with creativity and emotion - The playful side which seeks pleasure and happiness. Theory indicates that we tend to be primarily more left-or right-brained. A left-brained person is often said to be more logical, analytical and objective, while a right-brained person is said to be more intuitive, thoughtful and subjective. I'll leave it up to you to consider whether you've predominantly joined one club or the other. Herein lies the interesting phenomenon of categorizing ourselves and drawing conclusions based on these categories. *"Oh, you're a Libra; therefore, you are X, Y and/or Z".*

Your brain has five frequencies or waves (electrical impulses given off by brain tissue) that are measured in cycles per second, or Hertz (Hz). We'll surf these waves briefly to get an idea of how they work and how we can best utilize them.

Delta (0.5-4Hz), is the Deep Sleep Wave where your unconscious resides and healing and rejuvenation occur. Delta allows you to be more perceptive of information that isn't available to your conscious mind - what we refer to as 'gut instinct' such as intuition and psychic skills. These skills are made consciously possible when Delta waves are present in the waking state along with Beta, Alpha, and Theta waves.

Theta (4-7.5Hz) is the wave you drift upon during deep meditation and light sleep, including the REM (Rapid Eye Movement) dream state. Theta is where your creative inspiration and imagination come to life. This is also where your programming resides. At this frequency, you can make a deep Spiritual connection with The

Universe and play with its 'magic' as Theta is the wave on which you consciously create your reality.

Alpha (7.5-14Hz) is the deep relaxation wave you glide upon when doing yoga or light meditation. This is the state in which your body and mind are able to relax and synchronize.

Beta (14-40Hz) is known as the busy or reasoning wave where you spend most of your waking, conscious time. It's also where your stress, anxiety and restlessness reside. *Hmm, wouldn't wanna doze off and miss any of* ***that*** *now, would you?*

My personal favorite is the fastest (or highest) of them all, the Gamma (above 40Hz). This wave was essentially unknown before the development of EEG (Electroencephalogram), a device discovered by Hans Berger in 1924 using electrodes placed along the scalp to record the electrical activity of the brain. While the other waves predominantly affect particular areas of your brain, Gamma influences your entire brain. It's associated with the feelings of blessings and connection with all things. Referred to as the Insight Wave, Gamma is linked with the brainwave state of being 'in the *Zone*' - The feeling that you can do anything. Every signal generated by the brain can not only be picked up by EEG machines, but also by the Universe itself. You may be thinking '*How can I get more Gamma*'? We'll discuss this in Chapter Eleven - *That's where the fun is!*

...Hey – Where are you goin'? Get back here, now – No Peekin' !

Your Body: Network Communication System - Your Spinal Cord and Nervous System

Your body is equipped with the most complex biological system known, your Central Nervous System (CNS) which consists of your brain and spinal cord along with nerve cells (neurons) which transmit and receive signals. You can think of your nerve cells as bio-electrical fiber optics which depart from your brain and spinal cord and extend to every point in your body. Your spinal cord is like a bundle of fiber optic cables. Your CNS collects, interprets and responds to the signals that it receives. This is your network communication system. All sensory and thought-based information and instructions in your body are delivered by means of these cables. The information is encoded in the form of electrical stimuli inside nerve extensions and transported in a wave state. Nerve fibers have electrical charges which are positive on the outside and negative on the inside. When stimulus is introduced, an electrical impulse is given off, causing the positive and negative charged fibers to produce an electrical current. These currents run your organ and muscle functions. They're also responsible for your thoughts, emotions and moods.

Your Vibrations: Symptoms and Conditions

Your Limbic System is the emotional center of your brain. It consists of Amygdala, Hypothalamus and Hippocampus. They comprise your ability to store and retrieve information and process your emotions. We won't go into these in detail; but basically this is your hard drive - a database where all of your data (history, memories - home movies of your life) is stored. It is your subconscious mind where your programming resides. Your conscious or thinking mind is like the screen on which you view the data contained within your database.

Everything you experience and learn builds a connection in your brain, referred to as neural pathways. Sensory nerves gather information from your environment and send it to your spinal cord, which forwards the messages to your brain. Your brain then filters these messages and returns a response. This filtering process is key to understanding your programming because what you do with the information that's received is what creates the physical sensations in your body, your emotions and perceptions...and ultimately, your reality.

It's estimated that your brain produces upwards of 50-80 thousand thoughts per day. It's further estimated that 70-80 percent of those thoughts are negative -*Now there's a rather disturbing thought!* Your brain's objective is to make sense of the overwhelming amount of information it receives. To accomplish this, it sifts through the information using filters such as your survival instincts, values, beliefs and your perceived identity. It then sorts the information according to relevance using generalization, distortion and deletion processes.

Your subconscious acts as your Network Administrator in that it will only accept data which supports your individual filters (your beliefs). Information which does not support your filters (what you *believe*), is deleted. Therefore, that which is not deleted is often incomplete and biased by subconscious defense mechanisms such as denial, minimization, magnification and rationalization.

Once this distorted data has entered the subconscious mind, it's compiled into memories or what's referred to as mind movies. Your subconscious reviews these movies to interpret their meaning before sending it along to your Limbic System to be emotionally charged, catalogued and stored in your long term memory as an honorary member of your belief system. This is known as compartmentalization. When you experience a situation even remotely similar to one already stored in your database, the emotional charge is triggered, confirming and strengthening the reality of it which is encoded within your neural networks. This is where your patterns and habits are created. When you accept this, unknowingly by default, and maintain it by re-presenting these mind movies, you allow them to limit you, creating the illusion of feeling stuck.

This process is similar to a stored procedure, a built-in function within software for which the same code is used over and over. While variable property values for an object within the stored procedure (i.e. people, places and things) - or more importantly, our perceptions of them - can be altered, they typically hold default values which are used when these parameters are not changed. When the stored procedure is triggered, it performs the same function and produces similar return values or results.

All of this work is done on the server (your subconscious mind); and the results are not always returned to the client (your conscious mind). They can be stored on the server or provided to the client for utilization within the software at a later time. These stored procedures are the neural pathways of your brain, and they're basically just constructs, or implanted points of view.

Your judgment of something creates your point of view. Your point of view creates your belief system which in turn creates your reality. Keep in mind that all of this data was initially run through your filters. The point I'm making here is that things may not always be as they appear.

The Cookie Thief, a poem by Valerie Cox, demonstrates this beautifully:

A woman was waiting at an airport one night,
With several long hours before her flight.
She hunted for a book in the airport shop,
Bought a bag of cookies and found a place to drop.

She was engrossed in her book, but happened to see,
That the man beside her, as bold as could be,
Grabbed a cookie or two from the bag between,
Which she tried to ignore, to avoid a scene.

She read, munched cookies, and watched the clock,
As the gutsy "cookie Thief" diminished her stock.
She was getting more irritated as the minutes ticked by,
Thinking, "If I wasn't so nice, I'd blacken his eye."

With each cookie she took, he took one too.
When only one was left, she wondered what he'd do.
With a smile on his face and a nervous laugh,
He took the last cookie and broke it in half.

He offered her half, as he ate the other.
She snatched it from him and thought, "Oh brother,
This guy has some nerve, and he's also rude,
Why, he didn't even show any gratitude!"

She had never known when she had been so galled,
And sighed with relief when her flight was called.
She gathered her belongings and headed for the gate,
Refusing to look back at the "thieving ingrate."

She boarded the plane and sank in her seat,
Then sought her book, which was almost complete.
As she reached in her baggage, she gasped with surprise.
There was her bag of cookies in front of her eyes!

"If mine are here," she moaned with despair,
"Then the others were *his* and he tried to share!"
Too late to apologize, she realized with grief,
That *she* was the rude one, the ingrate, the thief!

Our perception is a key component in the creation of our reality. This woman's limbic system combined her thinking with the emotional and visual aspects of the situation, compared them with the records in her database, rationalized and concluded them as truth. The process which occurred in her subconscious is what created her belief and ultimately, her reality. As it turns out, the accuracy of this woman's conclusion was skewed and biased due to her subconscious filtering, sorting and defense mechanisms. However, you see how the process works.

I'd like you to try something here: Close your eyes, and say the following to yourself out loud ten times:

"Everything is the opposite of what it appears to be.
Nothing is the opposite of what it appears to be."

Now, open your eyes, and try to have a rational thought. ~The Divine Paradox in the Law of Polarity.

The circuitry of your brain is constantly changing. This is known as Neuroplasticity, the brain's ability to reorganize itself by forming new neural pathways in response to changes in the environment of the neurons (nerve cells). This means that you can intercept and build new neural pathways to accommodate new software. The more they're used, the stronger these new pathways become, providing your intended reality a foundation on which to grow.

Your thoughts and emotions radiate out as vibrations (energy) which are returned to you as experiences. By spotting the limitations within your thoughts and emotions and switching out the energy, you challenge your map of reality and the programs you're running. By upgrading your software and blazing new neural pathways, you open yourself to more possibilities by which to redesign your life. If you don't like what you're getting and are asking yourself questions like: *Why does this keep happening* or *How can I change this*, you now have an answer and a place to begin.

Now that you've seen the hardware of your brain and how it works in relation to and with the various systems in our body, you may be wondering whether the brain and the mind could be two separate, or different, entities. Regardless of the true answer to that question - which the jury is still kibitzin' about - when you take into consideration the factors of awareness and free will, you can appreciate that you're not a slave to your hardware, and the software you choose to run – the reality you create - is entirely up to you.

The majority of your autonomy and influence lies within your subconscious mind. In order to create your life purposefully, it's necessary to integrate an awareness of and faculty for working with your subC by living mindfully. Your body is an amazing vehicle within which your Spirit lives. Your Spirit (your heart), is the GPS (Global Positioning System) for the journey of your life. When you follow the directives of your GPS, all systems function in harmony; and life is experienced with ease and joy. We'll discuss this in more detail during Chapter Five.

If your lineal mind could solve all of your problems, it would have done so already; *Right*? Well then, let's try something different now, shall we?

For more information, please visit Resources.

Musings…

"Can you remember who you were before the world told you who you should be?" -Danielle LaPorte

Chapter 3

Are You a Programmer or a Subscriber?

In this Chapter, you'll review the various influences in your life and the effects they have on your autonomy and well-being.

From the age of pre-birth to seven, your brain functions at a low frequency (Theta) which is considered a hypnotic state. Basically, you were in record mode; and everything you were exposed to during those years became a program inside of you. These programs are based on how you *learned* to respond to stimuli. They're anything from your manners at the dinner table or the reverberation of your parents' clichés to the choices you make throughout your life.

While the first seven years imparts the most foundational, programming and conditioning continues throughout your life. Have you ever gone on auto pilot as you travel the same route to and from work - arriving at your destination with little recall as to the details of your journey? You may have the radio on in the car or overhear a conversation on the train not realizing that the advertising or expressed opinions of others planted seeds within your subconscious. These influences are contributions to your programming and your belief system.

Science has shown that 95% of our thinking is subconscious while only 5% is conscious. Our emotions, decisions and behaviors are born of and rely on this 95% of our brain activity. Up to 99% of the day, our nervous system and cognitive behavior that controls our life is operated from our subconscious programs, not our conscious mind. Therefore you're not entirely operating from your own conscious objectives; you're operating from the subconscious collective conditioning you've received from external influences. Psychologists say that 70% of this conditioning is negative, disempowering and self-sabotaging which explains why we can occasionally feel like victims of circumstance. We can circumvent this misconception by taking an active role in our capacity as co-creators of our reality. First, let's have a look at how these misconceptions are generated.

The science of memetics, a controversial new field that transcends psychology, biology, anthropology and cognitive science, is the science of memes, the invisible but very real DNA of human society. The term meme was first introduced by Richard Dawkins in his book, *The Selfish Gene.* The concept of memes is likened to a replicator akin to the gene that would be at the center of the evolution of culture - the way that genes are at the center of the evolution of organisms. Memes are ideas, beliefs and behaviors that are transmitted through writing, speech, gestures, rituals and other imitable phenomena. They are cultural analogues to genes in that they self-replicate, mutate and respond to selective pressures. Memes are pieces of mental programming or conditioning that people acquire throughout their lives.

The programming in your mind is run by the code behind your software. Richard Brodie refers to the undesirable or detrimental species of this code as '*Mind Viruses*'. In his book, *Virus of the Mind*, he asserts that as memes evolve, they become better and better at distracting and diverting us from what we'd really like to be doing with our lives. They're a kind of 'Drug of the Mind' which spread mental programming among people the way viruses infect computers. He also asserts that they've evolved to the point where we've become immune to their existence and are impervious to antibiotics. While this is true, within mindfulness lies the antidote.

Where does your programming come from? The main streets, back roads and the vehicles which traverse your mind are as diverse as your thoughts, feelings and emotions. There are, however, maps and methods to the madness / magic. When you feel that there are too many cooks in your kitchen and embrace that *You* are the CEO (Chief Enjoyment Officer) of your life, things begin to shift. So let's have a look at some of them and realign the hierarchy a bit.

The initial source of your programming stems from inheritance. You may carry it with you in your muscles and cells; you may bring traces from past lives or inherit them from your family, friends and the cultures within which you live.

Muscle Memory is synonymous with motor learning - a form of procedural memory that involves consolidating a specific motor task into memory through repetition. When a movement is repeated over time, a long-term muscle memory is created for that task, eventually allowing it to be performed without conscious effort. This process decreases the need for conscious attention and creates maximum efficiency within the motor and memory systems. Riding a bicycle, playing a musical instrument or typing on a keyboard are examples of every day muscle memory.

Body Memory is a hypothesis that the body itself is capable of storing memories, as opposed to only the brain. This is used to explain having memories for events where the brain was not in a position to store recollections and is sometimes a catalyst for repressed memory recovery. These memories are often characterized by phantom pain in parts of the body whereas the body appears to remember the past trauma. This phenomenon has often been observed in amputee patients wherein the patient experiences pain in a limb which is no longer physically present. The idea of body memory is associated with the idea of repressed memories wherein memories of incest or sexual abuse can be retained and recovered through physical sensations. The idea is pseudoscientific as there is no known (*yet*) means by which tissues other than the brain are capable of storing memories.

Cellular Memory is a variation of body memory. In Epigenetics, the idea is that non-genetic information can be passed from parents to offspring. It's an additional hypothesis that memories can be stored outside of the brain. Unlike body memory, the cellular memory hypothesis states that these memories are stored in all cells of human bodies, not in the body's organs. The idea that non-brain tissues can have memories is also believed by some individuals who have received organ transplants.

Osmosis, the slang definition of which is the picking up of up knowledge unintentionally without actually seeking that particular knowledge, is another avenue by which software is downloaded to you from stimuli in your environment.

Richard Brodie discusses the memetic, viral and often stealth genre of programming. The 'Meme Pool' is known as the sum total of all memes which consist of varying types. Three of particular interest that he discusses in his book are the Distinction, Association and Strategy Memes:

Distinction is the manner you perceive that which you experience. You're presented with a tremendous amount of sensory information every second of every day, and the objective of your brain is to make sense of it all. This daunting task is achieved with the assistance of your Network Administrator's sifting, filtering and cataloging tools. It's the distinction memes you're programmed with that create your 'buttons' which, when pushed, influence your behavior. Advertisers understand this and fully employ it to their marketing advantage.

Association Memes are those which associate with one another. When one is present, so too are those associated with it. A clear illustration of this is Pavlov's dog. Ivan Petrovich Pavlov was a Russian physiologist famous for his conditional reflex experiments while examining the salivation of dogs. When he rang a bell as he provided food to a dog, the dog would salivate. The dog then associated the sound of the bell with the arrival of food and would salivate simply as a result of hearing the bell. Association Memes influence your choices and behavior and are used relentlessly in marketing and sales.

Strategy Memes are based on the beliefs that you trust and hold true. Lies, lines and manipulation (LLM) are tools of cause and effect. A lie is something that's not true but something you may tell a person because you know it's what they want to hear. Lines are used to convince others of something that will work for you. Manipulation is utilizing possibilities to get the most beneficial outcome. LLM tend to be viewed as evil tools with which to control others. While this may be true in some circumstances, the causality need not always be a disadvantage to either side. For example, if a product successfully pushes one of your buttons with their advertising and the result of utilizing that product renders positive effects, then any covert meme strategy involved in attracting you to the product is insignificant. It's the memes you absorb unknowingly which reap undesirable affects that you want to be mindful of. Richard notes three methods of memetic penetration within our software:

> Conditioning and Repetition are useful when preparing for a marathon, an exam or learning a new skill. Of concern, however, are the variations of this method that affect us without our knowledge which may not serve our best interests. When we

see and hear something enough times and/or from multiple sources, we tend to deem it as true, even though it may not entirely be true for us. It can then become one of our own beliefs or values.

Where religion is concerned, one can go from zero belief to full blown faith with conditioning and repetition. The messages of many religious documents are delivered as metaphors in order to download their true meaning into our subconscious. Unfortunately, dogma has a way of manipulating and encrypting these messages. Entertainingly, reversing the letters in the word dogma produces AmGod. Fortunately, mindfulness and free will allow us to discern what is true for us and what is not.

There are two types of conditioning: *Passive*, which is often utilized in advertisements; and *Operant* wherein the motivation is a reward provided for proper behavior. Passive conditioning is listening to a song and later having the tune or lyrics reverberate through your mind long after the song has ended. Advertisers take advantage of this by showing pictures of happy people consuming their product, creating the association (Association Memes) of being happy as a result of the consumption of that product while repeating their slogans and jingles… which can also become ear worms. Operant conditioning is when little Johnny gets ice cream for bringing home a great report card.

The Trojan Horse method of meme penetration is the procedure by which your attention is drawn to one topic or meme while a bundle of additional memes are snuck in. This is referred to as 'Bundling' which, in marketing terms, is packaging two or more products or services in a single bundle for one price. The term *Trojan Horse* originated from the manner by which a surprise attack was accomplished by constructing a huge wooden horse within which soldiers were hidden and later emerged to attack their opponents once the horse was upon enemy territory.

Richard provides a great example of bundling frequently used by politicians and trial attorneys wherein they state a bundle of memes in decreasing order of believability with the intention of the credibility of the most believable carrying over to the least. For example:

We all want freedom!
We all want democracy to work for everyone!
We all want every American to have the opportunity to pursue the American Dream!
And we all want a national health-care system that makes that possible.

By juxtaposing the statements, the questionable memes ride into your mind inside the Trojan Horse of the acceptable ones. Can you think of any Trojan Horse experiences of your own?

Anchoring and Embedding are members of this method in that an idea is anchored into your subconscious using an image, sound or sensation that your mind cognitively relates to which is embedded using NLP (Neuro-Linguistic Programming). NLP is an approach to communication and psychotherapy developed by John Grinder and Richard Bandler based on their theory of a connection between neurological processing, language and behavior learned through experience.

In his book, Richard notes a line from Raymond Shaw, the protagonist in the movie, *The Manchurian Candidate*: "*There are two types of people in this world: Those that enter a room and turn the television on and those that enter a room and turn the television off.*"

Television is very low on the list of choices with which to utilize my time. I consider it one of the broadest sources of conditioning and programming there is. The worst thing you can do is fall asleep with the television on as your brain drifts into Theta. Do you really want to marinate your subconscious in material which is unbeknownst to you all night? I suggest turning the TV off and making a mental list of all that you are grateful for and intend - a far greater *Secret Sauce* for the dream state, me thinks.

The function of the mind is to take your thoughts and beliefs and make reality out of them. Cognitive Dissonance is the filtering process of your mind. Cognition is a group of mental processes such as attention, memory, learning and reasoning. Dissonance has several meanings - all related to conflict or incongruity. Your brain's objective is to make sense of the overwhelming amount of information it receives. When your brain encounters something that does not compute based

> on your filters, it will either discard it, create a way of making sense of it to conform to your current programming or – through neuroplasticity and with your *intentional focus* - it will create a new neural pathway and program to accommodate it ~ within the latter lies the impetus for change.

Our DNA is the connection between the physical and Spiritual realms. With this in mind, I'd like you to consider what your understanding, points of view and beliefs currently are regarding your own DNA, your genes. For instance, if diabetes '*runs in your family*', are you anticipating your body having to deal with this condition at some point in your life or are you of the belief that it's a choice for your own Mind/Body to make for itself?

You may consider yourself a victim to the legacy of your genes. However, heredity is not inevitably your fate map. When you believe that it is, you disempower yourself by relinquishing your role in the co-creation process, and your destiny. Your perception and beliefs, your free will, plays a key role in this process. If you believe that life happens *To* you, your life will be lived as a victim of circumstance. However, when you believe that life happens *For* you, you're able to discern and create for yourself. Fate is the cards you are dealt within the game of life; destiny is how you choose to play that hand. This is true with regard to every aspect of your life.

While there are many factors which can contribute to dis-ease, one component that's often overlooked is that every condition of the body is influenced by the beliefs in the mind and that our Mind/Body operates from the choices we make based on those beliefs. It's essential to look at all components of any problem, not only the symptoms and mechanical aspects. The *whole* person must come under review when dis-ease of any kind presents itself [hence the term Holistic (*Whole*-istic)] because the body speaks the mind.

Bruce Lipton, PhD, an American Biologist and best-selling Author, is well known for his research of the concept that DNA and genes can be manipulated by a person's beliefs. He says the new science of Epigenetics shows that our genes are, in fact, controlled and manipulated by how our minds perceive and interpret our environment. Genetics is the blueprint of the cells. Epigenetics is the study of changes in gene expression or cellular phenotype, caused by mechanisms other than changes in the underlying DNA sequence. Phenotypes result from the expression of an organism's genes as well as the influence of environmental factors and the interactions between the two.

In his book, *The Biology of Belief - Unleashing the Power of Consciousness, Matter & Miracles,* Bruce tells us that our cells read the environment and dynamically adjust their biology and genetics to complement their environment. Between the environment and our cells is a layer of interpretation, our mind; and the chemistry of our beliefs drives this process. Our mind reads and interprets the environment and sends signals to our cells via our nervous system which is the interpreter for communication. Interpretation is key, as it is based on our perceptions, and our subjective perception of reality overrides our objective experience.

Cells respond, not so much to the *real* world, but to our interpretation of it (their environment) in one of two ways: Protection or Growth; but both cannot be cultivated at the same time. When threat is detected, you move away and close yourself down for protection. There are two aspects related to protection: Inside protection which is our immune system and Outside protection, our adrenal system which deals with outside influences such as threats by producing our fight or flight response. When threat is detected, all of our energy is directed toward protection. The stress induced shuts down our internal immune system. Protection mode can be short lived; and once the threat is removed, you can open back up. However, when we live in a chronic state of stress, we are constantly shutting down. To foster growth, you must be open to moving toward and receiving positive, empowering nourishment.

It's a universal law of nature that truth feels light, while anything that feels heavy is not true for you. You learn early on to judge and categorize your experiences and feelings into light or heavy: right or wrong and good or bad. These are filters, compiled from your perceptions which form your beliefs based on your experiences. Although choice is ever available, it may not be readily apparent at times. Conformity is born of observation and assimilation due in part to our default objective of acceptance and survival. Have you ever encountered someone who tends to take the side which appears most socially acceptable? Perhaps you've done it yourself on occasion. It's amazing how quickly we can form a perception or belief with very little, often biased, input or simply conform to the masses without conscious consideration. We can mistakenly take for granted that we know the whole story, judging a book by its cover or reading selectively between the lines.

Although our default objective may be acceptance and conformity for survival, it's not the only objective to cultivate. There are other possibilities from which to select and create, regardless of the points of view of others. One of the greatest freedoms is not allowing the influence of others to overshadow your free will in choosing for yourself.

"As long as you are worried about what others think of you, you are owned by them. Only when you require no approval from outside yourself can you own yourself." -Neale Donald Walsch

Learning to harness the mind to promote growth vs. protection is the secret of life. Beliefs are your perceptual filters, and they are the key to programming, and reprogramming your consciousness. The first step in retraining your consciousness is to examine your perceptions and beliefs, determining whether they are true for you and then identifying the programs that you're running based upon them. Your life is basically a printout of your programs. Things that come easily and are enjoyable for you are those for which you have supportive and encouraging programs. Those which you may struggle with are those for which there are subconscious programs which do not encourage and support them. These are the ones to identify and adjust. To this intent, I offer an exploratory exercise in the back of this book.

There exists a notion that we're only capable of using 10% of our brain. If you're a current subscriber to the belief that 90% of your brain's resources are untapped, it may come as a surprise that there's no scientific basis for this belief. Publications such as *Scientific American* have conveyed testimony that optimal brain usage is inhibited only in a brain encountering damage or disease. The proliferation of this myth is a prime example of the memes and mind viruses that Messrs. Dawkins and Brodie speak of.

It's rather interesting that we've created our computers and internetworking in the likeness of our own design. Still, a computer can only do what we program it to. Its capabilities are governed by the functionality of the software which is installed upon it and the manipulation of its operator. There is a certain inherent control structure to which code is executed and when, as well as the return value of the functions within the code. With this in mind, I have a question for you: *How much control over the condition of your life do you feel you currently possess?* Should you feel that a disproportionate amount of your circumstance is beyond your jurisdiction, I ask you: *Truth*: Is it; *Really*?

We gather and discuss the mire in our lives, comparing and licking our wounds. We often choose to keep our own troubles without considering possibilities for the resolution of the issues presented on either side. It's been said that what you complain about is something you have an unconscious intention to produce, or reproduce. As Laurie Buchanan so eloquently summed it, "*Whatever you are not changing, you are choosing.*"

Everything is a matter of awareness and choice. When I began to review my life, I asked many questions: *Why did I get married so young? - Why didn't I go to college? - Why did I leave my career'?* What elements (limitations and/or expectations) contributed to my choices? If I'd chosen otherwise, would it have been different? Sure. Would it have been *better*? In some ways, perhaps; in others, maybe not so much. Is there an essence of blame underlying the causes and effects of my directions? While external influences play a role and can explain many things, ultimately the responsibility for our lives lies within ourselves; and it is never too late to make new choices. Do I have regrets? I did for a while. However, the way I now choose to perceive my life can be summed by the following from Dr. Wayne W. Dyer:

> *"With everything that has happened to you,*
> *you can either feel sorry for yourself*
> *or treat what has happened as a gift. Everything*
> *is either an opportunity to grow*
> *or an obstacle to keep you from growing. You get to choose."*

All we can do is our best with what we have to work with at any given time. This is not an excuse or a justification, it is reality. With this in mind, we can consider: What if Problem/Program X is nothing more than an implanted point of view and a series of choices based on that point of view which can be altered with expanded awareness and choice?

Although your perception of alternate possibilities may currently be somewhat hindered or slightly beyond your present level of awareness, as we progress through the upcoming chapters, you'll come to appreciate that you're not nearly as limited as you may currently think or believe. Your potentiality is governed only by the boundaries constructed with what you tell yourself. Endless possibilities exist just beyond your current awareness and belief system.

"Life begins at the end of your comfort zone." -Neale Donald Walsch

For more information, please visit Resources.

Musings…

"The best teachers are those who show you where to look, but don't tell you what to see." -Alexandra K. Trenfor

Chapter 4

Metaphysics and the Universal Laws of Nature ~ Living Purposefully in Possibility

In this chapter, you'll gain a deeper understanding of the Natural Laws and appreciation for their practical use.

Have you ever wondered whether there's a method to the perceived madness of life - A system to the perceived subjective randomness - one which could be used purposefully to your benefit? There is. It's called Metaphysics - The branch of philosophy involved with the fundamental nature of reality as well as abstract concepts such as being, knowing and that which is outside of objective experience.

Before we proceed, I'd like to discuss two books written by Napoleon Hill, an American author of personal success literature. Andrew Carnegie, one of history's greatest philanthropists, wanted to publish a book that would provide the masses with the secrets to success. He commissioned Napoleon Hill to interview and study 100 of the most successful millionaires in the United States. Twenty years of Hill's research was compiled into his first book, *The Law of Success.*

Purportedly, when millionaires (the likes of which included Henry Ford, J. P. Morgan, John D. Rockefeller, Alexander Graham Bell and Thomas Edison) realized the power of the information contained within this book, they protested its publishing in 1925. Instead, a purportedly watered-down version was published under the title *Think and Grow Rich* in 1928.

A statement on the Napoleon Hill Foundation site indicates that Hill was unable to obtain a publisher for the 1925 version, consisting of fewer than 500 pages. He was encouraged to expand on the principles, resulting in the 1928 edition of more than 1,400 pages. The Foundation has compared the two versions, stating that nothing of any consequence from the first was omitted from the newer version. Conspiracy theorists asserted that *Think and Grow Rich* was a form of Crippleware, containing just enough content to benefit some with key information omitted in order to maintain control of the masses. I'm inclined to maintain a bit of skepticism on either side because with the resources of someone like Andrew Carnegie, I find it difficult to believe that a publisher could not initially be acquired for such an extraordinary masterpiece and gift. However, these principles are freely available for everyone; and they can be found interwoven within most self-help books available today. Napoleon Hill's work outlines *17 Principles of Success*, the steps by which to achieve success and *The Master Key - 12 Great Riches of Life* to be derived from that success. The Universal Laws of Nature are the foundation of Hill's work.

"Whatever the mind of man can conceive and believe, he can achieve." -Napoleon Hill

Natural Law is the system of nature, and is thus universal and absolute. These laws apply to all things. They exist and operate whether we accept them or not. While there are some variations on the names and descriptions of these laws, the premise throughout is the same. Some are considered *subordinate* in that they support the foundational law which they corroborate. For simplicity, we'll focus on the foundational seven.

"The Principles of the Truth are Seven;
he who knows these, understandingly, possesses the Magic Key
before whose touch all the Doors of the
Temple fly open." -The Kybalion

The Kybalion is a book from 1908 outlining the essence of the teachings of Hermes Trismegistus, a legendary author of literature embodying alchemical, astrological and magical doctrines. Hermetic Philosophy is based on The Seven Hermetic Principles, referred to as the Universal Laws of Nature. This book was originally published anonymously under the alias of *The Three Initiates*. Works of this kind, particularly when published anonymously, are imbued with mysticism, yet there's really no secret to the wisdom they hold.

When I was learning the languages of programming, it seemed a bit intimidating at first. I came to realize, however, that - as with various interpretations of Spirituality, through them runs a common thread: Pure logic and truth. These laws, and their applications in our lives, are no different. The following are brief descriptions of the foundational seven laws/Kybalion principles along with some of their subordinates. As you progress through the remaining chapters, you'll see how these laws come into play within your everyday life and how you can use them purposefully to your benefit.

<u>The Law of Perpetual Transmutation / Principle of Mentalism</u>:

Everything is energy vibrating at a certain frequency which is constantly changing and moving into and out of physical form. Everything manifest begins as a thought or an idea. Higher vibrations consume and transform those of lower vibration.

The Law of Relativity / Principle of Correspondence:

Everything simply *is*. This law, not to be confused with The Law of Polarity, declares that nothing is big or small, good or bad. It simply *is*...until you relate it to something. Basically, your perception determines the relevance of all things in your life. There is correspondence between the three planes of being: Physical, Mental and Spiritual. As above, so below. As within, so without.

The Law of Polarity / The Principle of Polarity:

All exists in duality. There are two sides to everything; and they are identical in nature, yet differ in degree. Without darkness, there would be no light. This is contrast. The Divine Paradox: While the Universe is not, still it is. Negativity or undesirable attributes may be transformed by first accepting and allowing that they simply *are* and then focusing on their polar opposite per the Law of Perpetual Transmutation (Noted above).

The Law of Gestation / Principle of Gender:

All things have a gestation or incubation period before they manifest. Gender manifested as Feminine (Yin) and Masculine (Yang) is evident on all planes.

The Law of Rhythm / Principle of Rhythm:

Everything has a natural cycle. There's an ebb and flow to all things in life. There is night, and then there is day; and change is ever constant. There is rhythm between every pair of opposites (Polarity). These rhythms are manifest in cycles as patterns such as seasons, stages of development, etc.

The Law of Cause and Effect / Principle of Cause and Effect:

Action and Re-Action are opposite but equal. That which you sow, you shall reap.
Causation: There is no such thing as chance or outside of Natural Law.

The Law of Vibration and Attraction / The Principle of Vibration:

Everything vibrates, and nothing rests. Motion is manifest in everything. The Law of Attraction decrees that vibrations of the same frequency resonate with each other ~ Like attracts like. The Law of Attraction being a popular focal point of late, included below are subordinate laws relative to purposeful co-creation with the LOA:

- The Law of Polarity: The side of the pole on which you focus is what will actualize.
- The Law of Sufficiency and Abundance: Supply is infinite. There is enough for everyone. Source (*You*) is the provider of all abundance. All else (your work, investments, etc.) are the channels by which it is received.
- The Law of Pure Potentiality: Pure consciousness seeks to express itself. There are no limits, other than those you place upon yourself through doubt and fear. *~Anything is possible.*
- The Law of Deliberate Creation: That which you focus your energy upon grows. Thoughts attract; however, thoughts imbued with emotion attract quicker.
- The Law of Entrainment: When two closely related rhythmic cycles interact with each other, they will synchronize.
- The Law of Detachment: Change what you can, yet have the wisdom to accept that which you cannot. Be in allowance, and trust that you will receive what is in your best interest, knowing that you are well regardless.

- The Law of Allowance (The Law of Non-resistance and The Law of Receiving): Anticipate that which you are creating, and be open to receive it.

The Law of Vibration & Attraction and The Law of Attraction & Repulsion are not the same, nor are they polar opposites. Due to magnetism (electro-magnetic force), vibrations move in relation to opposing poles: A positive pole projects energy and a negative pole attracts energy. Due to the vibratory nature of all things, that which you vibrate out is reflected or returned to you at that frequency. You vibrate at the frequency of your beliefs; therefore, you will attract what you believe. This is how energy is manifested by, through, from and to us.

The above are the foundational seven. Below are several supplementary laws which are noteworthy for our purposes here:

- The Law of Divine Oneness: All that we think, say and do affects everything around us. We are all connected at the level of the Collective Unconscious or the Universal Mind.

- The Law of Conservation of Energy: Energy can neither be created nor destroyed; rather, it transforms from one form to another.

- The Law of Resistance: That which you resist you draw unto you. *"What you resist persists. ~Carl Jung*

- The Law of Action: The fundamental laws can only be facilitated by action. You must take a proactive role in creating your life.

- The Golden Law / The Golden Rule / Ethic of Reciprocity: One should treat others as one would like others to treat oneself. *I'd like to note the polar:* One should treat oneself as one would treat others.

- The Law of Fellowship: When two or more of similar vibration are gathered for a shared purpose, their combined energy is further multiplied.

- The Law of Reflection: The aspects you respond to in others are those you recognize within yourself.
  ~So be careful when throwing stones at a mirror.

- The Law of Compensation: You receive that which you give.

- The Law of Gratitude (The Law of Expansion or Increase): That which you appreciate appreciates you.
  When you live in the vibration of gratitude, you appreciate more to be grateful for.

- The Law of Unconditional Love: The acceptance of that which exists without judgment or expectation.

- The Law of Divine Order: Everything is as it should be.

- The Law of Comprehension: Suffice it to say it as Einstein had: *"The eternal mystery of the world is its comprehensibility… The fact that it is comprehensible is a miracle."*

From "Physics and Reality," Journal of the Franklin Institute 221, no. 3 (March 1936).

- The Law of Free Will: Choice is universal, and we are responsible for the results of our choices and actions.

The following laws are relative to Soul Evolution:

The Law of Reincarnation and Karma: You will reincarnate to sequential life until you have resolved your Karma by fulfilling your Dharma (Dharma is the meaning, purpose, principle or law that orders the universe).

The Law of Harmony: Harmony is the ultimate balance. The purpose of Karma is to attain harmony.

The Law of Wisdom: Lessons may be learned through love and wisdom, rather than pain and suffering. When we have embraced this and absolved our Karma, we have evolved within; therefore, it is no longer necessary to reincarnate.

The Law of Soul Evolution: By overcoming fear and loving unconditionally, we raise our vibration and our Soul to a state of harmony.

The Law of Bodhisattva: A Bodhisattva is one who is free from the need for earthly incarnation. However, a Bodhisattva is one who *chooses* to reincarnate in order to assist others in freeing their own Souls.

During my research, I discovered the works of Joseph Murphy and came to understand the simple manner by which we can work with our subconscious mind, using these laws to purposefully create the realities we prefer. While he cites the foundational seven, he also speaks of supplemental laws which can be employed in successfully doing so.

Murphy asserts that The Law of Your Mind is the Law of Belief: Whatever is in your belief system, whether with feeling and conviction or not, becomes your reality. From a seed planted in your subconscious will grow a belief. Murphy attests that utilizing

The Law of Inverse Transformation with your subconscious mind is the way to actualizing your objectives.

The Law of Inverse Transformation (Law of Reversibility/Polarity) affirms that if a physical fact can produce a psychological state, then the polar is also possible in that a psychological state can produce a physical fact. This means that when you create and sustain within yourself the feeling of *having* your objective fulfilled, it becomes a belief in your subconscious mind. The law of the subconscious mind is compulsion. Therefore, your objective will then actualize itself - The belief will be realized. *-You'll see it when you believe it.*

Everything that's in existence began as a thought, an idea. In order to actualize an idea, the belief that it is possible must be firmly planted within the subconscious mind. However, your beliefs and feelings must first be in line with your ideas. We'll discuss the process of shifting and solidifying your beliefs to align with your objectives when we get to Chapter Eleven. Suffice it to say for now that embodying the state of *being* associated with your objectives having been fulfilled - living it as part of your reality - activates the compulsion of your subconscious creative capacities. This does not mean that you should go on a shopping spree and max out your credit card as if you've received a huge cash win fall. While retail therapy has its merits, this will not accomplish your ultimate goal. Embodying your intended state of being means living in the feeling and having the demeanor that you will by actualizing your objective.

Incidentally, virtual shopping sprees, using visualizations and affirmations are effective ways to anchor a new belief into your subconscious - *Fake it till you make it!* We'll discuss the optimal use of these techniques and other methods in detail during Chapter Eleven as well.

I'd like to clarify that manifesting and actualizing are not one and the same. Actualization is the showing up of that which you objectified while manifestation is the manner by which your objective shows up - It is the *how*, if you will. Nurturing your beliefs, utilizing the laws and expressing gratitude for their actualization by living in the vibration of their existence are your part in the co-creation process. The details of manifestation, the how's, are for the Universe to handle.

The Universe delivers that which is for the highest and best of all concerned in divine time. When utilizing the Law of Attraction, detachment is essential as it demonstrates your willingness to be in the flow of life and your faith in its process. The more attached you are to a particular outcome, the more likely you are to be disappointed. When you affirm your beliefs and embody the feelings associated with them, you're able to detach from the outcome and embrace gratitude for the gifts in your life. You may not always get precisely what you want or what you may *'think'* that you want, yet through mindfulness, trust and gratitude, you will come to realize that you receive all that is required in the interests of your highest and best. When you live in this manner, you'll be amazed how things will come together as if by magic to actualize within your life, better than you could imagine.

Have you ever had a passing thought like *'Gee, it'd be nice to not have to cook tonight'* and then receive an impromptu invitation to dinner with a friend? Perhaps someone crosses your mind and you wonder how they're doing - Then you unexpectedly receive a call from them. This is the laws of detachment and attraction in motion. These laws are always working automatically whether you're consciously aware of it or not. Consider the Law of Gravity: You know it exists (belief), but you may not give it much attention (detachment) - unless, of course, you're playing a game such as Jenga☺. Having a gracious understanding of the natural process of life, aligning your beliefs with your objectives and selecting your choices accordingly is all that's required to utilize these laws purposefully.

I'd like to mention the Spiritual Law of Grace as it is the *Secret Sauce* within all others. When you live your life guided by the principles of compassion, forgiveness, kindness and unconditional love, it is a life of grace. Anne Lamott articulates this by saying, *"I do not understand the mystery of grace – Only that it meets us where we are and does not leave us where it found us."*

I couldn't move on without mentioning Murphy's Law: *Anything that can go wrong will go wrong.* This isn't so much a law as it is an adage occasionally used in sarcastic humor. In keeping with The Law of Polarity, however, the inverse is also true. Therefore, I suggest focusing on the implementation of the polar: *Anything that can go well will go well.* Please note: There is no association of this law with the Joseph Murphy mentioned above.

By embracing that these laws are the *Source Code of Your Soul* which governs your role in the process of co-creation, you are empowered by the magic of life. Michael Bernard Beckwith, an American New Thought spiritual teacher, author and founder of the Agape International Spiritual Center headquartered in Los Angeles, describes the four stages of this process in his book, *Life Visioning*:

In Stage One, *"To Me,"* an individual lives from a consciousness that life is happening *'To'* them by outside sources for which they are not responsible and is typified by "Victim Consciousness."

In Stage Two, *"By Me,"* an individual begins to consciously understand and participate in the co-creative process, one of the fundamental laws governing the universe, and is described as "Manifester Consciousness."

In Stage Three, *"Through Me,"* an individual maintains a spiritual practice of meditation, affirmative prayer and life visioning, leading to a "Channel Consciousness", meaning that this state of awareness consciously catches intuitive guidance from Spirit.

In Stage Four, *"As Me,"* an individual lives in "Being Consciousness", an unbroken awareness of oneness with Source and an absence of ego. In this advanced stage, meditation or any other spiritual practices are not by necessity but rather by choice.

The fourth stage may initially seem rather bold to some. However, this is the state wherein you take responsibility for your life. It is where you come to a visceral understanding that you are the one who creates you and everything about and around you to be what it is. Truth: Only you have the ability to create the best version of yourself and your life.

This responsibility can initially be unsettling, especially if you've ever felt victimized to any degree. It was for me. As the saying goes, *The truth will set you free, but first it may, indeed, piss you off.* This understatement covers a lot of ground. I can assure you, however, that once the piss and vinegar settle - and with your acceptance, they will indeed settle - you will find the game of life to be so enjoyable that you'll come to forget all about them. Never doubt that your subconscious already knows this truth.

It is my assertion that Goddess/God is not any one thing, nor a being. Goddess/God is an essence, one which we all possess collectively. As the title of Joan Osborne's 1995 song invokes, *What if God was one of us?* What if, indeed?

The phrase *"I am that I am"* is said to have been God's response to Moses when asked who God was. Neale Donald Walsch shares his inspiration regarding the message within this phrase. He considered what it would be like to see everyone as another part of himself and to see everything as part of all that is. Neale spent some time observing the world around him, pointing out people, places and things, while consciously saying to himself *"I am that, I am"*. The placement of a comma within this phrase enabled him to see the true meaning of these words: God is everything, and everything is connected. I recommend trying this yourself. Doing so provides a refreshing perspective on the world and life in general to say the very least.

Georges Lemaître, with his Hypothesis of the Primeval Atom ~ *The Big Bang Theory*, was the first to propose that the creation of the Universe occurred billions of years ago as a result of an enormous explosion from a single point of nearly infinite energy density. Lemaître referred to the creation of the primeval atom as a divine act outside the realm of scientific knowledge. This hypothesis provides a viable answer to the universal questions: *Where did we come from?* and *Why are we here*? It also lends credibility to a supposition regarding the *purpose* of our life in that we're infinite energetic beings having a physical experience. We simply are.

~ Living Purposefully in Possibility ~

What if the willingness to be out of definition and in question is the gateway to freedom and the capacity to create and experience a phenomenal life?

Over 95% of your thoughts, feelings and emotions are born of external influences and the conditioning you've been exposed to. These elements formulate the beliefs on which you base your choices and create your life. Truth feels light while heaviness is born of untruths ~ most of which originate from these external sources which aren't yours to begin with. They may seem to be if you've chosen (albeit unconsciously) to subscribe to them. However, things of this nature are simply on loan to you unless or until you choose otherwise. You can think of them as lines of text within a file or code within a program which can be commented out for reference, rewritten or deleted entirely.

Your lineal brain bases its deductions on what is already known or in place ~ the key word here being *already*. However, the realm of pure potentiality exists just outside of this box. You can choose to view any situation either from an unremitting viewpoint of limitation or a transitory perspective of possibility, choice and change. As Greek Philosopher, Heraclitus was quoted, *"The only constant in the world is change."*

The impetus of anything you'd like to change is held subconsciously and energetically. Your best interests are paramount to your true self. It knows what is at the core of everything you embody, intend to change, create and experience. You can inquire and require your true self to shift anything ~ whether the source and details of which are consciously known or unknown to you ~ that may stand in the way of your alignment with your objectives. When you identify something of this nature through the process of enquiry, you can compel your true self to transmute its energy.

The process of shifting begins with query ~ probing into your subconscious and energetic files. By revealing their content and function, discerning what does not serve from what is true and ideal for *You,* their components can be reverse engineered and their negative influence alleviated. By basing your choices on the foundation of these findings, you can initiate change and embrace being the purposeful creator of your own life, regardless of any circumstances which may exist around you.

Bearing in mind the vastness of our receptivity, enquiry is the greatest tool in the discovery process. We can begin inquiring around the where's and how's of our situations and subsequently open the door to shift and change. For example, if you are or have a history of experiencing financial difficulty, you likely hold limiting beliefs around money. Perhaps you consider (either consciously or unconsciously) money as difficult to come by, that it's only obtainable through hard ('hard' meaning unenjoyable or unfulfilling) work or that having an abundance of it is meant for some but not others. Consider where these limiting beliefs may have been instigated by asking some questions: *Where did this originate (from whom did I learn this) ~ my parents, teachers, friends? When did I adopt this viewpoint, decide to believe it and opt to base my choices upon it? What have I created or not created in my life because of it? Is it true? Would I like it to be true for me as I move forward?* When you experience a sense of lightness as a result of such inquiries, it is confirmation that you are shifting it. While 'X' may have originated from a source outside of yourself, you can choose not to hold on to it as your own.

Peeling the layers of a proverbial onion where beliefs and the situations around them are concerned can seem daunting at first glance through the lenses of limitation created by them. However, what if all that is required to bring about change is a shift in perception? What if you could clear all of the layers with one slice simply by acknowledging them and sending those files to the recycle bin for transmutation of the energy into something more desirable? *You Can.* You have the capacity to compel your true self to clear it with a directive such as: *"Everything this is and brings up, whether known or unknown consciously or unconsciously that is limiting me where X is concerned, I choose to release and transmute its energy to a higher vibrational frequency across all timelines and energetic fields under grace with ease. And so it is."* This process is tremendously empowering. You can then begin asking more open-ended questions, choosing, creating and experiencing something different.

When questions are posed, the compulsion of your brain is to search for answers to them. However, it can only search for answers within the database of that which it is *already* aware, which can place you into limitation. *Open-ended* questioning is simply *asking*, but *not* looking for the answers. An open-ended question such as '*What else is possible*' changes the energy of any situation by challenging the filters of your subconscious belief systems and expanding your consciousness to the infinite possibilities which are available. This expansion can lead you to ask more purposeful questions such as: *What shifts could I make to…; What actions could I take to…; What vibrational energy could I be that would guide me to actualize these possibilities and see them manifest in my life?*

To demonstrate the expansion that asking such questions can provide, I'll paraphrase Anita Moorjani's *Flashlight Exercise,* a metaphor of the enlightenment gifted to her during a near death experience which she shares in her book, *Dying To Be Me.*

> Imagine there's a huge warehouse which is dark, and that you live in this warehouse with one small flashlight. Everything you know about this warehouse is what's in the beam of your small flashlight. Outside of the beam is darkness. This is your current awareness. Whenever you look for something, you may or may not find it; but it doesn't mean that it doesn't exist. It's there, but you just haven't flashed your light on it.
>
> Then one day, someone flicks on a light switch; and for the first time, you can see the whole warehouse. The vastness of it is almost overwhelming. You notice how many different things there are in the warehouse which you never noticed or even conceived existing, yet they do – simultaneously,

> alongside the things you know existed (those you found with your small flashlight). When the light switch goes back off, nothing can take away the understanding and clarity of your experience. Even though you're back to the tiny beam of one flashlight, you know what is possible and how to look for it. You start viewing things differently, and it is from this springboard that new experiences begin to happen.
>
> ***Anita Moorjani, Dying to Be Me, Copyright 2012, Hay House, Inc., Carlsbad, CA***

For fun, try this exercise:

> Look around the room you're in. Make note of the things that are the color red. Now, close your eyes.
>
> Keep them closed and try to recall as many things in the room that are the color *blue*. Now open your eyes.
>
> Look around the room and see how many blue things you missed while your flashlight was focusing only on the red items.

Anita says that in her daily life, she refers to the various aspects of her experience at different times, understanding things in a different way and finding that there are things that she now feels she knows or understands that she hadn't realized she'd known before. During her near death experience, Anita saw people as vibrating energy. She says that depending on where our energy level is, that is the world we've created for ourselves. Anita goes on to say that we are energy first with the physical being the expression of our energy; and that we can change our physical reality if we change our energy, our vibration.

Anita came to understand that in order to keep her energy level up, she only had to live in the moment, enjoy every moment of life and use each moment to elevate the next moment (which then elevates the future). It is in that moment of elevation that you can change your future. She says that this may sound very simplistic, but it felt very deep when she was experiencing the understanding of it. Anita's message is an exquisite expression of the transformative nature of perception and confirmation of the ease and joy with which life can be created and experienced. She shares the details of her amazing experience and journey in her book, which I highly recommend.

Anita Moorjani, Dying to Be Me, Copyright 2012, Hay House, Inc., Carlsbad, CA

I believe that our free will is the dimmer switch to our awareness, and that we have the capacity to choose the lighting of our lives.

My intention in in this chapter is to provide you with a means by which to re-member and utilize what you already know as truth. Truth is the Universal Law. Incidentally, stating the word *'Truth'* before asking a question compels honesty of your subconscious mind. Consciousness obeys the laws of physics, and there is no mystery or secret to these processes. They are the foundation of life itself, the *Source Code of Your Soul.*

It is my personal belief that while it may have its place in University, the wisdom of these laws, principles and methods, especially due to their non-secular, universal nature, should have their place in every curriculum early on. We study mathematics, history, economics, sociology and psychology ~why not the Universal Laws of Nature and their contemporary, practical applications? Implementing these concepts and practices as an integral part of our lives elevates and fosters our well-being, ease and enjoyment of life, providing a conscious foundation for future generations.

I conclude with a quote from Joseph Murphy:

> *"The law of life is the law of belief; and belief could be summed up briefly as a thought in your mind. As a man thinks, feels and believes, so is the condition of his mind, body and circumstances."*

For more information, please visit Resources.

Musings…

"Happiness is when what you think, what you say and what you do are in harmony." -Mahatma Gandhi

Chapter 5

Happiness Is...

In this chapter, you'll explore what happiness is for you and embrace an enduring, visceral union with its intrinsic nature.

If you were asked by a creature from another galaxy what happiness is in your reality, what would your answer be? Having only 60 seconds to provide a brief reply, consider the feelings, emotions, images and/or objectives which come to mind. What words might you choose to compose your response?

____

____

____

If you drew a line down the middle of a blank page and listed in the two columns the elements which contribute to your happiness as well as any unhappiness in your life, which column could you fill the quickest and which would contain the most items? Would some of the items in the happiness column be a result of eliminating items from the unhappy column?

The amount of material available relative to decoding, acquiring and sustaining happiness is astounding. -Seems like an awful lot of energy around something intended as intrinsic to our nature. Benjamin Franklin was quoted as saying "*The Constitution only gives people the right to pursue happiness. You have to catch it yourself.*" To pursue is to chase, and to catch is to capture. Do you consider happiness a commodity outside of yourself which must be pursued and caught?

When Thomas Jefferson included *Life, Liberty and the Pursuit of Happiness* in the Constitution of the United States as *Unalienable Rights*, his perception of the word *pursuit* was to practice - Not in a rehearsal sense, but as a living norm - which was the original descriptive intention of the word.

After visiting the tiny country of Bhutan, wedged in a Himalayan crevice between China and India, Chip Conley came to a visceral understanding of happiness. The following is in paraphrase of an article he wrote entitled *The Pursuit of Happiness*:

> While the pursuit can be alluring, quite often the obtaining of a goal or gratification leads to some disappointment. In other words, it's the act of winning that gives us a high rather than the carrot that we were pursuing. In sum, happiness comes from appreciating what you have in your life, not to the detriment of your pursuit of dreams, but instead as a healthy balance. Strangely enough, we often aren't grateful for something until it's taken away from us. Happy people bathe in gratitude, and they don't wait until something is gone to appreciate it.

We are born with intrinsic happiness. Unfortunately the mires of life may attempt to infringe upon our capacity to sustain this fundamental element. As with many aspects of living, happiness is personally subjective. While some prefer a high-profile lifestyle, more moderate options are ideal for others. Too often we're prompted or pressured by society to present certain appearances to the world. Many of our expectations, disappointments and perceived limitations are born of our subscription to these pressures and a compulsion to prove ourselves in some ways. Incidentally, when you feel that you have something to prove, it indicates that you don't believe it yourself. The only one to demonstrate anything to is *You.*

We tend to observe various components within our environment and go about mimicking them. We create airplanes in the likeness of birds and I/T (Information Technology) infrastructure parallel to our own design. In some ways, using mimicry as a tool can be beneficial. Yet in others, it may only generate mimicry which is one of the ways we invite limitation into our lives. While protocol and decorum have their places, approaching anything in your life, particularly where your happiness is concerned, with mimicry that is limiting to your objectives and intentions is neither creative nor generative. For instance, making your choices from within the perimeters of memes such as *'It's always been done this way'* and the beliefs built around them.

What if you chose to shift some of these per***i***meters to par***a***meters? In I/T, a parameter is an item of information. It's used as a selection option, the value of which is passed to a program which affects the operation of the software that is utilizing them. What might be possible by adopting this type of perspective, using your own *in*spiration vs. *ex*ternal approval as motivation for your choices and actions within the realm of your free will?

Can you think of any ways which you're conducting your life from a place of mimicry – particularly those where doing so is not serving your best interests and generating happiness? To begin shifting this paradigm, ask yourself: *What creation am I using to invoke and perpetrate the biom**e**metic* mimicry of other people's realities am I choosing?* Inquiries such as this will dissipate your reference points and open you to more creative and generative possibilities. Imagine the depth of change and freedom that's possible when you no longer mimic the points of view and limitations of others!

*Biom***e***metics are human-made processes, substances, devices or systems that imitate nature ~ things like vitamins, robotics, artificial intelligence, etc. In the opinion of prominent researchers, our neural network is a hypothetical biom***e***metic computer that works by making associations and educated guesses, and one which learns from its own mistakes. Please Note: While the typical spelling (as of this writing) of bio***meme***tic utilizes an 'i', I've used an '***e***' in reference to m**e**mes.

When measuring happiness, many researchers use a ratio of positive to negative emotions, indicating that the frequency of the emotions matters more than the intensity. Having 3 or more positives for every negative emotion constitutes the best recipe for happiness. This appears to be true for approximately 20% of people. Having 2 positives to 1 negative is the norm for most, while the minority are said to be languishing at or below a one-to-one ratio. A quote by William Penn comes to mind here: *"The secret to happiness is to count your blessings while others are adding up their troubles."* What percentage of *your* energy is spent on the former vs. the latter?

We tend to relate our quality of happiness with our sense of well-being, which is subjective in that it consists of our individual thoughts, feelings and perception of our life in relation to our expectations - *Expectation* being comprised of *belief* and *anticipation*: Belief being your current choice of perception with anticipation as supposing to receive something which you believe you're currently lacking. Not only does expectation tend to produce disappointment, it also takes you out of the present by placing your focus into the future. The seed of your expectations is -*You guessed it*, your programming ~ more succinctly, your beliefs, which we'll discuss in depth during Chapter Eleven. It's no surprise that expectation is a major culprit behind disappointment, perceived limitation and a less than exuberant quality of happiness.

"Happiness is reality minus expectations." ~ Warren Buffet

In his 2001 best-selling book, *Authentic Happiness*, Martin E.P. Seligman, Ph.D. proposed that we all have a particular Happiness '*Set Point*'; and while we can improve or hinder our well-being, we aren't likely to take long leaps in either direction from this set point. His initial theory and equation asserts that 90% of our level of happiness is a combination of a genetic set point and our individual choices with the remaining 10% relating to life events and our capacity for adapting to good and bad fortune.

We saw earlier that although we may (*albeit unknowingly*) hold the belief that genetic heredity is a, if not 'the' key determining factor where physical dis-ease is concerned, we also saw that we can influence that factor by choosing whether to subscribe to that belief or adopt another. In my mind, choosing to adopt another would significantly increase the percentage of our voluntary control where our happiness is concerned. It would also be more in line with the utilization of the Universal Laws of Nature.

Authentic Happiness launched the revolutionary new science of *Positive Psychology*, a recent branch of psychology, indicating that while traditional psychotherapy focuses on our troubles, positive psychology focuses on our strengths. Further studies yielded evidence that this set point can, indeed, be manipulated, indicating that almost half of our happiness is dependent upon our discretion and that it can be cultivated.

In his 2011 book, *Flourish*, Dr. Seligman surmises that real, lasting happiness comes from focusing on one's strengths. He provides readers with exercises to explore their own understanding of happiness as well as their virtues, providing tools for working with them in order to bring more positive meaning and enhancement to all aspects of one's life. He emphasizes that in doing so and living with flexible optimism, our happiness flourishes.

An important aspect of happiness is having an understanding of ourselves and the nature of our purpose. The manner by which each of us goes about doing so can be understood by considering what Caroline Myss refers to as our *Sacred Contract.* Caroline is a New York Times best-selling Author whose material conveys that each of us is guided by a *Sacred Contract* that our Soul made before we were born. This contract is comprised of the experiences we'll have and our relationships with the people who will help us learn the lessons we've agreed to work on. Each of these relationships represents an individual *contract* which is part of our overall *Sacred Contract.* Our free will plays a key role within our contracts. Caroline refers to this role as our *choice point* wherein we are provided with opportunities for growth which can come in the form of challenges at work, dissolutions of old relationships, the formation of new ones, etc.

She asserts that we're encoded with a set of 12 primary archetypes (*personality prototypes or traits*). These are like beta versions of ourselves. In software development, *beta* is a test version of a program. Four of these archetypes are universal and related to survival: Child, Victim, Prostitute, and Saboteur. The other eight are drawn from a vast storehouse of archetypes dating back to the dawn of human history which play key roles in relation to living at our highest potential. Caroline says that although archetypes are impersonal patterns of influence that are both ancient and universal, they become personalized when they are part of our individual psyche (our mind, Soul or Spirit).

Since your *Sacred Contract* is embodied in a support system of twelve archetypes, it's best to think of them as intimate companions as they provide the foundation for your personality, beliefs, motivations and actions. They take an active role as guardians and inner allies, alerting you when you are in danger of falling into destructive or *shadow* behavior. The Saboteur, for instance, warns you when you're in a situation where you tend to sabotage your own best interests.

Once you learn to recognize such a pattern and heed its signal, your Saboteur becomes your friend, assisting you to avoid selling out.

Caroline explains that our contract is made up of all of the elements and components of our lives, yet it can't be reduced to any one of them by itself. She says that you can view your contract as your overall relationship to your personal and Spiritual power in that it determines how you work with your energies. Finding and fulfilling your *Sacred Contract* also depends on how much you're willing to surrender to divine guidance. Caroline's experience of working with people led her to develop an insightful and ingenious process for deciphering our *Sacred Contract* using a new theory of archetypes that builds on the works of Jung, Plato and many other contemporary thinkers. In coming to know your archetypal companions, you begin to see how to live your life in ways that make the best use of your personal power and lead you to your greatest potential.

It is my belief that this describes our purpose ~ to learn, grown and evolve through our experiences and the path we have chosen for doing so in this lifetime. Our Soul knows its purpose; and there is confirmation in the heaviness of deviating from it and the lightness experienced by following our heart along that path. In addition to her book, *Sacred Contracts*, Caroline also provides an on-line course of the same name. I have personally found Caroline's work brilliantly profound and instrumental in helping me identify and understand these archetypes, my sacred contracts and the roles they play in my life – an invaluable asset from any perspective, yet particularly where purpose and happiness are concerned.

In her New York Times best-selling book, *Happy For No Reason*, transformational expert, Marci Shimoff discusses what she calls '*The Happiness Continuum*' as illustrated below:

Unhappy	Happy For Bad Reason	Happy For Good Reason	Happy For No Reason
Depressed	High from Unhealthy addictions	Satisfaction from healthy experiences	Inner state of peace & well-being

◄────────────────────►

EXTERNAL **INTERNAL**

Marci notes that many of us may seek to raise our level of happiness and make ourselves feel better through developing and partaking in escapes or addictions such as eating, shopping, sex, alcohol or drugs. Unfortunately these temporary escapes not only do not cultivate authentic, enduring happiness, but tend only to compound *un*happiness. We also expend a tremendous amount of energy achieving or acquiring things that we believe will bring us happiness, such as financial prosperity. However, this is only half the story because if these things are lost, so too is the happiness they prompted.

During her research, Marci found 21 common habits integrated within the lives of the people she interviewed who considered themselves to be essentially happy. She incorporates these habits in her *Seven Steps to Being Happy from the Inside Out,* illustrating them with her *Building a Home for Happiness*:

1.	Foundation, Your Personal Power	Take Ownership of Your Happiness
2.	Pillar of the Mind	Don't Believe Everything You Think
3.	Pillar of the Heart	Let Love Lead
4.	Pillar of the Body	Make Your Cells Happy
5.	Pillar of the Soul	Plug Yourself In to Spirit
6.	The Roof	Live a Life Inspired by Purpose
7.	The Garden	Cultivate Nourishing Relationships

Marci elaborates on these in her book and provides practical methods and tools for developing each of them. She enlightens us to the manner by which we can achieve internal, unconditional, enduring happiness independent of external influences by offering a breakthrough approach to being happy from the inside out - No matter what's going on in your life.

The compelling accolades and endorsements for Marci's book are many. Bill Harris, Director of Centerpointe Research Institute, says that Marci has *'cracked the code for being happy'.* I second that sentiment and highly recommend her book. Not only will it change the way you perceive happiness and provide you with practical habits for happy living, *just reading it will help you feel happier!*

Consider what your personal *Secret Sauce* Recipe for Happiness consists / would consist of. What key elements from the banquet of life would you choose to embellish? As you compose your recipe, I'd like you to make note of a few elements which tend to muddle our perception and encumber our capacity for authentic happiness.

Control (Stubbornness, Flexibility): Consciously choose not to waste your energy focusing on that which is outside of your control. Remember our discussion on allowance, keeping in mind that persistence is not synonymous with stubbornness.

"When being happy is more important than being right, you won't have to pretend anymore." -Ricky Williams

Remorse (Living in the Past) - Being Present: Express gratitude for your past and the wisdom it bestowed, but don't languish there.
"Life is only available in the present moment." -Thich Nhat Hanh

Perfection (Jealousy, Admiration, Appreciation):
There is no such thing as perfection. There is only ideal, which is unique to each of us.

"Happiness is not getting what you want; it's appreciating what you have." -Michael Josephson

Insecurity, Judgment & Negativity (Approval, Points of View):
Things to keep in mind:

- The only approval required is your own.
  Everything else is just an interesting point of view.
- *"What others think of you is really none of your business."* -*Martha Graham*
- *"The highest form of human intelligence is to observe yourself without judgment."* -*Jiddu Krishnamurti*

~ *Anything is possible in the mind of a positive thinker.* ~

Anger, Frustration, Conditions and Expectations: Simply put in the words of Elizabeth Kenny: "*He who angers you conquers you.*" By allowing the influence of others to determine your state of being, you surrender all of your power to them. By living your life to please others, you place your happiness into their hands. Allowing your happiness to be expectant or dependent upon someone or something external is a futile pursuit. Happiness is an internal state of being.

Excuses (Procrastination): We'll discuss this in detail during Chapter Six. For now, the proverb: *There's no time like the present* sufficiently sums it.

Money: The way money is coded - more accurately, *mis*-coded - within our belief system is often the culprit behind our misgivings around it. The Hedonic Treadmill Theory likens the pursuit of happiness to a person on a treadmill who has to keep working just to stay in the same place. According to this theory, as a person makes more money, their expectations and desires rise in tandem, resulting in no permanent gain in happiness. So, although it can subsidize many comforts, pleasures and distractions, increasing your income doesn't necessarily raise your happiness level. It simply puts you into a higher tax bracket.

Money does not afford happiness or virtue, nor does it avail unhappiness or evil - unless your belief system leads you there. Some wealthy people are regarded as evil by others because of these types of belief systems. The adage *Money is the root of all evil* is a misinterpretation of an entry in the bible which reads: *For the love of money is a root of all kinds of evil. Some people eager for money have wandered from the faith and pierced themselves with many griefs." [1 Timothy 6:10]* The subtle changes of *money* (substituted for *Love of* money) and *root of all evil* (substituted for root of *all kinds of evil*) generated quite a Meme. In a biblical sense, sin is the root of evil, not money itself. Money is neither good nor evil; it's simply a medium of exchange. The manner by which you acquire and utilize money is a reflection of who you are and what you value. Whether it's good or evil is a matter of judgment – either yours or those of others – based on the underlying beliefs.

While financial condition can affect our level of exuberance, happiness and unhappiness are not prejudiced regarding financial specifications. They are elements unto themselves governed by internal influences. It's interesting to note that many lottery winners lose most of their winnings within a relatively short period of time. This is because their belief system does not support that level of abundance leading them to make choices that bring their life back into alignment with their beliefs. It has been said that you will only allow yourself to have up to your level of self-worth - a topic we'll discuss further during Chapter Ten.

Think of all the good you could contribute to the world
with an abundance of financial resources!

While it is wise to consider the financial aspects of your choices, money alone ought not be the ultimate determining factor regarding any aspect of your life, especially happiness. Consider this: *What if money weren't an issue?* Allow yourself to embrace this fully. Feel what this would be like on all levels. Once you're in that space, ask yourself: If money weren't an issue,

- What would I choose?
- What reality would I create as my life?
- Who are the people that I would have or not have in my life?
- What would living in this reality actually be like?

With this in mind, how about editing the code or deleting the files associated with the limitations you perceive relative to money being the primary obstruction holding your happiness hostage?

Everything this is and brings up and anything that stands in the way of my creating and living this reality, whether known or unknown consciously or unconsciously that is limiting me where this is concerned, I choose to release and transmute its energy to a higher vibrational frequency across all timelines and energetic fields under grace with ease. And so it is.

Regardless of what you may currently *think,* abundance is infinite and there is plenty for everyone. Money is like air - you breathe in, you breathe out, and there is always more. We limit ourselves by thinking that money can only come from certain sources when in fact, *We* are the source of our abundance. Our jobs, investments and other avenues from which we derive money are merely the channels by which it's delivered – All of which are governed according to our belief system.

"More gold has been mined from the mind of man than the earth itself." -Napoleon Hill

Something to consider: What if you chose to remove the pressure of any judgments, conclusions or expectations related to what happiness is or perceptions of what it *should* be, insuring that you never fell short of any *standard*? What if you set *ease* as the primary focus of your living, intrinsically experiencing more happiness as a result?

Now let's have a look at some of the more desirable ingredients. While individual preference and taste may vary, any recipe for Happiness optimally includes these essentials:

Passion: What are you passionate about? What do you love to do? What are you really good at? Many of us have difficulty answering these questions definitively when it comes to revealing purpose in our lives. I'd like to assert that passion and purpose are not synonymous. Purpose equates to reason while passion equates to enthusiasm. Referring back to my comment in Chapter Four - supposing that the purpose of our life is to have a physical experience, it is our passion which influences the lightness, fulfillment and expansion of that life. It is simply a matter of *what* we prefer to experience.

Janet Bray Attwood and Chris Attwood's New York Times best-selling book, *The Passion Test: The Effortless Path to Discovering Your Life Purpose,* is rated the world's #1 tool for discovering your passions and finding your purpose. *The Passion Test* is a simple, powerful set of tools for discovering your passions and aligning your life with what matters most to you. The Attwoods provide a free *Personal Passion Profile* on their site. By answering seven simple questions, you'll be presented with a detailed analysis of your answers demonstrating where you stand in living your passions and what you can do to go to the next level.

"If you don't build your dream, someone else will hire you to help them build theirs." -*Dhirubhai Ambani*

"I honestly think it is better to be a failure at something you love than to be a success at something you hate." -George Burns

Forgiveness: Forgiveness is the act of choosing freedom from the toxicity of *un*forgiveness. It is a gift of grace and freedom -See *Remorse* above. We'll discuss this in detail during Chapter Seven.

Allowance: As we saw in Chapter Three, acceptance is a place of non-judgment where you are in total allowance of all things.

Gratitude: Gratitude is the currency of the Universe. Cultivate an *attitude of gratitude*. When you live in the vibration of gratitude, you appreciate more to be grateful for.

"In our daily lives, we must see that it is not happiness that makes us grateful, but gratefulness that makes us happy."
-Albert Clarke quoted in *Speak Peace in a World of Conflict* From *What You Say Next Will Change Your World* by Marshall B. Rosenberg

Love: We'll discuss this in detail during Chapter Ten. For now, though, consider this:

Love is all there is.
We are love.
Through love - ease, well-being and happiness are alive.
Love is all there is.

Now there's a flavor of circular logic that's worth looping through!

I'd like you to take a few moments to recall a time in your life when you considered yourself to have been in a place of happiness, perhaps even a state of bliss. This could be a time from your distant or recent past or referring to your state at present. See the sights, hear the sounds and feel the feelings. Close your eyes if you like and allow yourself a few moments in that space, being that version of yourself and enjoying the lightness of its essence. Once you're fully engaged in this energy, make note of the aspects:

- What's going on in my life - What am I doing?
- Who are the people in my life, and what are my relationships like?
- What key elements are prominent in my life at this time?
- What inspires me to get out of bed in the morning and takes my mind to reflect upon with gratitude in the evening?
- Do I feel loved? Am I *in* love?
- What is it about this energy, space and consciousness which quantifies it as happiness for me?

Make note of everything that comes to you:

____
____
____
____
____

Would your response to that alien differ, even slightly, now from the one you'd initially composed?

Once you experience them, the sensations of memories and states of being become and remain part of you. Those of high vibrational frequency are your *Secret Sauce.* You can whip up a batch and partake of them at any time of your choosing to nurture a graceful, enduring affiliation with intrinsic happiness. It's been said that happiness is like breathing; it cannot be taught or learned, it can only be practiced. Happiness is a vibration that you send out to the Universe. The more you feel good, the more the Universe provides to you to feel good about.

When I was growing up, my Mother always told
me that happiness was the key to life.
When I went to school, they asked me what
I wanted to be when I grow up.
I wrote down 'Happy'. They told me that I
didn't understand the assignment.
I told them that they didn't understand life.

For more information, please visit Resources.

Musings…

"Change your thoughts and you change your world." -*Norman Vincent Peale*

Chapter 6

Shiny Things & Addictions ~ The Art of Distraction & Self Sabotage

In this Chapter, you'll consider what may be detracting you from living your full potential and personal best.

We are all subject to habitual patterns in one form or another. They are learned behaviors derived from redundant thoughts and emotions. Habitual patterns are not so much about the forms they take as they are about the energy behind them. As with our native tongue, we learn the language of habit in that we pick up the energy of not being present – not acknowledging or addressing, avoiding or escaping what *is* in some ways. So let's have a look at the various forms of this energy.

The Diversion ~ When the Subconscious Goes Cyber Shopping

"Self-sabotage is when we say we want something yet go about making sure it doesn't happen." -*Alyce P. Cornyn-Selby*

During the course of my *me-search* on this topic, an acronym emerged:

Distraction:	Diversions preventing you from giving full attention to something else
Sabotage:	Deliberate action aimed at weakening through subversion, obstruction, disruption or destruction
Procrastination:	Intentionally and habitually delaying

In I/T, *DSP* (digital signal processing) is the representation of digital signals by a sequence of numbers or symbols and the processing of these signals. Although I'd been receiving them, overlooking these signals brought me to the same frustration at the end of every day. In spending the bulk of my energy attending to everything and everyone else around me, I consistently ran short of bandwidth for myself and the things I wished to bring about.

While you can't change something you're not fully aware of, I decided to take a long, hard look at mine – A lovely collection of elements such as blame, shame, anger, regret, fear and doubt - a mere few of the things that remove our choice and make us non-functional by masking what's really going on in our life. While my mind itemized the excuses and did its finger pointing, I knew on some level that ultimately the sabotage was self-inflicted. There's nothing more humbling than an *Aha* such as this.

"To be aware of a single shortcoming within oneself is more useful than to be aware of a thousand in somebody else." -*Dalai Lama*

In the midst of my review, I encountered an interesting pothole – a writer's block (one of a few) which lasted for several days. I'd been diligently working on this book for almost a year. There were days along the way when I allowed my focus to be redirected; but at this point, I was in the flow and working at a steady pace…until I hit this topic. I began considering my choices thus far, pondering their alternatives had I known then what I know now; and I could see the influences of distraction, undesirable programming and allowing myself to be covered in *'should'*. It's been said that when you write a book, particularly one of this nature, all of your stuff comes up. *Boy is That an understatement!* I tended to a few other things while kibitzing about this. Unfortunately, each time I returned to writing, the block accompanied me. How ironic that this would occur while I was focusing on the very subject itself.

I began asking *What's my purpose here? What am I 'doing'? What footprint will I impart, if any, on this world?* As if a thunder clap suddenly broke the eerie silence, it struck me. I was doing it – *being* the change I wanted to see; and I was sharing the wisdom of my experiences in a book. I felt a sudden rush of excitement. Yet it quickly subsided when I realized that, as far as my writing was concerned, I was still blocked.

I thought *Who am 'I' to write a book? What do I have to say that anyone would be interested in hearing or that hasn't already been said? What if it's terrible; What if I fail?* In my frustration, I *Googled* 'Writer's Block'. Per Wiki: *It can manifest as the affected writer viewing their work as inferior or unsuitable when in fact, it could be the opposite.* Well, then, which is it?!

I decided to visit my Son's ferret, Charlene. She cheerfully greeted me, and I watched as she did what we refer to as her 'Happy Dance'. She'd pivot and scamper about like a pinball, exploring and enjoying her vibrancy for life. This little creature embodies presence and joy and is the epitome of shiny thing – with one key exception, she *Is* the shiny thing. She doesn't distract, procrastinate or *pursue* happiness. She lives happily in the present moment without limitation - the same way we do as children. As I watched her, I recalled my Son's first ferret, Blizzard. A heart condition resulted in a very short life for him. However, in the time he was with us, Blizzard thoroughly enjoyed his life and brought us all so much joy. Reflecting on how fragile and precious life is brought home the true meaning of the saying *There's no time like the present*, which is all we really have. With this, I eagerly returned to the keyboard – yet the inertia persisted.

As I listened to the rain on the roof – one of my favorite soothing and meditative pastimes, I closed my eyes and thought *Well, if I'm the only person helped by writing this book, then it's worth it.* Quite a statement of self-worth, I thought. As I opened my eyes, they fell upon a small plaque a friend had given to me – A starfish bearing the words *Making a difference, one life at a time.* I picked it up and read the full text:

A little boy walked carefully along a crowded beach
where starfish by the hundreds lay within his reach.
They washed up with each wave, far as the eye could see.
Each one would surely die if they were not set free. So
one by one, he rescued them. Then a stranger called
"*It won't make a difference...You cannot save them all*". Yet he
tossed another back toward the ocean's setting sun, responding
with deep compassion: "*I made a difference to that one!*"

I thought: What if this book *does* help others, perhaps countless others? What if I *am* a contribution? In that moment, I realized what the block was about: *Fear.* I would be vulnerable – seen and heard, likely judged as well - not so comfy for a behind-the-scenes support type. I had my doubts but also a sudden enthusiasm. I felt as though I was on a roller coaster - *sitting in the front row no less.* Incidentally, I'm not fond of roller coasters. I've experienced the sensation during a rogue adventurous streak or two, but I'm typically the stuff holder/picture taker where they're concerned. I could hear the click-click-click as the cart made its way up the incline. While the prospect was exciting, I had that sudden rush of *"I want to get off!"* At this point, though, failure, success or perhaps a combined fear of both, I was not turning back.

I was at a precipice of ambitious proportions. A number of significant aspects of my life were beginning to shift in a positive direction based on my recent guided choices and actions. I felt as though I was standing at a door, knowing that on the other side of that door was everything I desired or perceived as missing. It was that pretty box under the Christmas tree with my name on it. All I had to do was open that box, take hold of the key and open that door - So simple and exciting; yet at the same time, so excruciatingly frightening. Fear and excitement being the same physiologically, I thought *What if there's no such thing as failure - or fear for that matter? What if I haven't missed a thing and it's all been beautifully orchestrated according to my Sacred Contract?*

I surmised that there will always *appear* to be speed bumps or perceived limitations in life; and that they exist to provide contrast, choice and growth. All that's required is viewing them as interesting points of view and choosing what feels lighter. Follow your heart from there, and you can't possibly go wrong; *Right?* Just then, my little Saboteur pipes up with *"What a lovely bunch of frou-frou. Sure, just click your heels and make a wish."* Although I was infused with a level of enthusiasm, I surmised that the Universe would simply have to prove it to me. On a deeper level and more accurately, though, I knew that I would have to demonstrate it to myself.

The sarcasm of our Saboteur may be entertaining, and they may not always deliver their messages in a gentle manner. They have their directive; period. However, keep in mind that your Saboteur is actually a well-intentioned friend, your *Guardian of Choice.* When your Saboteur contributes their two cents, it's their way of reminding you of your capacity of free will and cautioning you not to sell yourself short.

It's been said that folks who purposefully create their lives employ the Universal Laws of Nature, often without consciously realizing it. Marci Shimoff said it best in *The Secret*: "*The only difference between people who live in the magic of life and those who don't is that the people who live in the magic of life have habituated ways of being, and magic happens with them wherever they go.*"

After relocating to Washington State, colleagues of mine from Massachusetts recalled me saying "*When I get to Microsoft, I'll have my Lexus®.*" Noting that I'd used the word *when*, not *if.* Honestly, if anyone had told me prior to my doing so that I'd leave everything familiar to me and move across the country, I'd have told them they were nuts. In hindsight, though, my higher self was speaking, and I was listening, taking inspired action and utilizing the natural laws without consciously realizing it. I employed a similar approach when purchasing the home I currently live in, although a bit more purposefully after discovering *The Secret* and the Laws of the Universe*;* but that's a story for another day. I followed my heart, doing what felt lighter and enjoyed every minute of it. Now *that's* how to play the game of life! However, *You can't' win if you don't play.* Well then, let the games begin!

My life to that point had been all about work before play. Yet there was very little play; and as they say: *All work and no play makes Jane a dull girl. Oooh* - I just flashed on a scene from *The Shining,* where Jack's wife discovers that rather than writing his novel, he's been typing this idiom over and over onto countless reams of paper. *Talk about writer's block - Yeesh!* At this point, though, I went back to my notes and was able to continue writing.

I'd like to note that while there are times when you feel that you *should* be focusing on X, yet inspiration and motivation are MIA, there's a lot to be said for allowing yourself to re-focus temporarily, particularly where creative matters are concerned. I've received some of my greatest inspirations regarding my *shoulds* while allowing myself to do so. Note, however, that is not the same as procrastination.

Procrastination is a fabulous tool for self-sabotage. When you understand your mind, you can utilize it vs. being governed by it. So let's have another peek at your brain to get a sense of how this creature operates and how we can minimize its unfavorable influence. Procrastination is the outcome of a conflict between your Limbic System and your Prefrontal Cortex, and the neuroscience behind it is actually rather interesting.

Your Limbic System, being the hard drive where your memories and software reside, is also the storage area of your survival instincts. It's your Limbic System that signals you to pull your hand away from fire to avoid getting burned. It's also the pleasure center of your brain in that it finds ways of evading unexciting tasks in favor of more pleasurable ones. To make matters worse, it runs on autopilot.

The Prefrontal Cortex (PC) is where your planning and decision-making processes are managed. It's in charge of your impulse control. Unlike your Limbic System, you must deliberately put the keys in the ignition, kick it into gear and pay attention to the road. When your PC's not fully engaged in a task, it will go into sleep mode. When this happens, your autopilot can, and will, take the wheel. Before you know it, your focus is AWOL (absent without official leave) and your time literally evaporates while your auto pilot has a field day clad in a t-shirt sporting its motto:

> *"Never put off till tomorrow what may be done the day after tomorrow just as well." ~Mark Twain*

Neuroscience discusses the evolution of our brain and subdivides it into three parts, Reptilian, Middle and New. The reptilian is the most primitive, consisting of the brainstem and cerebellum, similar to that of a reptile. It's responsible for our survival instincts; and it only has two responses: On or Off. The Middle Brain is the Limbic or Mammalian Brain which evolves as we become more complex. It's responsible for your judgments and emotions which tend to influence, if not drive, your behavior. It has a modulating effect on the Reptilian Brain in that the Limbic System is brought into a primitive on again/off again response of gradation ~ You can be a little on or off or significantly on or off. The New Brain, which has evolved over the last couple hundred thousand years, is the Neocortex. Neo means new, and it's the covering of the brain which is responsible for your higher mental functions. It enables you to choose whether to react at all and how. These three parts of the brain communicate with each other through the interconnections of neural pathways.

One would *think* that because of evolution, Neo would be the Chief. However, it's the Lizard who wears all the feathers. With safety and comfort as its directive, it translates all incoming information into one of The Four F's: Food, Fight, Flight, Fornication - something to eat, something to fight, something to run away from or something to have sex with. It feeds on distraction because its purpose is to keep you in your *Happy Place.*

Your thinking brain (PC) feeds on logic, having the ability to rationalize and make decisions or choices. However, the information it bases these choices on is first filtered through the bottom two brains. This filtering process sends chemicals throughout your body which create sensations - stress, overwhelm, dread. These sensations are the escape hatches through which you lose focus in avoiding conflicts such as *'I'm afraid'*, *'I should'* or *'I don't wanna'*.

This is all very interesting, from a technical standpoint, but how can we utilize this information to motivate us in accomplishing our goals and actualizing our objectives?

Susan Jenkins is a gracious Shamanic Healer, and I love her analogy of procrastination and resistance. She likens them to a young child in that the more we overlook them, the more persistent, demanding and disruptive they become. When we stop and turn our undivided attention to them, meeting them in their essence with unconditional love, magic happens. They automatically calm down and center because they are receiving what they want and need.

Procrastination is fueled by resistance. When resistance is present, procrastination blocks your path. Procrastination and distraction are self-sabotage's best friends – with habitual escapes providing the entertainment – so don't let them gang up on you. If you ignore them, they will stalk you. So let's turn our attention to procrastination and get to the root and purpose of the resistance which lies beneath it.

Resistance is described as the refusal to accept or comply with something; the ability to be unaffected by something or someone, especially adversely. Resistance, however, provides an opportunity to explore our inner world and make adjustments to our software. That being said, we'll look to uncover the benefit(s) it may be providing for us. Perhaps it's a matter of rebellion wherein you're resistance is to authority, control or convention. Perhaps you're dragging your feet on your partner's request to clean out the garage because you were punished as a child for not completing your chores within the imposed timeline. Your resistance may be a matter of rebellion in some way. Postponing such a task until next Saturday because it's been raining for two weeks and the weather is conducive to playing golf with your buddies is one thing. However, when the endeavor is of significance (i.e. adopting a healthier lifestyle) and the procrastination turns from days into weeks into months and years as a habit or pattern, there's an obstruction that you'll want to examine.

Perhaps the procrastination stems from fear - of failure and/or success or perhaps of the unknown. Failure and success are a matter of perception - points of view and judgments. Keep in mind, though, that the actualization of success becomes elusive when you're blocked by fear while the outcome remains unknown. It's not fear itself that keeps you stuck; it's choosing to hold on to it that does. It causes you to limit yourself and lose your soul. Deepak Chopra once touched on this by reminding us that what is known has already happened and that the unknown is where we live, breathe and move; and yet, we're afraid of it. Perhaps if the unknown were known, there would be no fear. The unknown, however, is the field of possibility – which we'll discuss deeper in Chapter Eleven. When we are blocked by fear, we close the door to possibility. In actuality, fear is a messenger – typically indicating that you're on the brink of a breakthrough. Keeping in mind that fear and excitement are physiologically the same energy, by facing fear and stepping into your power, you open the door to possibility.

"Our deepest fear is not that we're inadequate. It is that we are powerful beyond measure." -Marianne Williamson

With this in mind, it's essential to uncover the essence behind your procrastination and self-sabotage. To this end, I offer enlightening exercises in the back of this book.

Resistance - whether resulting from past trauma or fear of the unknown and the limiting beliefs and emotions they create - is held in every cell of your body energetically. A technique known as EFT (Emotional Freedom Technique) a.k.a. Tapping can assist with acknowledging and clearing the heaviness of these emotions. EFT provides access to the subconscious energy of your beliefs (fears, programs and patterns) vs. consciously thinking and/or talking about them. Nick and Jessica Ortner, creators of *The Tapping Solution,* describe it as a combination of Ancient Chinese Acupressure and Modern Psychology. EFT utilizes the body's energy meridians by tapping on them with your fingertips, restoring balance to your body's energy.

Sanskrit traditions work with your energy field, consisting of energy centers known as Chakras which are considered both receivers and transmitters of energy. Meridians are the pathways in the body through which your energy flows. An article on Acupressure.com* explains the Acupressure and Acupuncture points and Meridians:

> An acupressure point actually has two identities and ways of working. When you stimulate a point in the same area where you feel pain or tension, it's called a local point. That same point can also relieve pain in a part of the body that is distant from the point, in which case it's called a trigger point. This triggering mechanism works through a human electrical channel called a meridian.
>
> The meridians are pathways that connect these points to each other as well as to the internal organs. Just as blood vessels carry the blood that nourishes the body physically, the meridians are distinct channels that circulate electrical energy throughout the body. They're thought to be part of a master communications system of universal life energy, connecting the organs with all sensory, physiological and emotional aspects of the body. This physical network of energy also contains key points that we can use to deepen our spiritual awareness as we heal ourselves.

This material is available more in depth through online courses and trainings available at Acupressure.com. Michael Reed Gach, Ph.D.

The EFT Tapping Points are at the ends of your meridians:

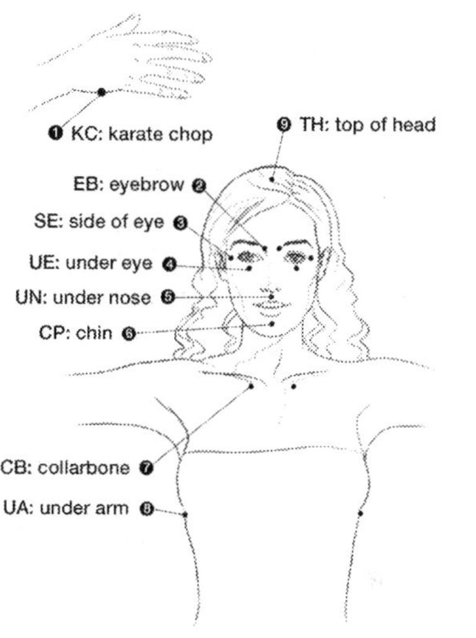

This EFT Tapping Points image is provided courtesy of Nick and Jessica Ortner – The Tapping Solution http://www.thetappingsolution.com

Dr. Dawson Church, Ph.D. performed a randomized, controlled trial to determine the impact of EFT on stress by measuring Cortisol levels in the body. He found the average cortisol reduction was 24% - almost 50% in some subjects with no significant cortisol reduction in those undergoing an hour of traditional talk therapy. Dr. Church's *Stress Project* teaches Tapping to veterans suffering with PTSD. Results show an astounding 63% average decrease in symptoms after six rounds.

Emotional freedom comes from being at ease with your emotions. When you allow them to rise up and be present with them, you can process them and harness their energy to heal, transform and create.

With Tapping, you're not just reading a book, listening to a lecture, discussing your problems or *thinking*, you're interacting with yourself and your energy system, which goes to the cellular level. By gently tapping on these points, you can tell the whole story – identify your feelings and beliefs around X where you've been sabotaging yourself. Tapping brings awareness and allows you to acknowledge your Saboteur. Without criticizing or shoulding all over yourself, you can acknowledge what's going on and get to the root of it so that you can nudge the inertia without chastising yourself. For example: While tapping, you can use statements such as *"Even though I've been procrastinating and sabotaging because of my fears, I accept who I am and that I'm doing the best that I can."* Once you've identified your fears, you can use statements such as *"I'm afraid of X. No wonder I've been procrastinating, limiting and sabotaging myself. I forgive myself for doing so. I'm just trying to stay safe. I understand it now, and I choose to accept who I am and love myself anyway. I can choose to release my fear and let go of the sabotage. I feel better already."*

It's not necessary to identify every incident around X or do any tedious onion peeling around any *Why's*. You simply bring up the issue and the beliefs around it. This is how you can open files within your system and edit their code. Tapping produces a calming effect, bringing your system back on line. When an issue becomes nothing more than an interesting point of view, you can then rewrite and rewire it. You can consider "Maybe I *can*..." vs. being stuck like a deer in the headlights.

Clearing your blocks and raising your vibration positively affects every aspect of your living. EFT is a free, simple technique that you can implement in relation to any issue either on your own or in the company of like-minded folks. Tapping is educational, expansive, healing and empowering; and it's fun. I highly recommend implementing this practice within your life. The Ortners provide a multitude of information and guidance on their web site (See *Resources*).

The Procrastination Equation: How to Stop Putting Things Off and Start Getting Stuff Done by Dr. Piers Steel provides a mix of psychology, science and self-help methods explaining why procrastination is dangerously on the rise and how we can overcome destructive patterns that affect our health and happiness to create more positive lives. Dr. Steel provides a *Procrastination Survey* on his site which offers a detailed diagnosis of your procrastination profile, along with some scientifically proven tips for taming your tendency to put things off. These tools can provide you with a foundation from which to evaluate and proceed.

I suggest taking at least one step, no matter how small, in the direction of your objectives every day. You can neutralize the temptation of falling prey to overwhelm by focusing on that one step and acknowledging yourself for taking it. As you do, the next step(s) will be revealed to you. By trusting the process, your journey will unfold organically.

Have you ever had the experience of simply beginning or perhaps completing something you've been procrastinating and find yourself thinking or saying things like *Well, that wasn't so bad* or *Why didn't I do this sooner?* ~ Funny that. I offer some of my own tips for navigating through procrastination in the back of this book.

"Do not wait. The time will never be 'just right'. Start where you stand, work with whatever tools you have at your command, and better tools will be found as you go along." ~Napoleon Hill

Dis-traction is a lack of traction to proceed. Affirm to yourself that *Today, I will not allow myself to be distracted. I will focus only on my objectives and intentions.* When you choose to be steadfast on your path, you won't allow yourself to be distracted by anything or anyone – no matter *how* shiny they may be.

In closing this portion of the chapter, I'd just like to say that the only limitations are those that you perceive and allow; and there is no time like the present to perceive other possibilities and allow yourself to make a different choice.

Oh, and if you'd like a snack whilst coasting off into the wild blue yonder of distraction, procrastination or waiting for the other shoe to drop, might I suggest a sampling of your *Secret Sauce* from the previous chapter.

"Never put off till tomorrow what you can do today." -Thomas Jefferson

The Escape ~ Path to Affliction or Portal to Reflection?

"I am a work in progress." ~Violet Yates

Autobiography in Five Short Chapters

~ Portia Nelson

Chapter One
I walk down the street.
There's a deep hole in the sidewalk.
I fall in.
I am lost…I am helpless.
It isn't my fault.
It takes forever to find a way out.

Chapter Two
I walk down the same street.
There is a deep hole in the sidewalk.
I pretend I don't see it.
I fall in again.
I can't believe I am in the same place.
But it isn't my fault.
It still takes a long time to get out.

Chapter Three
I walk down the same street.
There is a deep hole in the sidewalk.
I see it is there.
I still fall in…It's a habit…but
my eyes are open.
I know where I am.
It is my fault.
I get out immediately.

Chapter Four
I walk down the same street.
There's a deep hole in the sidewalk.
I walk around it.

Chapter Five
I walk down another street

~

In this section, you'll consider addictions that may be present in your life; what they are; and more importantly, what objective they serve within your life. Typically when you hear the word *Addiction*, images that come to mind are of those afflicted by substance abuse. However, there's a plethora of non-substance, pattern and process addictions we subscribe to whether we're consciously aware of it or not

Addictions are coping mechanisms we adopt as means of survival. Some may be inconsequential in moderation and the overall scheme of things - shopping, video gaming, gambling, dieting and exercise, the internet and television to name but a few. Many of us have convinced ourselves that we can't possibly function without that first cup of coffee in the morning. *~Grin~* The scene from the movie *The Bucket List* where Morgan Freeman informs Jack Nicholson of the origins of Kopi Lewak just came to mind here. If your addiction(s) aren't affecting your life in negative ways, then keep 'em if you like. Just know that they are not the truth of who you really are. However, when an addiction is a behavior that you continue despite the negative consequences it may be bringing into your life and the lives of those around you and you have surrendered your power of choice to these behaviors, it's time to re-evaluate.

In 2011, The American Society of Addiction Medicine (ASAM) released a new definition of addiction, stating that it's a chronic brain disorder and not necessarily a behavioral problem. Addiction is described as a persistent, compulsive dependence on a behavior or substance; the state of being enslaved to a habit or practice or to something that's psychologically or physically habit-forming. Associated descriptions are Infatuation, Compulsion, Obsession and Dependence. While these may represent the symptoms of addiction, they don't disclose the source of their manifestation, nor their purpose. Our objective in discussing this topic is to identify the function and reward you derive from them which keeps you going back for more.

All addictions, regardless of their labels, are the same in that they are expressions of what's going on within. There are energetic and emotional components to them all. The following are from Louise Hay's '*List*' in her book, *You Can Heal Your Life*:

Problem:	Addictions
Probable Cause:	Running from the self. Fear. Not knowing how to love the self.
New Thought Pattern:	I now discover how wonderful I am. I choose to love and enjoy myself.
Problem:	Alcoholism
Probable Cause:	"What's the use?" Feeling of futility, guilt, inadequacy and Self-rejection.
New Thought Pattern:	I live in the now. Each moment is new. I choose to see my self-worth. I love and approve of myself.

Louise L. Hay, You Can Heal Your Life, Copyright 1999 by Louise Hay, Hay House, Inc., Carlsbad, CA

Addictions keep us occupied, focusing on the tasks involved in the maintenance of these disorders, distracting us from living at our full potential. Our species is classified as Human *Be*ings, yet we've become Human *Do*ings in this world and to some degree have forgotten how to *Be*. Workaholism is a common demonstration of this phenomenon. Amidst the busy work of getting it all done, we can become hypnotized into limitation, losing our connection with our true self. All too often, we perceive ourselves as victims, losing sight of our free will and becoming enslaved to habitual limitation. We allow distorted software to validate the restrictions of biased data and manipulate us into believing that we cannot be, do and have everything that we desire. As we saw in Chapter Three, much of our software runs in the background somewhat inconspicuously. *That is, until now.* So let's have a look at the various labels we've prescribed to the species of viruses that elude our cognitive awareness and muddle our perceptions.

OCD (Obsessive-Compulsive Disorder) covers a wide range of addictions: over or under eating, desires to gain muscle or lose fat, various fears and phobias, perfectionism, martyrdom, codependence, the need to be right, win or be in control, to name but a few.

OCD is an anxiety disorder characterized by intrusive thoughts that produce uneasiness, apprehension, worry or fear. Variations of this dis-order are those where perseveration is a possible feature. Perseveration is the repetition of a particular response, such as a word, phrase or behavior, despite the absence or cessation of a stimulus - meaning that although the initial trauma or influence may be in the past, the symptoms or behaviors cultivated by it are maintained and perpetuated.

Examples are: OCPD (Obsessive-Compulsive Personality Disorder), PTSD (Post-Traumatic Stress Disorder) and ADHD (Attention Deficit/Hyperactivity Disorder).

OCD can be considered the base for many addiction stews as it provides a broad range of flavors with which to create and cultivate your particular customized recipes - my little *Cleaning Lady* being one of them. It's difficult for her not to be doing *something* all of the time. Her ingredients include cleaning, organizing and assisting. I'd spend hours putting things away, dusting off, sweeping up and keeping track of everyone's *stuff.* I swear they named that character, M-O, in the movie, Wall-E, after me. My 'house' was always in order, even if it meant not having the time or space for more meaningful things.

Don't get me wrong, it's nice to be organized, have a clean, comfortable home and contribute to those you love, but these need not be gifted to the detriment of self-care and the achievement of your own goals. My validation for Ms. Cleanaholic is that I have difficulty functioning among clutter and that cleaning is a form of meditation for me. *I do some of my best thinking during that activity!* While there is some truth to this, it's basically shiny thing justification.

Oh, my mind was always working. Among all that thinking, however, was a pot of resentment simmering on the stove...until that pot would boil over. What's that saying? *If Mama ain't happy, ain't nobody happy.* It was everyone else's fault for not cleaning up after and taking care of themselves or not contributing more once in a while. It was '*they*' who were not watching the pot. *Truth?* I'd created a fabulous recipe for self-sabotage. It had all the ingredients: Perfectionism, Blame, Shame, Guilt, Codependence, Control, Distraction and Procrastination...*Talk about Martyr Soup!*

Eventually, I reached a point where I'd had enough of that empty feeling at the end of the day. Poor Cinderella was tired, and she had to get up tomorrow and do it all over again. I began to wonder what I was '*doing*'. Why wasn't I moving forward with some of the things I intended to create, like starting a business or writing a book? I finally realized where the bulk of my energy was being spent. *Light Bulb*: By focusing on the organization of everything around me externally, I could make sense out of the chaos, control my environment and fill the voids I'd not been able to as a child and in some of my adult relationships. As long as it *Looked* good, it must *Be* good; *Right*? ***Not!***

Having graduated from Workaholic's Academy, I'd been programmed and fine-tuned for this from the beginning! While my upbringing boasts countless merits, I began to recognize the misguided directives of what was needed. Having invested so much energy to the external, I'd abandoned and numbified the internal. I had learned to escape.

At this point, I realized that it was time for a D&C (Dusting and Cleaning) - *How ironic*. I seriously needed to defrag and reformat my hard drive. *FDISK to the rescue!* Defrag (Defragmentation) is an operating system utility that reorganizes fragments of data on a computer's hard drive to maximize disk space and improve performance. FDISK is a utility used to format your hard disk by partitioning it into sections and specifying those sections for various uses.

Meditation is an incredibly powerful way to defrag your Mind/Body which we'll discuss in depth during Chapter Eleven. *My Advice*: Always ensure that you are not only *on* the list, but at the top of it, as often as possible. There's a reason why they instruct you to put on your own oxygen mask before assisting others on an airplane. *You aren't much use to anyone, including yourself, if you're not breathing!*

While my intention is to focus primarily in the non-substance realm, I'd like to share two accounts relating to this topic that resonated with me. The first is Dyan Cannon's description of an experience with her Husband, Cary Grant, under the influence of LSD. Cary considered himself very Spiritual and asserted that LSD offered a path to truth and enlightenment as a gateway to God, through which he'd found the key to ultimate peace of mind; and he wanted to share it with her. Dyan recounted an LSD experience wherein they were eating cake and ice cream, saying that she could not taste the sweetness or feel the texture of them. Cary's summation was I *am* the sweetness and texture, adding that he wasn't using LSD as a party thing; he was utilizing it to reconnect with his inner peace and presence, the *I Am*.

LSD, an abbreviation of the German term Lysergsaure-Diathylamid for Lysergic Acid Diethylamide (a.k.a. Acid), is considered a hallucinogen; and the characteristics of its effects apply to other hallucinogens: i.e. mescaline, ibogaine and psilocybin.

The second account is that of Ram Daas. During his time as a Harvard Professor, under his birth name of Richard Alpert, Ram Daas was part of the *Psilocybin Project* in the early 1960's along with Professors Timothy Leary, Aldous Huxley and Allen Ginsberg. They conducted their explorations of human consciousness experiments amongst themselves with the use of Psilocybin (psychedelic mushrooms) which he referred to as '*Gifts left by God*'. Psilocybin was used to supplement their practices of transcendental meditation and altered states of awareness in the quest for knowledge regarding consciousness.

During one particular episode, Ram Daas describes himself as having no body yet being aware of the bodies of various aspects of himself in the assorted roles he'd played throughout his life to that point. During this episode, he had an awareness of his true self with all the veils of these identities stripped off. He described the experience as having realized his consciousness.

After one particularly profound experience, Ram Daas received a book entitled *The Tibetan Book of the Dead* which would be read by one monk to another as he was dying. He discovered that what was described in the book - what happens when we die - was strikingly similar to a recent experience he'd had with psilocybin.

During a trip to India, Ram Daas met a Hindu guru, Neem Karoli Baba, whom he called "Maharaj-ji". It was Maharaj-ji who gave him the name Ram Dass, which means Servant of God. One evening, while looking at the brilliant sky of stars, Ram Daas felt his Mother's presence. She'd recently passed away of spleen complications. Maharaj-ji, who only spoke Hindi, made a statement in Ram Daas' direction which he did not understand, albeit for the English word 'Spleen'. He realized in that moment that this guru knew everything about him, feeling that he was in awareness of his Soul. Although he'd only planned to spend two more days in India, Ram Daas did not leave the company of Maharaj-ji for another six months. He shares that although his guru has since crossed over, their relationship has not changed; and their connection remains the same. Ram Daas has fostered his capacity for this level of intrinsic connection to this day.

In 1965, Professor Timothy Leary was noted for commenting that he'd learned more about his brain, its possibilities and psychology in the five hours after using Psilocybin than in the preceding 15 years of his study and research.

We arrive in this world with an intrinsic sense of consciousness and truth. Unfortunately, our mind and heart can become disconnected from this birthright due to the infiltration of bugs and viruses within our system. The experiences of these men are intriguing in that the introduction of mind-altering substances re-opened a channel for them. However, the capacity to do so ~ without the aid of external substances ~ is intrinsic within us all. This connection can be reestablished and nurtured through the choice to consistently practice meditation and mindfulness. WiFi is ever present and infinite in its bandwidth.

What if incorporating this practice could bring you to a perpetual state of ease? Would there then be anything to be distracted by, from or addicted to? What would future generations be like with early integration and proliferation of these practices? What would our world be like with this state as a commonality among us?

"You see things; and you say Why?
I dream things that never were; and I say
Why not?" ~Robert F. Kennedy

~ Everything is possible. It is only our choice that keeps us from it. ~

When what you intend varies from what you're experiencing, it's a sign of disconnection. You may, for instance, vow not to become your parents in some ways. Yet at some point, find yourself saying and doing the very things your parents said and did that were objectionable to you. Perhaps you enjoy a fulfilling yet time-consuming career which affords very little personal time. You may discover that you've inadvertently become the somewhat absent parent you felt neglected by. *What's that song? Cat's in the Cradle ~Harry Chapin.* Through choice and mindfulness, however, things of this nature can be amended.

You may discover that a career path or relationship you've invested a great deal of energy into no longer resonates with you. You may perceive limitation when initially considering a stretch outside of the box or proverbial corner you feel you've painted yourself into. However, disassociating from your purpose and sacrificing your Soul is not a solution. It will only produce more limitation, frustration and misery. Making a stretch, albeit temporarily uncomfortable (and I stress *temporarily*), will enlighten you to possibilities available on avenues beyond any intersection at which you find yourself. It's happened to me. Whether it be careers, relationships or behaviors, at the end of the day, it's never too late to make a new choice.

While the experiences of Cary Grant and Ram Daas demonstrate one perspective, habitually escaping into *Gifts left by God* is considered substance abuse and addiction – especially when no adjustments in your life are made as a result of any enlightenment gained from entertaining them. While medicating the symptoms of distress may provide the temporary illusion of relief, ultimately it serves only to exacerbate and prolong suffering and perpetuates denial. Denial is a trick an addict's mind plays on itself to excuse their behavior. Addiction is a thinking problem before it becomes a process or substance problem. Habitual or addictive thinking is a form of denial in that it deceives you and keeps you from a place of mindfulness and presence which wreaks havoc in your life as well as those around you.

Codependency is another interesting base for addiction stew. I've personally found it quite complimentary with OCD as white wine with fish or red with tenderloin. My team of administrators has engineered multiple productions of this lovely combination which I affectionately refer to as *Cody*. This blend was an encryption of patterns so intricate that it was not only difficult to decipher but initially impossible for me to identify.

Encryption is the conversion of data into cipher text that can't be easily understood by unauthorized people. Decryption (or deciphering) is the conversion of encrypted data back to its original form. It's used for security purposes to protect the integrity of data when in transit over networks (Bank transfers, mobile devices, etc.). It's also used by your subconscious mind.

I'd been on a treasure hunt of sorts for clues to unlock some of the patterns in my life when a friend handed me her copy of Melody Beattie's book, *The Language of Letting Go,* which provides daily meditations for those struggling with the issues of codependency. It seemed as though every passage had been written specifically for me. I'd never even considered this entity, yet realized how it had overlaid so many aspects of my living.

Codependency is a learned behavior, the competence of which is typically adopted during childhood in response to some sort of pain - This competence being a collection of survival and coping skills which congregate alongside your pleasure center in your auto pilot Limbic System. While these particular skills may have been somewhat suitable during the early years, they can be, and often are, problematic in adulthood.

Codependency is a psychological condition or relationship in which a person is controlled or manipulated (or allowing themselves to be) by another who is affected with a pathological condition, typically narcissism or substance addiction. Codependency involves placing a lower priority on one's own needs while being excessively preoccupied with the needs of others. *Well now, this certainly explains a lot.*

Incidentally, Narcissists - characterized by egotism, vanity, pride, or selfishness - are considered natural magnets for the codependent. *Now there's an interesting demonstration of the Law of Attraction!* Not all narcissism is the same, however. The healthy flavor is described as a structural truthfulness of the self, which is contrary to insecurity and inadequacy. *A most interesting display of polarity.*

While researching this entity, I was like a sponge finding hydration in an oasis after crawling through the dessert for what seemed an eternity. Among a sea of information, support and assistance, I came to light on *CodependencyQuiz.com* which inquires, "*Wondering if*

You're Codependent?" and proposes: *"The fact that you're asking this question, taken the time to do some research and are now on this web site leads to one logical conclusion: We have no idea. There's no easy answer to this question. Codependency is not like a physical disease. You can't just get a blood test and have some guy in a white coat look in his microscope and tell you, "Yep, you've got codependency." The best way to decide for yourself is to take the quiz."*

As you can see, they have a sense of humor which is an invaluable ingredient for ease in the process of life, particularly in relation to issues such as these. Incidentally, their content includes a list of *Symptoms of Codependency,* taken directly from another book by Melody Beattie, *Codependent No More.* Interestingly, the first one listed is 'Caretaking'....*I know, right?!*

It was comforting and enlightening to be able to identify what I'd been experiencing in regard to some of the patterns and relationships in my life. The quiz is part of *The Codependency Project,* a comprehensive program developed by Paul Elmore, M.A., M.S., LPCi and Dave McGuire based on experiential transformation techniques. The content is rich, effective and invaluable. I highly recommend connecting with this oasis.

While you may have the best intentions in mind, providing too much support to others, particularly within codependent relationships, often contributes not only to their downfall but to your own as well. Herein, I'd like to make mention of the term 'enabling'. In a negative sense, it relates to dysfunctional behavior intended to help or resolve a problem which actually exacerbates it. It's a relationship wherein one takes responsibility or makes accommodations for another's harmful behavior, shielding them from the harm they're doing and the necessity for amends and change - doing so out of good intention or from fear and insecurity. This is a common theme within relationships where addiction is present.

As an example, a partner may make excuses for and cover the messes created in the wake of an addict's choices and behaviors. Doing so, however, only compounds the problem and blocks the healing, growth and well-being of all concerned. The butterfly story provides a great analogy here. The following is a summation:

> A little girl, seeing a butterfly struggle to emerge from the tiny opening in its cocoon, snipped the cocoon open to assist. Unfortunately, doing so hindered rather than helped the creature. The little girl was disappointed when the butterfly emerged with a swollen body and shriveled wings.
>
> Struggling to emerge from the cocoon is part of its transformational process. The struggle pushes the fluid out of its body and into its wings. Without the struggle, the butterfly would never fly.

In the negative sense, enabling can promote and/or propagate codependency. In a positive sense, however, it is the fostering of healthy patterns which encourage development and growth.

The most prominent, all-inclusive addiction is Polarity - an addiction to contrast, intensity and adrenaline. We tend to function from thoughts, feelings and emotions; and polarity keeps us operating from the trauma and drama, upset and intrigue of those emotions. We can allow ourselves to be sucked in by the gravitational pull of another's planet without consciously being aware of it, which is the incubator for codependent relationships. These affiliations allow both parties to mutually elude their own issues by making those of their partner the focus and priority. These relationships can become toxic for one or both parties as well as those around them, creating an endless loop of codependency, chaos and despair.

Codependency comes in many forms – habitual behaviors, relationships and substance abuse. In order to alleviate codependency, you must first be willing to identify your beliefs around the events, patterns and triggers that push your buttons, prompting a desire to satisfy unmet needs. When you are triggered and experience a charge from that trigger, you'll know that you're in a pattern. Sometimes we think that we don't know what our patterns are. The truth is that we *do* know on some level, yet are often in denial.

> *"Denial is the shock absorber of the Soul. It protects us until we are equipped to cope with reality." -Melody Beattie*

It's important to understand that while polarity and codependency are *Not* one-sided, you can only address your side of the equation while allowing the other side to choose for themselves. While the push of a button can trigger us in the direction of destructive chaos, through conscious mindfulness, it can also trigger us in the constructive direction of healing, change and the manifestation of our preferences and dreams. The most powerful antidote to polarity is allowance, which is the elixir of change.

When you are willing to acknowledge and address the reality of your patterns, find the feelings of the pattern and allow yourself to experience them fully. It can be helpful to write them out. For example:

When X happens or when Person X says/does X, I feel __________, _____________, _____________.

Consider when/where this may have begun. Allow yourself to uncover the true thoughts, feelings and emotions that you may not have felt safe fully expressing initially and be with them fully. Acknowledge and thank them for holding space until you were ready to convene with them.

For each, ask:

- *What do I hate about this?*
- *What do I love about it?*
- *What do I want that I'm not getting or getting that I don't want?*
- *What is the meaning that I've given to this?*
- *What are the underlying beliefs which created, or re-created it?*

Consider what choices and actions brought you into this pattern or addiction. Ask yourself:

- *Who would I be without this?*
- *Who do I prefer to be?*

Questions bring awareness which is the first step to healing and change where beliefs and coping mechanisms can be released. You can then choose to adopt new beliefs, make different choices and exhibit different behaviors. When you get your mind and body working together to match your intentions and begin to have different experiences, these experiences will affirm your intentions; and conscious choice then becomes a new, refreshing pattern.

Let's look at an example: You've experienced betrayal or abandonment in the past. When the shock occurred, the survival instincts of your Limbic System came to the rescue, encouraging you to build a brick wall around your heart in order to prevent further damage. To maintain security, utilizing self-sabotage as the mortar, you fortify a barrier against being subject to vulnerability, receiving love and experiencing intimacy. This wall helps you feel safe, and this safety is your reward. As a bonus, when the repeating pattern occurs, you can say things like "*See, I knew it!*" Then you get to be right...yet another reward.

This is a false sense of security that will not work, though, because it's grounded in fear.

Although traumas of the past may come flooding back to you as you begin to look at your patterns and triggers, it's not necessary to visit every occurrence in detail. Simply identify the feelings of the pattern and consider what you prefer and the changes you're willing to make toward the actualization of that objective. As you do, identify the risks and rewards: Sadness (a broken heart) vs. Happiness (a healthy relationship).

Do I want to be a prisoner of the past or a pioneer of the future? ~Deepak Chopra

During this process, you may go to a place of allowance and choose forgiveness (a topic we'll discuss in the next chapter) for those who have hurt you, as well as for yourself. The word allowance may initially evoke an essence of resistance; therefore, allow me to elaborate. Allowance is the acknowledgement of what is, i.e. 'X happened/is happening or Person X is X" vs. resistance of what is, a.k.a. Denial. You can allow something or someone to be and accept that they are; yet based on what is, you can choose not to subscribe to or integrate their traits as your own or invite them to be part of your life going forward – i.e. holding on to the energy of it, hence attracting and/or recreating similar issues in the future.

Keep in mind that there's no room for guilt, blame or shame in allowance or forgiveness. Guilt is an invitation for punishment. Blame is a distraction from your responsibility in the co-creation process, and shame destroys your sense of worthiness and self. When codependency is eliminated, you're empowered by knowing that you are in charge of your life and not at the mercy of forces outside of yourself.

It's not so much the situations in our lives as it is our beliefs and the expectations built around them which provoke our challenges. Joe Vitale tells us that *"The meaning you give an event or a situation is the belief that attracted the event."*

Understanding these concepts is the first step in freeing yourself from patterns and codependency. When you have a neutral response to a trigger vs. a re-action, you'll know you've healed the pattern. When you have mindfulness around codependency, you can view all of your experiences, even those you've been angered and deeply hurt by, as lessons and opportunities to grow ~ contributions to your evolution.

Addiction is anything you do to avoid the intensity of the energy that you're experiencing. With substance abuse, the intensity is increased not only for the addict, but those around them as well. Addiction is a choice that leads to a seemingly 'no choice' position, a compulsion. It offers something that you *think* you don't have. Yet it will never be what you *think* you're going after – running to escape or chasing a high – which is just a hook. Buddhism calls this hook 'The Hungry Ghost'. Addictions are not so much about the particular behaviors or substances as they are about the escape we use them for, and the thought process of the belief system that takes us there. While addiction is a learned behavior and a coping mechanism, it is ultimately a choice – One that can always be transformed and changed.

A leader in mindfulness psychology, Dr. Elisha Goldstein is the best-selling author of, among others, *The Now Effect: How This Moment Can Change the Rest of Your Life*. Dr. Goldstein tells us that neurons which fire together are wired together in our brain. Our Mind/Body provides the *queues* which trigger our addictive behaviors. These queues raise Dopamine in the brain. Dopamine is the motivational chemical associated with pleasure that says *"Go do this right now"*.

When flooded with Dopamine, the brain is cut off from the higher reasoning and impulse control of the Prefrontal Cortex. This is when the reptilian brain takes the helm and heads in the direction of the Basal Ganglia, associated with recorded processes and practices. The brain looks for stored procedures and goes to the default recorded routine - Exhibit a particular behavior: have a drink, cigarette, drug, etc. A craving is the mind thinking *'I want this'*, and an urge is the physiological impulse which accompanies it.

Then there are the mind traps: rationalizations, justifications, bargaining and blaming: *I've had a hard day, I could use a drink; I did well, I deserve a decadent dessert; Well, just this once* or *It's their fault – They hurt me or made me so angry that I'm doing X.* When this happens, our impulse control is compromised, and we lose our capacity to consider, or re-consider the direction in which we're headed. What's needed is something to interject this process, an *Interrupt*, if you will.

In systems programming, an *Interrupt* is a signal that alerts the processor to a higher priority condition, requiring the interruption of the current code the processor is executing (the current *Thread*). The processor responds by suspending its current activities, saving its state and executing a small program called an Interrupt Handler or Interrupt Service Routine (ISR) to deal with the event. This interruption is temporary; and after the ISR finishes, the processor typically resumes execution of the previous thread. For example, while working on your computer, you may encounter a message similar to "*The program has encountered a problem and needs to close.*" This is an ISR. Some ISR's don't provide any information regarding the problem or whether it will resume after handling it though. This scenario is similar to the manner by which some addicts may pretend that nothing has transpired in the wake of their actions; and you may not know why, if or when another incident may occur.

It's helpful to understand the processes of your brain because at times like these, you don't necessarily have full control. Brain chemicals are driving the bus more than we ever knew or understood before. When you choose mindfulness and are aware of the functions of your mind and the compulsions of your body, it enables you to be more present in the space between awareness and response where you can observe and act vs. *re*-act. In that space, you can choose. You can take back your power, referred to as the *locus of control* - the extent to which you believe that you can control events that affect you. A person's locus (Latin for place or location) is conceptualized as either internal (the person believes they can influence their life ~ life happens *For* them) or external (they believe their life is controlled by factors they cannot influence ~ life happens *To* them). Feeling the locus of control is the opposite of feeling anxiety, depression or helplessness and provides a sense of option vs. attack.

"The most important decision we make is whether we believe we live in a friendly or hostile universe." ~ Unknown

In *The Now Effect*, Dr. Goldstein presents *The Stop Practice,* which is a fabulous ISR (Interrupt Service Routine).

S Stop
T Take a few breaths
O Observe your experience
P Pause. Bring blood flow back to the Prefrontal Cortex before proceeding.

This practice is part of his Mindfulness work. It's one of the most popular practices because it's short, simple and can be applied to any circumstance. Our brain loves to chunk away at things, and this acronym makes it easy to remember. You can use this practice throughout your day and challenge yourself to employ it during the most difficult of scenarios. Dr. Goldstein provides a free demonstration of this practice on *YouTube®* (See *Resources*).

The present moment is the time to choose to respond differently in order to work with new neurons in your brain and have them fire in a different direction. So, before you return to your regularly scheduled programming, *STOP* to consider your capacity of choice and free will.

There is a breathing exercise that can be of great assistance in this process. It can be employed anywhere at any time to assist you in finding and remaining calm and centered even in the most stressful of situations. It only takes 16 seconds – or longer if you so choose.

> Close your eyes if possible.
> Inhale deeply for four seconds – Counting 1, 2, 3, 4.
> Hold that breath for four seconds – 1, 2, 3, 4.
> Exhale to the count of 4 – 1, 2, 3, 4.
> Relax for four seconds before taking the next breath.

Tools such as these provide a manner by which to bridge the severance between your brain and your heart to bring your Mind/Body into balance. A complete transformation may not be immediate; but with persistent consistency, results will be rewarded. It's similar to choosing to adopt a healthier lifestyle. When you begin making healthier eating choices, you may initially feel deprived in some way. When you begin an exercise routine, your muscles may be sore. However, after regular intervals and feeling more energetic, junk food and a sedentary lifestyle become unappealing. The more often you widen the space within which you can choose your response, the more automatic conscientious choice becomes as you cultivate mindfulness and create new neural pathways to support your objectives.

Mindfulness provides countless benefits for addiction therapy, particularly where some may feel a resistance to traditional twelve-step programs or experience less than exultant or enduring results with them. Mindfulness is a subtle, autonomous approach. It provides a sense of personal control, bringing you back in touch with yourself to the place where you'd lost that connection and chose to fill the void with an addiction.

Addiction is not something that happens *To* you. It's a choice and a learned behavior consequential to a culmination of choices which often began in childhood resulting in a place which *seems* to offer no choice. Low self worth and the negative beliefs which birth this perception can be a self-fulfilling prophecy in that it can lead to a myriad of coping mechanisms and addictive behaviors. Addiction is not only about a behavior or a substance. An overwhelming sense of wrongness (judgment ~ a wrongness of self) is often the primary addiction with the secondary being the behavior or substance used to escape it.

When you go into escape mode, particularly with substance abuse, you put a *"For Rent"* sign on yourself, inviting entities to run you. These entities could be Spirits of addicted souls who will find a body through which to use drugs or alcohol. When addiction is extreme, you invite demons as well. An addicted person often appears to have shadows about them or seem creepy. One moment the person is there and the next, their eyes are empty ~ as if another being is starring out through them. I can personal attest to this phenomenon as I have witnessed it myself.

Interestingly, the word Demon was originally spelled Daemon (Latinized from Greek). Most people are not aware that daemons were not always thought to be only evil. In the ancient world, there were two forms of daemon known as eudemons and kakodemons, originating from Greek meaning good and evil, respectively. The negative connotation of demons came with Christianity; and the original meaning and definition has been twisted and lost over time.

This term is utilized in the computer world - with the original spelling of the word. You may have encountered this entity in the form of an email message such as: *"MAILER-**DAEMON** @ SomeCompany. com: Delivery Failed."* The term was coined by the programmers of MIT's Project MAC. They took the name from *Maxwell's Demon*, an imaginary creature who works in the background sorting molecules created by Clerk Maxwell as part of his experiments regarding the Second Law of Thermodynamics. *Maxwell's Demon* is consistent with Greek mythology's interpretation of a daemon as a supernatural being working inconspicuously with no particular bias towards good or evil.

Many substance abusers refer to their vices as demons, using them as justification for their choices and actions as an excuse to avoid addressing their issues and taking responsibility for their behaviors. By utilizing substances, one may temporarily become unconscious of whatever it is they're attempting to escape; however, suppressing it only creates the temporary illusion that it's not there. Eventually it will burst out and manifest in all sorts of ways - heavy emotions, anger and depression - resulting in a truly tortured Soul.

Our point of view regarding addiction, which is typically adopted from others, is what holds the addiction in place. When you 'fight' against an addiction, you strengthen the bond to it. In some situations, while a substance may be relinquished, the energy of the underlying issue(s) and/or its constituents remains. For example, although an angry alcoholic or drug addict may renounce the use of a substance, their anger may persist - another phenomenon which I have personally witnessed. The process of recovery includes acknowledging all of the aspects of the energies involved – the emotional, physical and energetic.

What if recovery is not so much about renouncing the use of a substance or fixing something that's wrong as it is about remembering the parts of you that have been disconnected along the way? Often when the primary is acknowledged and addressed, the secondary falls away. Recovery is a willingness to choose to be all of who you are and the ability to be aware of everyone and everything without going to judgment or escape.

In many ways, I view addiction as a cry for help. Despite what you may have heard or think, you are not powerless over addiction, and it is not a permanent state. However, moving through it can only come from the choice of the addicted person. They must choose recovery for themselves, not as a bargaining tool or to appease the preferences of another. When you care deeply for someone and wish to assist them in traversing addiction and recovery, it is essential to be mindful of this, particularly regarding wrongness, blame, shame and/or enabling - as we discussed earlier in relation to codependency. While you may have the best intentions at heart, the gifting of your assistance must be provided from a place of mindfulness and compassion for all concerned.

When you acknowledge the patterns and addictions in your life, you can set about transforming them. Doing so may seem overwhelming at first; however, transformation is a process. Although spontaneous transformations do occur, don't tax yourself with any sort of expectancy or pressure. Doing so can bring about self-defeating notions which often lead to the demise of your intentions. You can approach any transformation with a ten-second choice technique and employ Dr. Goldstein's *Stop Practice*. At the end of a minute, hour or day, you may find that you're a completely different person - one who can make choices based on refreshed perspective and renewed empowerment. As Lewis Carroll wrote in *Alice's Adventures in Wonderland: "I could tell you my adventures, beginning from this morning; but it's no use going back to yesterday because I was a different person then."* With a gradual approach, a change or goal which may initially seem daunting becomes attainable. You only need to see the first few feet in front of you, and the next will unfold in due time under grace.

The process of choosing recovery involves a very real sense of loss and grief. Grieving is a visceral process consisting of several stages. Swiss psychiatrist Elisabeth Kübler-Ross introduced the concept of identifying these stages in her 1969 book, *On Death and Dying*, which was inspired by her work with terminally ill patients. Kübler-Ross later expanded her model to include any form of personal loss, including addiction. A commemorative edition of her book, *On Grief and Grieving: Finding the Meaning of Grief Through the Five Stages of Loss,* co-authored with David Kessler, expands on this topic. Identifying and acknowledging these stages can assist all concerned in traversing the process of *recovery.* Grief and recovery are as unique as you are. I have provided a library of reference material in the *Resources* section to assist in finding the recovery path which best suits your situation and preferences.

Patterns and addictions are the manifestations of messages from your Mind/Body. They are catalysts for change. Once you uncover the lesson(s) within the messages, you can choose to no longer play out the pattern. You can choose to embrace gratitude in acknowledging the healing and growth appreciated through the experience.

Many people find that their lives are better after going through a grieving process due to post-stress growth (Recovery). This growth refers to positive psychological change experienced as a result of the struggle with highly challenging life circumstances. This growth is not simply a return to baseline from a period of suffering. It's an experience of improvement which is deeply meaningful. Quite often many who have encountered a Dark Night of the Soul and/or a Healing Crisis (*which we'll discuss in Chapter Eight*) have found that once they've completed the cycle, they are healthier and happier than before it began as a result of what they gained in the process.

My Mother crossed over while I was living on the other side of the country. Shortly after her services, during which I'd been away from the office, I felt a calling to return home once again. This calling came at a time when I was engaged in a demanding part of my career; and taking more time from work was not conducive to my professional objectives. I recall a personal conversation with my Manager at the time wherein the little workaholic in me was justifying not taking additional personal time due to the increased backlog in my work which would be waiting for me upon my return - not to mention that burying myself in work was a comfortably familiar way to escape the internal turmoil I was resisting. I'll never forget the perceptive, compassionate and wise advice this man offered to me. He said that the work will always be there; that will not change. The distinction is that in honoring myself, although the work would be the same upon my return, ***I*** would be different and so to would be my approach not only to my work, but life in general. Fortunately, I heeded Kevin's advice; and he was absolutely right.

Regardless of how many cracks you've been tripped up by or holes you may have fallen into along the various avenues you've traveled, it does not mean that they are failures or dead ends. It simply means that there's a message that's been waiting to be heard. The term 'rock bottom' comes to mind here; and although it sounds like a terrifying and tragic place, it can be the space wherein you find the strength to see the truth beneath the damage that has been inflicted upon yourself and those around you, the beauty of which is the opportunity to heal, grow and evolve.

Denial may have become a familiar and comfortable place. However, when the comfort found in familiarity becomes objectionable and the fallout of the patterns become unbearable, you're ready to make a change. When you choose to be present with yourself and attend the engineering design meetings for your own software, you can implement tools which assist you in confronting entities when they surface. There may initially be times when the tools are not yet fully integrated and a falling off of the wagon may occur, especially when the *Frenemies* associated with patterns and addictions beckon. Ultimately, however, the choice is always yours; and persistence is the key to unlocking the door to change.

"The key of persistence opens all doors closed by resistance." ~John Di Lemme

Thomas Edison was asked whether he felt like a failure and considered giving up after accumulating over 9,000 failed attempts to invent the light bulb. His response was *'Why would I feel like a failure or ever give up when success is within my grasp?'* After 10,000+ attempts, Edison invented the light bulb.

"Our greatest glory is not in never falling, but in rising every time we fall." ~Confucius

"My past has not defined me, destroyed me, deterred me, or defeated me; it has only strengthened me". ~Dr. Steve Maraboli

"Our self-image and our habits tend to go together. Change one and you will automatically change the other." ~Napoleon Hill

"There is a power inside every human against which no earthly force is of the slightest consequence." ~Neville Goddard

~ Life is a process and a journey. Enjoy the ride. ~

For more information, please visit Resources.

Musings...

"Forgiveness is the fragrance that the violet sheds on the heel that crushed it." -Mark Twain

Chapter 7

Forgiveness ~ The Get Well Bouquet You Gift To Yourself

In this chapter, you'll explore the virtue of forgiveness at a visceral level. You'll contemplate what it represents for you and consider some tools and processes to assist you in appreciating more lightness and freedom in your life.

It's misleading to believe that forgiveness absolves responsibility. While it affords release, it is not absolution of accountability, nor a condonement of transgression. It's about the drawing back of personal worth devalued as a result of transgression. It is the act of choosing freedom from the toxicity of *un*forgiveness. While it may be imparted to others, at its core, forgiveness is something you do for yourself. That being said, let's observe the various elements surrounding this virtue.

When you have been violated and feel victimized, it's natural to experience a gamut of emotions from hurt to hate and everything in between. Depression and anger are the pinnacles within this range of emotions. Anger is the physical empowerment of pain. It is the result of an underlying emotion that we're trying to escape. When anger is directed at others, it's an expression of our own pain.

There are primal, physical elements to anger which are impossible to deny. They are part of us, and reactivity occurs whether we're in control of it in the moment or not. Unfortunately, we may not consider, much less employ, a viable manner by which to process them constructively in those moments, often saying and doing things we later come to regret.

When we encounter anger, our self-preservation (fight or flight response) kicks in. Experts at HeartMath® Institute have found that a five minute episode of anger depresses the immune system for up to 6 hours. Suppressing anger is not an antidote to expressing it in detrimental ways, however. Because of the physical nature of anger, it's best to process it with productive physical activity - a brisk walk, run or a workout at the gym. It is essential to tend to this energetic force, lest it fester and debilitate us further.

E-motions are energy in motion. They are intended to flow through us vs. being suppressed and accumulated. Raphael Cushnir, an expert in the dynamics of feelings, believes that there is a glitch in our brain which developed through the course of evolution. He says this glitch is the reason why it's so hard to feel our emotions the way they need us to. The following is in summary of an excerpt from his web site:

> Our limbic system generates a challenging emotion for us to feel. Our primitive (reptilian) brain considers that emotion life-threatening and blocks it. This battle leaves us cross-wired and stuck, creating stress and illness. An unfelt feeling cannot and does not go away. It lodges in our body as well as our unconscious where its mission becomes getting noticed. It has a particularly diabolical way of doing so in that it acts like a magnet, drawing into our lives people and situations that will cause us to feel the feeling that our primitive brain blocked in the first place.

> The cause of harmful patterns in our lives is unfelt emotion. The longer these emotions remain unfelt, the more intense the backlash. It's actually impossible for the primitive brain to block old emotions and any new ones that are magnetized. To fend these emotions off, the primitive brain calls in reinforcements. Its most powerful allies are compulsions and addictions.
>
> The good news is that all of this can be reversed. The primitive brain can be updated to understand that challenging emotions aren't life threatening so that when they come up, it doesn't shut down as hard or as long, enabling us to reharmonize and live life to our full potential.

Our emotions are the energetic expressions of our heart – our GPS. They are the compass of the heart which generates them to be acknowledged in order to provide guidance and choice points within the journey of our lives.

During my *me*-search, I discovered Dawn Clark. I immediately identified with Dawn while listening to her interview with Eram Saeed in her *From Heartache To Joy* series as she described her philosophy and approach to healing. Dawn speaks of our vibratory nature and that our Soul is encoded with an original underlying blueprint – a template for our body and our world. She refers to this template, our DNA and Morphogenetic Field, as our operating system for life in that it contains information regarding who we are and what our Soul came here to do.

During your life, traumatic experiences create what Dawn refers to as core fractures in your morphogenetic field which compromises your DNA. Fractures are a symptom of core energy loss, and this is where limiting beliefs and blocks infiltrate your operating system. When fracturing occurs, the hurt part of you becomes disassociated. Core fractures are like shattered mirrors which reflect fissured versions of ourselves causing us to re-create and re-live the patterns of the fractures - much like a scratched CD plays the same tone repeatedly when stuck at the speed bump of the abrasion.

Toxic emotions are like the fallout when the infrastructure of a nuclear reactor is compromised. Unless or until the damage is repaired and the fallout is cleared, your original frequency codes cannot broadcast clearly due to the interference patterns transmitted by them – similar to the chaos encountered when your computer's operating system is infiltrated by a virus. Core fractures and the toxic emotions that come with them can cause you to repeat undesirable patterns and engage in unhealthy behaviors - creating a playground for un-wellness on all levels.

Have you ever acknowledged, processed and embraced forgiveness around someone or something-surmising that you'd released it, yet later found that if the subject resurfaces, it brings along a residual degree of charge? This is due to a lingering fracture and/or its toxic emotions lurking within your system. As with some dis-eases, you can live without experiencing symptoms yet be a carrier, waiting for just the right host.

Acknowledgement, processing and forgiveness are the beginning of the healing process, which can be sufficient in many scenarios. In some, however, you may not reach deeply enough to fully resolve and clear all of the toxicity. Although surgery may remove a tumor from a compromised organ, it's possible that cells containing residual dis-ease could be present elsewhere in the body. When my thyroid gland was removed due to cancer, I was put on a diet to deplete my body of iodine in preparation for radiation treatment. I subsequently drank radioactive iodine. Any thyroid tissue or remaining cells would absorb the iodine and the radioactivity would eradicate these cells, thus eliminating the possibility of them metastasizing into new tumors. Along with the mechanical aspects, though, it was also necessary for me to process what my Mind/Body was presenting in the form of this dis-ease. The cancer was followed by a number of intensely acute bouts of Tonsillitis - demonstrating the determination of my Mind/Body in getting a message across. Once I did the internal, emotional work around the message, the frequency of tonsillitis diminished; and the cancer has never returned. We'll discuss this process in a bit more detail during the next chapter.

Implementing the material in Dawn's programs, *Repairing Core Fractures* and *Clearing Toxic Emotions*, was profound for me, particularly her *Seven Step Process.* This involves viewing what you intend to heal through three perspectives of understanding: The Victim's, The Clinical/Therapeutic and through Universal Understanding and Acceptance (A *Sacred Contract* perspective). The verbal expression of unresolved issues, initially directed to the other person (not in their physical presence, although you may choose that option, but in a therapeutic setting) and subsequently to yourself, is extensive; and the healing derived from this process is deeply fulfilling. Dawn's programs provided a channel through which I could allow myself to sweep away the crumbs I'd been carrying in my pocket and release them along my path – not to retrace undesirable patterns, but as stepping stones in a return to wholeness.

~ When *'Sorry'* isn't enough…

When you are wounded, your brain's defense mechanisms will express their self-talk: *"I don't deserve this"; "I didn't create this"*, etc. It does so in order to make sense of reality to appease your Administrators in compliance with your database integrity. This is the hardwiring aspect. When you are a victim, you often cannot see beyond the wound, a requirement for restitution or perhaps even revenge. When you find yourself in *'They need to pay for it'* mode, it's difficult, albeit inconceivable, to see other possibilities, especially forgiveness. However, an eye for an eye only equates to two wounds which do not amount to a whole. You may be so consumed by hurt or anger that accepting an apology – should one, genuine or not, come your way – will not suffice. Forgiveness may feel like a weakness in that it's as if you're renouncing the injury. This is a misconception of sorts, though, because prolonged *un*forgiveness only wreaks more havoc in your life.

There are times when forgiveness does not come easily. You may be contemplating issues in your life for which, although it would be to your benefit, choosing forgiveness may be a struggle. You can get stuck in the charge of judgment and polarity of right and wrong. You may feel that if you're not making something wrong, you're somehow making it right or letting the other person off the hook. It's impossible to make any sort of beneficial choice from within that polarity.

The reason many of us get stuck within things of this nature is due to our need for acknowledgement and validation. The depth of a victim's pain cannot and should not be underestimated. There are those, yourself included, who may judge and cover you in should – *"You/I should just let this go"* or *"You/I should be over this by now."* In the absence of acknowledgement, it's nearly impossible for a victim to even consider, much less begin to heal their pain and move on. A search for the *Why* often leads a victim to a wrongness of self in some ways (*"What did I do to attract/'deserve' this?"*) which only deepens and prolongs the pain. We may feel powerless against the affects that an experience or situation had or has over us, leaving blame, shame and pain the only power we feel we have left; when in truth, they are *dis*empowering. Blame limits your capacity to heal, shame devastates your sense of self and pain begets pain.

In these types of situations, it is essential to acknowledge and validate yourself – *even, and Especially, if no one else does.* Allow yourself to embrace all of your thoughts, feelings and emotions around a situation and those involved. Feel them fully – particularly those which were not safe to feel, express or perhaps even acknowledge initially. They are part of you, and there is nothing wrong or needing to be 'fixed' where they are concerned. Gift yourself permission to do so fully and honor yourself by giving it a voice. Dig in to the dirt and till the soil, as it is fertilizer for healing and growth. The most advantageous, and often the only way out is through. Thank that part of yourself for holding on until you were strong enough to process it. You can choose to forgive yourself for not being able to release it. You'll do so when you're ready.

It can be quite beneficial to write your sentiments out in a letter - whether those involved are currently in your life, in the distance, living or deceased. Doing so allows you to process your thoughts, feelings and emotions around the situation. You can express yourself freely without resistance, interruption, judgment or argument. This process can bring you to a place of allowance and acceptance ~ as we discussed in the previous chapter. Going there provides a space wherein you can view the situation for what it is, process your sentiments and make authentic choices for yourself. Once such a letter is completed, it is not necessary to share it with the addressee(s) or ever allow them to read it at all - although you can if you so choose. A letter such as this is primarily for you. You can tuck it away somewhere or you could opt for burning the paper on which it's written to release the charge of the emotional energy expressed therein.

Once you've acknowledged your thoughts, feelings and emotions, you can identify how they've served you and the negative power they have in order to find that power in a positive way somewhere else. It's important to know that you have this power, that you can claim it and afford yourself the choice to release things of this nature - otherwise it will be difficult to let them go. Dawn Clark's material offers some fabulous tools to assist you in this process.

Unforgiveness is a trap that will keep you imprisoned. As a victim, your survivalist will hold onto a wound in an effort to protect you from experiencing it again. Unforgiveness is resentment that spews all kinds of evil. It breeds distrust, fear, disconnection and depression; and it destroys your sense of self, closing you off from being present. *Holding on to things of this nature is like drinking poison and expecting the other person to die -Buddha.* Should you find yourself in such a scenario, ask: *Truth, Who am I hurting?* Unforgiveness closes your heart. Forgiveness opens it. When you draw back your power, you free yourself, making it easier to bring yourself back into a state of balance. Although it doesn't change your past, forgiveness absolutely changes your present as well as your future. This is the *re*-wiring aspect.

"As I walked out the door toward the gate that
would lead to my freedom, I knew
that if I didn't leave my bitterness and hatred behind,
I'd still be in prison." -Nelson Mandela

Have you ever encountered someone who ruffled your feathers – a family member, coworker or passing stranger in a store or traffic? Consider learning at a later time that this person was/is coming from a place of trauma, serious illness, financial difficulty or depression - perhaps a mixture thereof. *Who does that belong to?* By considering how they may have come to be the way that they are, your perception of and interaction with them may come from a different plane of energy. You may relate to them with compassion vs. contempt. While this awareness may not excuse their demeanor, it can assist you in choosing yours - Who does *that* belong to? Always keep in mind that you never know what a person is dealing with, where they are coming from or where they are at. All you can do is choose to be who and where *you* are. The following is a valuable affirmation from Louise Hay which speaks volumes:

"I did the best that I could with what I had to work with at the time."

When you can recontextualize a situation, you're able to expand your awareness and embrace a broader perspective which enables you to view a situation with compassion vs. contempt. Contempt is born of judgment which places us into wrongness – which is always present to some degree on both sides of any situation. Judgment begets blame which limits the capacity to heal. Stepping out of judgement and contempt opens the door to compassion where you can discover the potential positives within a situation; i.e., gratitude for not being the one having experienced or experiencing trauma, abuse, neglect, serious illness, financial difficulty, etc. You may even embrace a willingness to offer assistance in some way.

Everything is a matter of perspective, from which perception emerges. Neale Donald Walsch elaborates by saying that when you change your perspective, you change your perception. When you change your perception, you change your beliefs. When you change your beliefs, you change your behavior; and by changing your behavior, you change your experience and alter your reality. *-Cleansing Breath-* So True.

Recontextualization is the deliberate redrawing of your experience. When you look at a situation in a new way (recontextualize it), you allow yourself to experience it differently. In doing so, you also experience yourself in a different way. By recontextualizing you can ask what is true from the Soul level and receive clarity from your Soul's perspective of the human experience. Neale refers to this manner of questioning as *Soul Logic* in his book, *The Only Thing*

That Matters. The following is in paraphrase of an excerpt posted on his Facebook page:

> Using this remarkable device, you dramatically alter the data that gives rise to a truth that forms the thought which produces the emotion that creates your experience of any present moment. The process of recontextualization does just what its name suggests. It creates a new context within which to frame life itself, as well as any event or circumstance within life, virtually eliminating any reason or justification you might have felt to be angry or resentful with or about anyone.
>
> This remarkable tool involves a repositioning of your perspective, allowing you to see what is going on at any moment in your life within a new and startlingly different context. It should be clear at this point in your life that what brings you joy—the highest joy—is self-expression. It is through the fullest expression of Self that the fullest experience of who you really are is achieved. A person looking at life a certain way might feel that the fullest expression of self is very wonderful if it can be made to happen, but it doesn't happen very often for many; and life has more to it than this, and we must all go on, whether we feel fully self-expressed or not.
>
> Recontextualization, on the other hand, tells you that full self-expression is the experience you came for. This creates a not-willing-to-settle-for-anything-less thought in your mind. It reformulates the days and times of your life within the context of your

> Soul's agenda, not your mind's concepts. The Soul's agenda always exceeds the mind's concepts. This is not true some of the time; this is true all of the time.

As Neale suggests, you can find the path to your Soul, especially with regard to a particular life issue through Soul searching. Through this searching and embracing the logic of the Soul, one can see that there are no victims and no villains - There is only the mutual agenda of the Souls mutually held and mutually experienced. Neale provides an enlightening demonstration of his *Soul Logic* process in a *YouTube®* video which I highly recommend viewing (*See Resources*). As I watched, I witnessed a woman coming to a place of not only understanding, forgiveness and healing, but a place of unconditional love for her *Villain* as well as for herself (her *Victim* Archetype).

Everything we've experienced thus far has brought us to the present moment. While we can recall our experiences, we can choose not to become their story. It is not our experiences which shape us; it is what we choose to derive from them that does.

There is wisdom to be mined from every experience, whether windfall or wound. That being said, asking: *Truth: If X happened / is happening for the highest and best, what might that be?* puts you into a space of gratitude for the wisdom you may not be able to see, *yet* - even if you're unable to choose forgiveness or see any potential positives within the situation at the moment. Notice how you feel when you function from a place of question vs. conclusion. When you consider the Laws of Relativity (*Everything simply is*) and Polarity (*Everything has an opposite*), the question *Why* tends to become somewhat irrelevant within the objective of your overall journey. Asking open-ended questions takes you out of the *Why* and puts you in a place of *What If* ~ possibility and choice.

While time itself may not heal all wounds, it does provide a space wherein to re-evaluate and contemplate our options. Doing so is often the first step on the path to freedom. Our experiences are contributions to the journeys of all concerned in that they are opportunities to learn, choose and evolve. When we can appreciate the roles we play in the creation of each other's lives, we're able to see the broader picture. Consider those in your life who provide you with these opportunities. Life is a process; and all that any of us can do is our best with what we have to work with at any given time. With this in mind, I offer an enlightening exercise in the back of this book as a gateway to compassion, forgiveness and freedom. I'd like to note that *enlightenment* not only refers to acquiring wisdom and understanding. It also articulates the lightness of freedom from encumbrance.

New York Times best-selling Author, Iyanla Vanzant, reminds us that you cannot un-hear what you've heard, un-see what you've seen or un-feel what you have felt or experienced. In trying to do so or lingering within it, you lose the present as well as the future because you're stuck in an endless loop. What you can do, however, is choose to stop believing that what occurred has somehow left you wounded, damaged or broken. In her book, *Forgiveness: 21 Days to Forgive Everyone for Everything*, Iyanla invites us to liberate ourselves from the wounds of the past by embracing the power of forgiveness.

Expanded awareness enables us to view life from the big picture perspective, having compassion for ourselves and others. Compassion motivates us to move beyond the limitations imposed by unforgiveness. Our motivation to forgive is increased when we realize how important it is to free ourselves from the past so that we can live in and enjoy the present as well as the future. Although compassion has an emotional component, it's also regarded as an action, based on an intention to alleviate suffering among humanity.

The Biehl family is an exceptional demonstration of forgiveness and reconciliation. Amy Biehl was a white American graduate of Stanford University and an Anti-Apartheid activist in South Africa who was murdered by Cape Town residents in 1993. The four men convicted of her murder were sentenced to 18 years in prison. Amy's parents, Linda and Peter Biehl, created the *Amy Biehl Foundation* in their Daughter's honor to focus on supporting South Africans in their everyday lives. They made a statement asking the Truth and Reconciliation Commission (a court-like restorative justice body assembled in South Africa after the abolition of Apartheid) to grant these men amnesty. Two of them were subsequently released and now work on projects sponsored by the foundation. To say that this is a profound expression of forgiveness and reconciliation is an understatement.

Although I can comprehend it, I'm not certain how long, if at all, it may take for me to come to that level of forgiveness and reconciliation had I lost my beloved child -especially in that manner. However, when I see the contribution that the Biehl family are to us all in, as Mahatma Gandhi suggests, *Being the change that you wish to see in the world*, I'd like to intend that I, and perhaps all of us, could.

We are all worthy of compassion, forgiveness and new beginnings – especially when awareness and fresh perspective are introduced. The following is an excerpt from Jack Kornfield's book, *The Art of Forgiveness*, about a South African tribe that treats people who step out of line in an extraordinary way, ministering with compassion and gratitude vs. judgment and punishment:

> When a person in the tribe acts irresponsibly or unjustly, they are placed in the center of the village, alone and unfettered. All work ceases, and every man, woman and child in the village gathers in a large circle around the accused individual. Then

> each person in the tribe speaks to the accused, one at a time, each recalling the good things the person in the center of the circle has done in their lifetime. Every incident, every experience that can be recalled with any detail and accuracy, is recounted. All of their positive attributes, good deeds, kindnesses and strengths are recited carefully and at length. This tribal ceremony often lasts for several days. At the end, the tribal circle is broken, a joyous celebration takes place and the person is symbolically and literally welcomed back into the tribe.

Compassion is an usher to forgiveness which lifts the burden of limitation and opens the door to peace and freedom. Meditation (*which we'll discuss in depth during Chapter Eleven*), in and of itself, is a form of forgiveness as it frees you from the past and future by providing enlightenment and balance, anchoring you in the present. I have found Ho'oponopono and Metta meditations profoundly beneficial in relation to compassion and forgiveness.

The ancient Hawaiian practice of Ho'oponopono is a simple, yet profound technique for opening the flow of forgiveness and reconciliation. Traditionally, Ho'oponopono is practiced by healing priests or Kahuna Lapaʻau. Modern versions are performed with a guide or by an individual alone. Ho'oponopono involves repeating a Mantra comprised of these four short statements:

I love you. *I'm Sorry.* *Please Forgive Me.* *Thank You.*

Ho'oponopono can be directed toward yourself, to others, a situation or all of the above inclusively.

Metta is a Buddhist practice of benevolence – kindness or an inclination to be kind. Metta is about compassion - focusing on the intention for the well-being of all. Metta is first directed toward yourself and then toward others. While the practice is versatile, the following is a basic Metta Meditation:

Make yourself comfortable and close your eyes. Take two to three deep breaths with full inhale and slow exhale. Allow yourself to let go of any preoccupations or concerns and simply feel your breath within your heart center. As you breathe, slowly repeat the following to yourself:

May I be happy. *May I be safe.* *May I be peaceful and at ease.*

Then, focus on a good friend as you slowly repeat these intentions:

May you be happy. *May you be safe.* *May you be peaceful and at ease.*

Focus on a neutral person and repeat the same. Then focus on a difficult person and repeat these intentions, gradually extending the intentions toward the entire Universe.

Although softness is the intention of Metta, feelings of anger, grief, fear or sadness may arise. These are signs that your heart is opening. Allow them to surface vs. judging or resisting them; and direct loving kindness toward them. While Metta can be considered a meditation practice, it is intended more as a manner of being - with yourself, others and life in general.

Utilizing these techniques has endowed significantly profound and enduring results for me as well as many of my clients; and I highly recommend opening yourself to the gifts they bestow. It may be interesting to compare your energy surrounding a chosen issue after applying these techniques in relation to the exercises in previous chapters.

When you choose to make a transition, whether it's forgiving past transgressions, moving away from people and situations or relinquishing objects, it's essential to be clear about the incentive and purpose for doing so. Ask yourself: Am I willing and ready to let this go? When your mind is ready to take this path, you'll want to insure that your heart has given consent. Only then can it be released on a soul level. I suggest making a solemn vow with yourself never to muse over your choice. Embrace gratitude for its lesson(s) and contribution(s) as well as the transition and allow yourself to move forward without second guessing or looking back.

I had a number of shares in Microsoft stock which I'd intended to gift to my Son at some point in his adult years. Their value had been languishing for some time, yet I had faith that they would eventually elevate to an appreciated level. During the purchase of our home, I chose to sell the stocks to contribute to our overall financial well-being at the time. When I discussed my intention with a dear colleague and friend, he cautioned me that once I sold the stocks, it would be wise to refrain from tracking their value and simply let them go. Shortly thereafter, just out of curiosity, I looked them up on the NYSE (*New York Stock Exchange*). After all the years I'd held them, the value of those stocks had nearly doubled in the few months since I'd sold them. *Oh, if I'd only waited just a little longer... or heeded Ed's advice - Arg!* Albeit a mild example, especially when considering the intensity of transgressions and wounds being sought to heal, you see the concept. At the end of the day, though, once you've made your choice, on all levels, allow bygones to be bygones and treasure the strength and wisdom gifted through the process.

~ *Living well is the best revenge.*

Esther Hicks is an American inspirational speaker and a best-selling co-author with her Husband, Jerry Hicks, of books and workshops relative to the teachings of Abraham. In their book, *Ask and it is*

Given, they remind us that our true vibration is one of very high frequency. They describe forgiveness as the process of releasing yourself from the excuse you're using to be in a lower vibration – likening it to a cork bobbing on the surface of water in that while you may hold it under water for a while, its compelling objective is to bob back up.

Resurfacing is what you do energetically when you make a transition. If you're not doing something that puts you in a lower vibration, such as holding vengeance, placing blame or harboring guilt, your vibration rises intrinsically. Forgiveness is the letting go of the cork. Abraham-Hicks validate that doing so is not always easy; and that you must choose to really care about feeling good in order to be able to deliberately observe other things. It's about deciding to be in alignment with who you really are; and the best way to get there is by choosing higher vibrational thoughts and feelings.

Abraham-Hicks provides an *Emotional Grid* as an illustration of emotions on a gradient scale in a downward or upward spiral. This scale can assist you in transitioning from a lower to a higher vibration. By seeing where you are on the scale and choosing thoughts that feel a bit better, you can make gradual steps to a higher vibration. It's a matter of caring about how you feel, choosing to feel good and the vibration that you send out to the Universe. The more you feel good, the more you will appreciate to feel good about.

The wisdom of knowing that it's never too late to make a new choice for yourself while allowing others do the same enables you to be present with gratitude. The best way to embrace this gratitude is by acknowledging the lessons, growth and wisdom acquired from your experiences through which you have evolved to a new level, choosing to create and live fully in the present. In its true essence, gratitude is an outlook on life. When you live in gratitude and vibrate at that level, life treats you differently ~ You appreciate more to be grateful about, experiencing more ease and joy as a result.

~ There is grace in compassion, freedom in forgiveness and love in all things ~

For more information, please visit Resources.

Musings...

"All Healing is first a healing of the heart." - Carl Townsend

Chapter 8

The Healing Response

In this chapter, you'll gain a fresh perspective on dis-ease, healing and rejuvenation.

A Healing Response, sometimes referred to as a Healing Crisis, is the process of releasing toxins in the body. It can often be the outcome of becoming conscious of the unconscious, a phenomenon referred to as a 'Dark Night of the Soul'. A dark night is a time when you experience desperation of some degree – You've been deeply hurt, diagnosed with a serious illness or feeling you've lost what you consider to be someone, something or perhaps what seems like everything of value in your life. During a dark night, your subconscious is undergoing a shift - one which could manifest as illness, yet one which can transform you and your life in the most extraordinary ways.

For reference, *Dark Night of the Soul* is a poem written by 16th-century Spanish poet and Roman Catholic mystic, Saint John of the Cross (*Juan de la Cruz).* It narrates the journey of the Soul from its bodily home to a union with its creator and the often painful experience endured in the process.

Please note that this is not necessarily referring to dying and death. Consider the transformation of a caterpillar to a butterfly. Although there may appear to be 'religious' connotations, the term 'Dark Night of the Soul' is metaphorical in nature.

'*BS*' has more than one interpretation. In the computer world, it's known as the 'Blue Screen of Death' (BSOD, or *BS* for short), affectionately describing a GPF (General Protection Fault). These occur when a computer encounters a problem and locks up, freezes or shuts down. *Ever have one of those times in your life?* Although there may be signs of a problem prior to a BS, once it occurs, there's not much that can be done to remedy it other than rebooting, hoping the task you were in the midst of completes successfully the next time around. Of course, if the system takes the same path on the do-over, the result will be of the same insanity...*Sound familiar, Einstein?* I liken this process to a healing crisis as your Mind/Body functions in a similar fashion. It presents you with nudges and signals constantly. When you chronically ignore these subtle messages, it will take matters into its own hands.

Our perceptions and emotions alter our brain functions which, as we know, triggers changes in the body. It is crucial to acknowledge, express and process emotions as they are intimately entwined throughout our physiology. Pent up negative emotions are toxic to the body. Left unattended, they can produce overwhelm and lead to serious dis-ease. This is not new-age mumbo-jumbo, it's hard science which is indisputable.

Every dis-ease that exists is basically chaos. Chaos at the atomic level leads to chaos at the molecular level which leads to chaos at the cellular level. When enough cells are in chaos, they metastasize and you encounter the offense in your body and experience the physical symptoms.

Every dis-order, at its core, has an emotional component. Let's say, for instance, that in exploring the signals you've received, you realize that something within your software (or your life) is not functioning optimally. When you redesign a program or modify your environment, as with any shift, there is also a period of adjustment. While your mind may be at ease knowing that the issue is being addressed, your body may require a period of convalescence to process, stabilize and rebalance. This fallout, if you will, can and often does manifest as a healing crisis ~ a physical manifestation and/or detoxification response.

Ever plan a vacation to retreat from your busy life, come down with a cold and spend the bulk of your holiday tending to its symptoms? When you modify your field, the stress begins to dissipate; and the toxicity is processed and released through your body ~ often resulting in these types of maladies. This is a mild example, but you see the concept. In the medical field, the term Herxheimer Reaction is described as a short-term detoxification reaction in the body. Although the symptoms of this process may be unpleasant, they are actually an indication that healing is taking place.

The physical discharge of the toxins caused by the release of disparaging cellular memories, negative beliefs and emotions can produce dis-ease within the body; i.e. headaches, fatigue, flu-like symptoms and/or perhaps a worsening of that which you're working on healing. The more muddled your system, the more refuse there is to dispense. If you've ever done a detox regimen, you may have experienced this process and the resulting symptoms within your physiology. These healing responses are natural. If you suspect that you may have a serious condition, you should seek the assistance of a qualified professional. That being said, it is essential to take a holistic approach to dis-ease and address the issue from all angles.

One of my experiences with this process occurred over twenty years ago before I was enlightened with the wisdom I now have. In reviewing this crisis from my current understanding and perspective, I'm able to appreciate the brilliant mechanism of our Mind/Body.

I was transitioning from an unhappy marriage; and I was in a place of new beginning. Then I was diagnosed with cancer. The news hit me like a ton of bricks. I was just beginning to breathe and experience a sense of self and happiness when I collided with what I perceived at the time as a death sentence. *How could, and why would, this happen?! What a cruel world!*

I went through all of the stages of grief: denial, anger, bargaining, depression, acceptance…in varying degrees and random, recurring fashion. Fortunately, I was blessed with an abundance of love and support. I will say, however, that there is no more desolate and frightening space than finding yourself faced with serious illness and/or sudden mortality. Under grace, though, I lived through it and have enjoyed a very healthy and full life since.

Through my subsequent enlightenment as to the manner by which our Mind/Body and Universe function, I came to understand that I'd experienced a Dark Night of the Soul and a Healing Crisis. When I came upon '*The List'* in Louise's Hay's book, *You Can Heal Your Life*, some years later and read the descriptions for Cancer, Thyroid and Tonsillitis, I came to fully appreciate the term 'Holistic'. These entries from '*The List'* are as follows:

Problem:	Cancer
Probable Cause:	Deep hurt. Longstanding resentment. Deep secret or grief eating away at the self. Carrying hatreds. "What's the use?"
New Thought Pattern:	I lovingly forgive and release all of the past. I choose to fill my world with joy. I love and approve of myself.
Problem:	Thyroid
Probable Cause:	"I never get to do what I want to do.

	When is it going to be my turn?" Also, Humiliation.
New Thought Pattern:	I move beyond old limitations and now allow myself to express freely and creatively.
Problem:	Tonsillitis
Probable Cause:	Fear, Repressed emotions, Stifled Creativity.
New Thought Pattern:	My good now flows freely. Divine ideas express through me. I am at peace.

Louise L. Hay, You Can Heal Your Life, Copyright 1999 by Louise Hay, Hay House, Inc., Carlsbad, CA

As far down the road as my revelation was, it all made sense. The realization that unaddressed issues resulting in a discontented lifestyle were holding me captive gave birth to a preference for freedom and happiness which prompted empowerment to take action. As I did so, my body began to flush the pent up toxicity which manifested as these dis-eases. Although they were painful and frightening at the time, I'm now able to view them from the rear view mirror. I see them as confirmation of the tremendous capacities of the Mind/Body and the healing and transformational empowerment which is possible through mindfulness.

One can wonder whether acknowledging and doing the inner work initially might have prevented the onset of these dis-eases altogether. You know where my vote lies. I occasionally have minor physical symptoms of an impending onset of tonsillitis. I am aware, however, that these symptoms are a reminder, a message that I'm not caring for myself or expressing my truth in some way. When this presents, I go within to see where this message applies so that I can address it. I then gargle with warm water and salt to flush the toxicity from my body with gratitude.

Incidentally, salt, particularly sea salt, is a fabulous tool for cleansing and clearing. Adding it to a bath and providing a candle for meditative focus is a heart-centered manner of self-care. You may already practice similar rituals thinking that the salt is just good for your skin and the candle a nice ambiance without realizing the full reach of their benefits.

As you experience stimuli, your brain creates chemicals - feelings and emotions. By allowing these to last for hours or days, you're memorizing them. This is referred to as a mood. When you continue this for weeks or months, it becomes a temperament. When Experience X causes you to live by the same emotional reaction by keeping the refractory periods running for years, it becomes a personality trait. In order to change some part of yourself, you must first look at the emotions that were memorized and stored.

It is vital to approach any situation in a *Whole*-istic manner - addressing the emotional elements as well as the symptoms of the manifestation. When we focus too much on the problem, we often can't see the possible solutions because all we see *is* the problem. ~ Recall the color exercise from Chapter Four. While medical intervention, therapy, etc. are components of the healing process, it is not entirely those contributions which heal you. It is the overall process as a *whole*. The possible solutions to any problems in your life already exist. It's simply a matter of being open to exploring and embracing them. I provide an exploratory exercise in the back of this book which I highly recommend contemplating.

I often explain to new clients that I don't heal people. I assist them in expanding their awareness, softening their resistance and re-connecting with their own capacities for healing themselves. You are the only one who can heal you because you're the only one who truly knows how – even if you don't currently *think* so. The *placebo effect* is an exquisite demonstration.

An article published in the *Wall Street Journal* entitled *Fake Knee Surgery as Good as Real Procedure, Study Finds* provides intriguing confirmation. Researchers found that a fake surgical procedure is just as good as real surgery at reducing pain and other symptoms in some patients suffering from torn knee cartilage. They studied two sets of patients – one that received the actual surgery and another that was led to believe that they had. The patients agreed to participate in the study prior to the procedure and were informed they would either receive the actual surgery or not. They underwent arthroscopy to confirm the tears, but for patients in the control group, doctors didn't remove the cartilage. Patients led to *believe* they had knee surgery saw results comparable to those who actually *had* the procedure.

The researchers observed no significant differences in improvement between the two groups after one year. In a related paper published in the *New England Journal of Medicine*, researchers found that while surgery provided a slight advantage early on, the differences disappeared by the end of 12 months. Jeffrey Katz, a Professor of Medicine at Brigham and Women's Hospital in Boston said *"The implications are fairly profound."* Teppo L.N. Järvinen, an Orthopedic Resident and Adjunct Professor at Helsinki University Central Hospital and one of the study's authors said that *"Doctors have a bad tendency to confuse what they believe with what they know."*

There was another study where fake radiation treatments were given to a group of patients. Although radiation was not actually applied to 1/3 of participants, they lost their hair nonetheless. Your perceptions and beliefs contribute to what ails you; and they also contribute to what heals you.

The placebo effect provides a clear demonstration of the capacity of the mind to heal. *No*cebo has the opposite effect. You can have the right surgery, medication, therapy, etc.; yet you don't heal. In both cases, people are using their beliefs, but in different directions. Something to consider: What if when a doctor says that something is *in*curable, it means that it's not curable by way of surgery or medication, etc., that it is only curable from with*in*?

Dr. Joseph Dispenza says that belief can be so strong that pharmaceutical companies use double- and triple-blind randomized studies to exclude the power of the mind over the body when evaluating new drugs. In his book, *You Are the Placebo: Making Your Mind Matter,* he tells of those who have gotten sick and/or died as a result of their belief in a diagnosis, mis-diagnosis and even curses and things of that nature. He shares scientific evidence of numerous documented cases of reversed cancer, heart disease and depression (among others) attributed to a belief in the placebo effect. He also provides a how-to meditation for changing beliefs and perceptions - which is the first step in healing.

When a Dark Night of the Soul and/or Healing Crisis occurs, all of your emotional stuff comes up. When you encounter such, allow yourself to be present with it - with no judgment where it is concerned. Set an intention not to resist or attempt to escape it... allow yourself to be there with it vs. falling apart in fear. This alone can set you on the path of healing and recovery. Consider this: What if everything that seems to be falling apart is actually everything preparing to fall together?

When you truly intend to create change, the structure that created that which you intend to change must be transformed. As it transforms, it begins to dissolve in order to make room for the change you prefer. While the process is a beautiful thing, it can be extremely uncomfortable. Asking questions can lighten the discomfort during this process in an amazing way by prompting you to consider the possibilities that exist which you may not be able to see when you're in the midst of the shift. For example:

- Is this falling apart or is it just falling together in a totally different way?
- Is this the change I've been asking for, showing up totally different than the way I thought it might?

"What the caterpillar calls the end of the world, the master calls a butterfly." -Richard Bach

"When one door closes, another opens; but we often look so long and so regretfully upon the closed door that we do not see the one which has opened for us." -Alexander Graham Bell

The Universe tends to deliver things in ways which we cannot begin to fathom ourselves because if our logical mind could have made the adjustments, it would have done so already. Instead of resisting and/or reacting and going to the wrongness of you or the situation, ask open-ended questions such as: *If this were happening for the highest good, what might that be? How is this happening 'For' me? What are the gifts that I may not yet be able to see?*

Take the opportunity to be grateful for the amazing capacities of your Mind/Body, and allow it to do its job. Re-mission is re-membering your mission. Enjoy the invitation to love and care for yourself through the transition; and in the future, don't wait until you are ill to do so. As we discussed in Chapter Six, many people have found that they are healthier and happier having gone through such a process as a result of the transformation and growth which is deeply meaningful in their lives.

"The worst thing that happens ***To*** *you may be the best thing* ***For*** *you if you don't let it get the best of you." -Will Rogers*

Before we move on from this chapter, I'd like to share an element for consideration: Because they may not conform to our established or socially accepted methodologies, some healings and transformations - particularly those credited to complementary medicine or energetic realms and modalities may seem to occur as if by magic or miracles - Yet they occur nonetheless and are more prevalent every day. *A Course in Miracles* teaches that all miracles involve a change in perception. As Morry Zelcovitch said: *If you can't measure or prove something, it doesn't mean that it doesn't exist. It simply means that we haven't yet discovered a way to measure, prove or explain it.* Just because we may not completely understand something doesn't mean we can't utilize it. For example, I don't understand how electricity works, but I can plug something in to a source and use it. Science can be viewed as a language by which to explain possibility. In the words of Augustine of Hippo (Saint Augustine): *"Miracles happen, not in opposition to nature, but in opposition to what we know of nature."*

"There are only two ways to live your life:
One is as though nothing is a miracle.
The other is as though everything is a miracle." -Unknown

"If you don't believe in miracles, perhaps you've forgotten that you are one." -Unknown

"Love is the great miracle cure.
Loving ourselves works miracles in our lives." -Louise L. Hay

Here's to more magic and miracles in your life!

For more information, please visit Resources.

Musings...

"A moment's insight is sometimes worth a lifetime's experiences." - Oliver Wendell Holmes

Chapter 9

Aha* Moments ~ You, Version Now.*Ohhh!

In this chapter, you'll mine the gems of your subconscious, expand on your *Aha's* and discover some new ones.

Have you ever attended a class or workshop, inspired and excited, only to encounter even more questions and frustration - listening to others share pyrotechnic revelations and breakthroughs, wondering *Where are **My** fireworks*? Have you read a book or watched a movie more than once and discovered that you'd missed something substantial the first or maybe even the second time around? Perhaps you've heard several sources deliver a similar message at various times in your life; yet on one occasion, you got the memo. We all have different access points. It's been said that you will only learn something once you already know it. *Yes, you read that right.*

"When the student is ready, the teacher will appear." -Buddhist Proverb

For fun, Epiphany is described as a sudden and profound comprehension about the nature or meaning of something. The term is typically used to describe scientific breakthroughs and religious or philosophical discoveries, but it can apply to anything where enlightenment brings understanding from a new and deeper perspective. An *Aha* Moment is described as one of sudden insight or discovery - Insight being sight from within and discovery the uncovering of the meaning around something that you likely already knew. It's where you instantaneously understand or know something without having to think about any details surrounding it. Your *thinking* mind tends to get in the way of your *knowing*. So rather than waiting for angels to fly down from the heavens to hand-deliver clarity, let's expand the mind to function a bit more from our knowing, shall we?

I've been reminded by friends many years later of something I was known for saying during the latter part of my high school years. With a mixture of trepidation and excitement of life before me as graduation approached, I'd say that I rather looked forward to my forties and fifties because by then, I'd likely have my s--- together ☺ I must have known on some level that it would be during that era of my life that clarity would emerge - that I wouldn't be muddled so much by what other people thought, and I wouldn't be living by anyone else's judgments, conclusions or expectations. *Talk about not being present, though!*

We all evolve at our own pace and in our own time. I may not have realized the implications of my words at the time, yet hindsight provides interesting perspective. It can be frustrating to realize that you've had the knowing and power to create your life as you wished all along. However, re-membering this capacity and appreciating that you can make new choices at any given time is exquisitely empowering.

"Our lessons come from the journey." -Don Williams, Jr.

Little did I 'know' (*cognitively anyway*) when I left the programming arena that my journey would take me in the direction that it has. Although I thrived in that environment for years, I see now that once I'd proven myself (or proven whatever it was *To* myself), it just wasn't fun for me anymore. When I became a first-time mother in my early forties, I realized that I preferred something different. I've often said that working in the programming field is not a job, it's a lifestyle. The same can be said for any occupation; and all too often we may identify and somewhat limit ourselves within these roles. I recall listening to Anita Moorjani speak on this. She said that *"Who you are is not your job title, and your job is not who you are - There's a difference. If you don't know yourself, following your passion is something that's outside of yourself."* I have found this to be quite true. While I enjoyed the corporate world for some time, I realized that on some level, I'd become my roles; and yet, they simply were not me ~ Something was missing.

"How many cares one loses when one decides not to be something but to be someone." ~Coco Chanel

Anita suggests that you get to know *You*. Ask yourself what you being your authentic self would be doing for your work or how you would *be* loving the work that you do. When we don't live from who we are, we settle. This is where Monday Blues, TGIF's, burn out and mid-life crises are born. We stay in jobs, relationships and patterns because on some level the familiarity feels safe. If you are being you, there would be no discontentment or need for escapes, retirement, and the like. The line between your job or relationships and who you are would be a blur, if there were a line at all.

Anita Moorjani, Dying to Be Me, Copyright 2012, Hay House, Inc., Carlsbad, CA

This may sound *airy-fairy* on some levels, but it is truth. Just look at some of the associated words:

Vacation: Vacate - move away from, leave, quit, cancel, annul.
~ Not to be confused with rejuvenation, expansion or exploring and enjoying desirable locations.

> Retire: Stop working, leave the grind, withdraw, go to sleep.
> ~ *Following your dreams doesn't mean going back to bed.*

During my *me*-search, I discovered a process called *The Disidentification Exercise,* developed by Roberto Assagioli, M.D., an Italian psychiatrist and pioneer in the fields of humanistic and transpersonal psychology. He founded the psychological movement known as Psychosynthesis, described in his book, *Psychosynthesis: A Manual of Principles and Techniques.* Dr. Assagioli was quoted as saying, *"We are dominated by everything with which our self becomes identified. We can dominate and control everything from which we dis-identify ourselves."* His Disidentification Exercise is a meditation that assists you in stepping outside of your identifications (roles, titles, etc.). It helps you to find your center and reconnect with who you are at your core. While there are various and expanded versions of this technique, the following is a brief synopsis which ideally is practiced every day, optimally in the morning. Repeat the following slowly and thoughtfully:

- I have a body, and I am not my body.
- I have emotions, and I am not my emotions.
- I have a mind, and I am not my mind.
- I have many roles that I play, and I am not my roles.
- I am a center of pure consciousness and love.

For some time, I've been a bit of a junkie for holistic and Spiritual material. An addiction in its own sense, but a beneficial one I felt warranted indulgence. I confess that for a while, I bought almost everyone's program. I'd listen to interviews of inspirational coaches, energy workers and motivational speakers, be inspired and purchase whatever package they were offering. With some, I'd go through the material and incorporate it for a while, yet ultimately resume the *me*-search. Some received but a mere surface review before I'd move on to the next shiny thing in the cyber mall. At one point, my shelves were so overflowing with Books, CD's and DVD's, I realized that it was time to either graduate to the next level in the school of the perpetual student or open a library...*I did a bit of both.* I continue to participate in this process, yet with a bit more selectivity these days. I'm not by any means discounting any of the programs I've personally utilized or that are available today as my rule of thumb is: *When you find something that resonates, Go For It.* What I am saying is that there is no single magic wand.

All of the material I've encountered, regardless of its level of impact, has contributed to where I am now...and I'm still evolving. My experiences and *Aha's* are the ingredients to the *Secret Sauce* of my personal best. In hindsight, I understand that some of these programs didn't '*work*' because I simply wasn't ready; but more likely, I was unaware of the manner by which to till the weeds and cultivate the garden of my subconscious before planting the seeds they provided. In the absence of understanding this essential element, my programming would kick back in - regardless of the content, quality of the material and/or my diligence in applying it. We'll discuss the optimal manner by which to integrate such material in detail during Chapter Eleven. For the moment, consider this a sharing of one of my many *Aha's*.

I recall reading and listening to the amazing people I've mentioned herein and silently wishing that I could be more like them - to embody their depth of wisdom, clarity, balance and peace in my own life. For some time, I went about my days experimenting on my own, sharing my experiences with clients and close friends. Delivering my first class on this material was a key turning point for me. I never envisioned myself teaching or writing about this stuff. I simply wanted to utilize it in my own life and share it with receptive, like-minded folks. I will confess that it took some nudging initially, but to my surprise and delight, I delivered my first class with little trepidation and great ease. Ordinarily, I'd fuss over the anticipation of delivering any sort of presentation. This time, however, I simply tended to the preparation and just did it. Thereafter, my confidence and conversations became more profound, my interactions more meaningful and the feedback I received was of a caliber I reserved only for the likes of my favorite inspirational mentors. *When something calls to you and you feel the nudge, follow your heart, make the stretch and take action. You'll quite often be very pleasantly surprised.*

For all of you healers (*and we all are*), whether you presently acknowledge and utilize your gifts consciously - privately, professionally or not, I'd like to share one of my more personal *Aha*'s. Although I'd made great strides with my inner work, there was a period wherein I began to wonder, *I help so many of my clients with similar issues, so why am I unable to fully do so with some of my own?* I felt as though I'd secretly become the queen of *Do as I say not as I do.* I'd discovered first-hand the truth in the adage: *The best way to learn something is to teach it.* When you stand up in front of a group of colleagues at Microsoft, many of whom were far more seasoned than I, you'd better know your sh--; or at the very least be humble enough to provide an honest "*I don't know, but I'll find out for you.*" Matters of this nature are no different, especially where authenticity is essential.

I often felt as though I was passing out on the airplane as I assisted those around me, having neglected to put on my own oxygen mask first. Perhaps it was one of those things where I wasn't willing to give up the rewards I'd been deriving from some of my patterns? I began going deeper with my inner work and journaling around it. Some of that work contributed to the format of many of the exercises in this book. I'm not entirely sure what the actual switch was that turned the key, but I began allowing myself to become more receptive to the healing work that I was doing and presenting. Once I did, everything began to shift; and my life has improved exponentially since. Richard Bach summed it beautifully when he said: "*We teach best that which we most need to learn.*"

Should you have similar inklings, my advice to you is this: Keep dipping your toe into the proverbial waters of change. Eventually your objective to be fully whole, authentic and free will grow and enable you to immerse yourself in the pool of forgiveness, healing and unconditional love. It may feel unfamiliar at first. You may even experience a Dark Night of the Soul and/or a Healing Crisis along the way. I assure you, however, that you will immerge energized, empowered and walking the walk of your objectives and preferences.

"Keep knocking, and the joy inside will eventually open a window and look out to see who's there." ~Rumi

It's taken me a number of years and milestones to feel that I've finally gotten it - or at least some of it. There have been many *Aha* Moments along the way, some more brilliant than others; yet somewhere within my journey, I came to understand that *getting it* is an ongoing, cumulative process - one which we traverse at our own pace in our own time. It's been said that when you acknowledge how little you know (or how little you choose to acknowledge) you are then ready to learn. I've personally found this to be true.

Realizing how I'd been creating my life was a tremendous *Aha* for me. I'd been allowing some people into my life who were unable to contribute to me in positive ways because in some respects, I wasn't first doing so for myself. They were distractions and shiny things. I wondered, why is it only when we get upset, frustrated or angry enough that we'll use the potency that we have to make changes and create what we prefer? I surmised that perhaps it's the outside motivation that we're waiting for to stimulate us to do what's going to make us as fulfilled as we can't possibly be. ~Yes, you read that facetious *can't* correctly. To this, a dear friend of mine commented: *"Ironic, though it is, how true. I guess we should be grateful for them (Upset, Frustration, Anger), as they too are gifts from the Universe - catalysts for change."* Well, everything that is and brings up.....

Aha's are the keys to opening doors to new levels of awareness. Each one an ideal ingredient for your *Secret Sauce.* So, let's have a look at some of your *What am I not getting's* and turn them into catalysts for change.

In-Sight is seeing from within. *Aha* Moments are insights where there's a sudden re-cognition, understanding or knowing. Sudden implying that there's no need to mentally scan your database for rationalization, validation, etc. Research has been conducted to discover what goes on in the brain when a solution to a problem is found analytically vs. by way of insight. John Kounios, Ph.D and Mark Beeman, co-authors of *The Eureka Factor: Aha Moments, Creative Insight, and the Brain*, conducted experiments regarding the cognitive neuroscience of insight. They found that analytical vs. insight solutions utilize different cognitive processes in the brain. The Gamma wave power of half the participants in the study was measured with EEG while and the other half with MRI. Mapping of the brain wave comparisons showed an area of increased activity in the portion of the brain above the right ear which was active during insight solutions yet inactive in non-insight solutions. This research indicated an increase in Gamma wave power in those participants finding solutions by insight vs. analytical means.

It's interesting to note that various factors can influence insight processing. For example, an MRI study showed that people are more likely to solve problems with insight when they are in a positive mood than a neutral or negative one. Positive mood was associated with greater activity in the Anterior Cingulate during the preparation period prior to each problem solving. This part of the brain plays a role in a wide variety of autonomic functions such as regulating blood pressure and heart rate. It's also involved in rational cognitive functions such as reward anticipation, decision-making, empathy, impulse control and emotion. This suggests that positive mood biases cognitive control mechanisms in ways that facilitate insight, with anxiety having the opposite effect.

Work in progress suggests that when positive mood is induced by having participants watch comedy videos, they not only solve more problems, they solve more of them with insight than they do after watching neutral or anxiety-inducing films. Herein lies more incentive to choose your television viewing options wisely and limit potentially negative external influencing factors. Choose not to subscribe to the doom and gloom of the daily news. Be mindful that within the same environment, while some are glooming, others are booming.

In their book, "*The Art of Insight: How to have more Aha! Moments*", Charles F. Kiefer and Malcolm Constable draw on years of research and experience to present a thorough, pragmatic approach to cultivating a mindset where insights come readily. The authors sight a difference between intellectual learning and insight learning. Intellectual learning being active and relying on accumulating facts, processing those facts, storing them in memory and connecting them in a methodical way. Insight learning works differently in that we look for insights, yet allow them to occur passively through a subconscious reflective process that's more receptive than active. Insight learning often involves taking diverse facts we already know and putting them together in a new way. The practice of insight thinking, termed '*The Art of Insight (TAOI)*' by Kiefer and Constable, is more of an art than a science, consisting of four key elements:

- Understanding what insights are and actively looking for them.
- Occupying a state of mind in which you're apt to have insights more frequently.
- Learning to listen in such a way that you hear insights in yourself and others.
- Growing your understanding of how thought works in your life.

Insight is about seeing something for yourself – having a thought or comprehension that you've never had before. To find these gems, it's necessary to look into the unknown - the vast realm of possibility. To productively till this realm, you want to approach with an open, relaxed or *insight* state of mind. Regrettably, life trains many of us out of employing this natural process, and we lose the habit of making insight a regular and expedient occurrence. The methods offered in *The Art of Insight* reconnect you with that ability and help you increase the frequency, strength, and value of the insights you experience. Kiefer and Constable provide *Insight Listening Tools* to assist in producing more insights. A link to detailed exercise reference materials and video demonstrations is available within their book from Berrett-Koeheler Publishers (*See Resources*).

Insight is the art of using your internal sight to gain accurate and deep intuitive understanding. Although we'd occasionally prefer the clouds to part, bestowing an undeniable lightning bolt *Aha*, when we're perceptive and mindful of the subtle messages that are available to us, we will find them. The key is to look for and listen to them. If something feels lighter to embrace, there's your confirmation. To explore this, I offer an enlightening exercise in the back of this book.

It's always beneficial to discuss your circumstances with others to gain their perspective and input. While it is valuable, be mindful that it is based on *their* perceptions, experiences and points of view. Your choices must come from your own known.

"A point of view can be a dangerous luxury when substituted for insight and understanding." -Marshall McLuhan

"The best vision is insight." -Malcolm Forbes

Developing and using your own personal insight where your objectives and choices are concerned is the optimal approach to creating and experiencing the life you prefer.

If I chose only one, my most significant *Aha* is realizing that life doesn't happen *To* me, it happens *For* me. Approaching life with this outlook and asking open-ended questions provides an open door to insight and the infinite possibilities which are available.

I'd love to create a positive news station. I'd call it W.***A.H.A.*** *- All Good News, All the Time.* People could call or write in to share the gems of their *Aha* Moments and positive experiences. Now *there's* something worth tuning in to!

"It is better to feel your way through life than to think your way through it." -Deepak Chopra

For more information, please visit Resources.

Musings…

"To love and be loved is to feel the sun from both sides." ~David Viscott

Chapter 10

What's Love Got To Do With It?

In this chapter, you'll consider the many aspects of love and the key roles they play in your life as an invitation to embrace unconditional love as your primary expression.

The creature from another galaxy that visited you in Chapter Five has returned with another question:

What is love? What sentiments would compose your brief response?

____

____

How much of the love that you've experienced or currently know is conditional or unconditional? How much of this love is determined by your perceptions and expectations, and how much of it is a reflection of the love you have for yourself?

The word *Love* has more classifications and descriptions than just about any word in any language. Wikipedia describes it as referring to a variety of feelings, states and attitudes ranging from pleasure to interpersonal attraction as well as a virtue representing human kindness, compassion and affection. Interestingly, Wiki makes the distinction of '*Human*' in their elucidation. They go on to state that love may be understood as part of the survival instinct, a function to keep human beings together against menaces and to facilitate the continuation of the species. They differentiate *conditional* love as that which is 'earned' on the basis of conscious or unconscious conditions being met by the lover; whereas *unconditional* love separates the individual from their behaviors and is given freely to the loved one - No matter what - Loving first. Buddhism describes love as the intention for happiness ~ its function being the unselfish objective for the welfare of all.

The *Law of Unconditional Love* is the acceptance of that which exists without judgment or expectation. It states that if you practice unconditional love, you automatically rise above fear; and as you transcend your fears, you automatically open to the expression of unconditional love.

What does it feel like to love? Do you remember the first time, or any time, you fell or were in love? Perhaps you currently are. What does it feel like? The permagrin on your face, the vibrancy, feeling that you are flawless in the eyes of another – acknowledged and accepted without judgment or heaviness of any kind while seeing them in the same light; being in a state of pure happiness and flow where everything in life is fine and fabulous. We come into the world with this natural temperament. *What if you could be that way most, if not all of the time?*

Let's have a look at some of the people, places and things that you love or are in love with and consider the aspects of this love from a conditional as well as an unconditional perspective. We'll start with something simple, a song, for instance. If you were to choose your favorite song of all time, what would it be? What feelings, emotions or memories does it conjure? What is it about the song that you love - the music, the message, the band that performs it, the feelings it invokes – a combination thereof? This being your favorite song, I'll surmise that it conveys lightness to you. With that in mind, what if you learned that the song was written to describe something opposing what it conjures within you - something heavy? What if you found that those who composed the song are folks that, for whatever reason(s), you might consider undesirable? Would you continue to love the song?

Consider *Helter Skelter*. What message does it convey to you? For me, it initially conjured the heaviness of the 1976 film of the same name based on the murders committed by the *Charles Manson Family.* In researching it, I learned that after hearing Pete Townshend of *The Who* describe their song, *I Can See For Miles*, as the rawest, loudest song they'd ever recorded, Paul McCartney of *The Beatles* was inspired to write *Helter Skelter* in response to critics accusing him of writing only ballads. Helter Skelter is a term used to describe disorder, confusion or disorderly haste. A Helter Skelter is also an amusement park ride with a slide built in a spiral around a high tower. Users climb up inside the tower and then slide down the outside, usually on a mat. The song, which was released in 1968, can be perceived as nothing more than a whimsical piece of music. When associated with the 1976 movie, however, it takes on an entirely different connotation. An interesting demonstration of how we can be influenced by filters and perceptions. Love is like music. A melody can provoke varying meanings to different people within assorted ambiances.

Depending on the relevance you prescribe to the various aspects of love, the love itself could be construed as conditional or unconditional based on your perceptions and expectations. This single concept applies to just about everything in your life - your relationships with yourself, others, jobs, hobbies, habits, food, etc. Do you discern based on the details of the package or are you one to focus on the package as a whole, regardless of the aspects woven within ~ perhaps a bit of both? Let's visit some of these aspects and their roles within three types of relationships: Children/Pets, Partner/Spouse and the most commonly overlooked, Self.

As a for instance, you acquire a new pet – a kitten you name Fluffy. You're thoroughly enjoying this addition to your life - loving her unconditionally, receiving the same in return. Then she coughs up a nauseating fur ball that stains your carpet, turns your bathroom into a war zone with her litter box activities and frays your drapes or furniture with her antics and claws. Does your love for her degenerate from unconditional to conditional? Do you stop loving Fluffy? Not likely. It's not so much diminished love for Fluffy as it is displeasure with the outcome of her actions which is the source of your discontent.

So you implement training strategies to alleviate these undesirable circumstances in a gently persuasive manner, and the love affair continues; or perhaps deteriorates. After a few unsuccessful attempts, you may find that you've encountered the mustang of the species and choose to opt out of the relationship. I'd like to express my empathy for any new cat owner - not only in your training endeavors, but in your overall feline relationship because the *Cat* is the one who will show *You* how it's going to be. One of my Sisters presented me with a plaque which says it all: "*Dogs have Masters; Cats have Staff.*"

With all due consideration of possible training and conditioning, while a dog may initially take preference to someone offering a snack, they typically greet all they meet uncategorically without all the filters we humans acquire during our lives. They really don't care what you look like, how much money you have or what your political views may be. They approach with exuberance, gift and receive some doggie love and continue along their way with no judgment or conclusion whatsoever. We could take a lesson or two from the animals, particularly those whose paths intersect with ours.

As with any relationship, there are times when one's behavior is cause for upset in the other. I try to be mindful of this overall, but especially as a parent. My Son, Boston, is eight years old as of this writing. He loves to draw, dissect and build. He's an engineer in his own right. He will sketch the specifications of his inspirations and set about constructing them using whatever he deems appropriate to manifest his masterpiece. He acquires the components for his inventions via the dissection of electronics – games, power tools and computer components (Mum's particularly fond of *those* reallocations of resources). Oh, and tape and glue…*Lots of 'em.* This little engineer is quite creative, ingenious and resourceful - articulate beyond his years as well. *M.I.T. - Are you listening? Can you say 'Scholarship'? -I digress.* His preference is the creation of robotic devices - many with aeronautic capabilities - a gift bestowed by his dearly transitioned Uncle Chuck, whom he asserts to have known in Heaven prior to his incarnation. Countless varieties of apparati took flight from the launch pad, a.k.a ceiling fan, in his playroom.

Boston's favorite drafting tool is a black Sharpie®, which is fine as long as the ink is transferred only to paper, not the furniture beneath…or anything else for that matter. However, our home currently exhibits two spectacularly permanent works of art. One of which graces the hardwood floor in his playroom – a race track designed to run his cars around on. *Well, that one's from a while ago and was rather amusing. It's now masqueraded with a strategically-placed area rug.*

The other *Boston Original* graces the wall in his bedroom - a seven-foot+ diagram of a beverage-dispensing machine. As it was explained to me by the engineer himself, this inspiration came to him one night when he awoke desiring a glass of milk. Having no inclination to descend the stairs to the kitchen, open the refrigerator and pour some into a glass, his deduction was that it would be far more efficient to have a device whereby the push of a button would deliver it to him. His design was not only a delivery mechanism; however, it was a cow-milking, filtering, packaging and dispensing system. Not only was he going for convenience, this guy was going for *fresh*! *"And the teenage years have yet to come"...she said with trepidation.* I mean anticipation, joyful anticipation ☺

When I encountered this work of art, while the location and permanency of the specs was met with disapproval, my esteem for the impressiveness of his innovative design was paramount. My point in sharing this story is to also share that I reinforced the latter, expressing love and encouragement to my Son. All of us, especially as children, need this type of reinforcement highlighted regularly - especially when we realize that we may have bestowed turbulence upon the village...*Recall the forgiveness intervention of the South African tribe from Chapter Seven.*

Research shows that children tend to absorb the responsibility of reproach and for the discontent of their parents, whether they contributed to it or not. The same tendency is true of pets who will take on their owners' physical ailments in order to relieve them of their suffering. When communicating with children, it is critical to be mindful of this because, as Peggy O'Mara was quoted as saying:

The way we talk to our children becomes their inner voice."

A quote from Lucille Ball also comes to mind:

*"Children internalize their parents' unhappiness.
Fortunately, they absorb their contentment
just as readily." - Love, Lucy (1996)*

It is essential, particularly as children, that our sense of love be nurtured, regardless of the circumstances of any situation. With the understanding that I now have at this point in my life, I recognize that had I received this type of nurturing and encouragement consistently early on, my adult life and relationships would have been quite different. While we're all doing the best that we can with what we have to work with at any given time, the more mindfulness we employ, the more ease filled and joyful our lives and those around us become.

In focusing on this aspect, I discovered what I call *Realized* Love. To realize is to give reality to; to comprehend it completely and obtain as a profit. In this context, it's the ability to see and experience love where it may have previously escaped our perception. This is the type of love that Dr. Wayne W. Dyer and Anita Moorjani were able to appreciate for her Fathers later in their lives. Looking at my parents from their circumstances and perspective provided clarity on many of my childhood experiences and much of the baggage I'd been lugging around. Viewing them in an entirely different light enabled me to embrace unconditional love and a deeper level of appreciation for them.

"Where there is no love, put love -- and you will find love." -Juan de la Cruz (Saint John of the Cross)

Love for a child is the epitome of unconditional love. Parenting is the ultimate contribution to the evolution of a Soul. Truly, the greatest gift and legacy one can bestow upon a child is healthy self-love and a positive consciousness…which optimally is embodied and demonstrated by the adult. Our relationships with others are reflective of our relationship with our self. That being said, let's talk about self-love.

Quite often during my I/T career, I recall saying that I felt as though I'd jumped into graduate school from kindergarten without acquiring my CEU's (Continuing Education Units) along the way. I later found that this statement's significance held more relevance to my life overall than merely in relation to my previous profession.

While I'd been acquiring them, I came to realize that I'd been somewhat remiss in their integration. Patience is, indeed, a virtue - one which I'd not been astute at embracing. Clearly I was in a rush to get here and neglected to pick up my *Owner's Manual* at the gate or forgone its review after discovering it in my pocket. My soul knew what was needed. I simply hadn't been listening.

Shortly after my Son was born, I left I/T and returned home. We stayed with one of my Brothers while we searched for our new residence. It was during one of the coldest, snowiest Northeast winters in some time; and my Brother made us quite comfortable. My entire focus was nurturing my child and family. It was the most beautiful period of my life. After some time, though, I began slipping into a state of overwhelm. Being a displaced new Mom, experiencing culture shock, sleep deprivation and a certain degree of seclusion escorted me into what I now understand was depression. I came to realize that somewhere along the line, I had become my job; yet could see that I'd been rather disengaged from it for some time. I'd now become a parent and was beginning to feel a similar disconnection. I found myself experiencing a severe identity crisis – feeling misunderstood, alone and confused as I had during my childhood.

I began recalling some of my unhappiest memories from those years, re-experiencing the toxic emotions they'd produced which had been stored within my subconscious. The happiest time of my life came to include a Dark Night of the Soul. In the still of that dark night, though, I found Dr. Wayne W. Dyer and Louise Hay. *Goddess/God Bless them both - Trillionfold!* I began to digest and integrate their material. I realized that I'd been living my life guided only by my programming and a tiny shaft of dim light described by Anita Moorjani in her *Flashlight Exercise.* I did a lot of Soul searching, reviewing my life thus far and came to realize that I'd been looking outside of myself for acceptance and fulfillment when the primary directive was to begin within. *Talk about lookin' for love in all the wrong places!* I'd been conducting my *me-search* in an obscure wing in the library of life. While the librarian in the dimly lit hall of wisdom was quite helpful, she could merely guide me to the general area of that which I'd inquired upon. When I followed my heart down an unfamiliar hallway and found the switch that turned on the lights, I discovered that there was so much more

I also discovered Rhonda Byrne's *The Secret,* and devoured the material of each and every avatar therein. I felt like a kid in a candy store! I began asking questions, doing energy work and meditating. This was my *secret sauce* recipe – It was the frosting for the cake which had been baking in the oven and was now cooling on the countertop. These tools enabled me to embody what I'd somehow known on a visceral level yet had been unable to consciously comprehend and employ.

I came to understand that, regardless of my past, I was responsible for my life and everything about it. I began to comprehend that regardless of my current circumstances, I could change it at will. With this enlightenment came empowerment. I vowed to always listen to and follow my heart, regardless of what the situation, potential judgments, perceived setbacks or fears may be. I also knew that doing so would involve some honest, significant adjustments and changes; and I was excited at the prospect. Shifts began immediately. At first, quite subtly; but as the days, weeks and months passed, the changes were not only tangible and empowering, they were enduring. This new energy seemed vaguely familiar, almost like a dream - yet more like a memory. When you acknowledge your own consciousness and choose to make a shift, magic emerges and miracles begin to happen. I was becoming me ~ stepping into my authentic self, and I began to embrace self love.

As the Universe in divine wisdom and timing would have it, I came across an audio version of Marci Shimoff's *New York Times* best-selling book, *Love For No Reason,* that I'd purchased some time ago but had not yet listened to. *LFNR* is about connecting to a state of pure, unconditional love within yourself - A love which is limitless, doesn't ask to be returned and does not depend on anything outside of yourself. Marci tells us that when you love and accept yourself completely, old patterns dissolve and fulfillment in life grows. You have a sense of well-being, satisfaction and fullness versus a fundamental void that many of us try to fill with shiny things or turning to unhealthy behaviors.

Marci asks the question, *What does it mean to love?* And says that all experiences of love can be divided into 4 distinct categories along a spectrum she refers to as *The Love Continuum*:

No Love	Love for Bad Reason	Love For Good Reason	Love For No Reason
◄	———	———	►
Hate, Fear, Resistance	Using others to fill a void inside	Healthy, mutually beneficial relationships	An inner state of pure unconditional love
CONDITIONAL		UNCONDITIONAL	

Listening to Marci's audio was inspiring to say the very least. It brought countless aspects of life and love into a whole new dimension of perspective and understanding for me, especially where self-love is concerned. Her book is brilliantly honest, exquisitely composed and incredibly enlightening. It includes techniques to assist you in expanding your ability to be in a state of unconditional love more of the time. Marci brings the spectrum of love from what we often perceive as complex back to its natural state. She asserts that living in this state is the ultimate cure-all and that happiness takes a back seat to love because when you love, happiness is present intrinsically.

> *"Wouldn't it be powerful if you fell in love with yourself*
> *so deeply that you would do just about anything*
> *if you knew it would make you happy?" -Alan Cohen*

I offer an enlightening exercise around this topic which is included in the back of this book.

~ Love begins with me ~

The universal symbol for love is the heart, so let's have a look at this amazing entity. The heart is the first organ to develop in a fetus and the last to shut down when we die. Most of us view the heart as a physical organ with a mechanical directive. However, it is so much more. The heart chakra is located in the center of the chest and radiates out to the arms and hands - which we use to express our gifting and receiving of love. The Heart Chakra joins the upper three Chakras (your thought and logic processes) and the lower three Chakras (your emotion and creativity processes) together. It is the entry point for the Soul, *and* it has a mind of its own.

Research in the field of neurocardiology has provided scientific proof that the heart is a source of intelligence that has a greater influence and impact on our lives than we may be aware of. During his research, Dr. J. Andrew Armour introduced the term *Heart Brain*. An article published by HeartMath® Institute entitled *Science of the Heart* states that the heart brain is an intricate network of several types of neurons, neurotransmitters, proteins and support cells similar to those found in the cranial brain. Research has shown that the heart communicates to the brain in four major ways: neurologically (through the transmission of nerve impulses), biochemically (via hormones and neurotransmitters), biophysically (through pressure waves) and energetically (through electromagnetic field interactions). Its elaborate circuitry enables it to act independently of the cranial brain – to learn, remember, feel and sense.

In fetal development, the heart forms and starts beating before the brain begins to develop. The heart is an electromagnet that trains the rest of the body. It communicates information throughout the body by means of electromagnetic field interactions and generates the body's most powerful and extensive rhythmic electromagnetic field. In *Science of the Heart Volume 2*, HeartMath® Research Staff notes that the heart's electrical field is about 60 times greater in amplitude than the electrical activity generated by the brain. Furthermore, the magnetic field produced by the heart is more than 100 times greater in strength than the field generated by the brain and can be detected up to 3 feet away from the body in all directions using SQUID-based magnetometers. SQUID (*superconducting quantum interference device*) is a highly sensitive detector of magnetic signals used to measure extremely subtle magnetic fields.

Professor Karl Pribram suggests that the cranial brain is primarily a pattern storage and recognition system which interprets signals and labels emotions, but that feelings are generated in the heart, not the brain. HeartMath® research shows that although communication travels in both directions, the heart actually sends more information to the brain than the brain sends to the heart. So, perhaps it's not so much *all in your mind* as it is *in your heart…* Trust your instincts as well, of course, yet be mindful that the inner wisdom of your heart is ultimately the barometer and GPS of your life.

In Louise Hay's film, *You Can Heal Your Life ~ The Movie,* Christiane Northrup, M.D. shares that when you think with your heart, your DHEA levels rise and balance your hormones. DHEA (dehydroepiandrosterone) is a steroid hormone made from cholesterol by the adrenal glands which is converted into testosterone and estrogen. The beat to beat variability of your heart normalizes and goes into a different wave pattern that can be seen on a heart rate monitor which balances the entire body. When you bring yourself to a state of relaxation that enlightens you, it results in a decrease in stress hormones and blood pressure, normalization of blood sugar, relaxation of all smooth muscles and a balance of the parasympathetic and sympathetic nervous systems. The Sympathetic Nervous System is like the gas pedal in your vehicle with the Parasympathetic being the break. When these are balanced, you can function more efficiently with beautiful Yin-Yang symmetry. This can be accomplished through heart coherence and meditation.

Louise Hay and Friends, You Can Heal Your Life ~ The Movie, Copyright Hay House, Inc., Carlsbad, CA

Research at HeartMath® has shown heart coherence to be instrumental, not only in the health of our bodies, but in the creation of our lives. Coherence is the quality of being logical, consistent and forming a unified whole. *In*coherence is a lack of cohesion, clarity or organization and is characterized by chaotic rhythms in the heart induced by stress and negative emotions. HeartMath®'s intention is to enlighten us as to the optimal path by which to become a master of our heart's rhythms so that we can positively influence our health. Their widely acclaimed book, *Transforming Stress,* explains that becoming a Rhythm Master is a lot like when you were a child learning to swing. You first started kicking and trying to make the swing go. Then someone gave you a push to help you get going and find your rhythm. Before long, you got the feel of how and when to pump, when to shift your weight and when to kick it up to control the speed. Rhythm Masters not only are adept at orchestrating the rhythms of their hearts and becoming coherent, they're also masters at orchestrating the rhythms of their lives. HeartMath® provides a free download of their *The Quick Coherence Technique®* to assist you in creating a state of coherence in about 60 seconds (*See Resources*) which I highly recommend implementing.

The rhythms of my life were clearly incoherent. Realizing that I'd fallen off the self-love wagon, I asked: *Truth: If I loved myself, then?* A profound question I learned from Karen Paolino-Correia, a wise, gifted and generous woman. Shortly after *The Secret* was launched, I met Karen when I attended her Vision Board workshop on *'Manifesting Your Best Year Yet'*, an insightful, inspiring experience. At the time, her book, *What Would Love Do? A 40–Day Journey to Transform Your Fears Into Miracles of Love*, was about to be published. In celebration thereof, Karen gifted me a spiral bound copy at the end of the workshop. It was not until a couple of years later during my *me-search* on this topic that I read and utilized its inspirational and empowering material.

At that time, I discovered that Karen was offering an on-line course, the description of which read *"If you're tired of searching outside of yourself for acceptance and approval and you're ready to spend quality time getting to know who you really are, then this journey is for you."* I signed up immediately. The title of this course is *A 40 Day Affair with Your Self ~ A Journey of Self Love and Owning your Divine Magnificence.* The depth of the journey this course took me on was profound. It provided a space of warm encouragement and incentives for opening to authentic self-love. When I find myself facing a challenge, I ask: *Truth: What would love do*? Asking this open-ended question bestows incredible clarity, direction and ease. Karen's material is an invaluable contribution in my journey to self-love. I highly recommend gifting it to yourself in yours.

My parents were not freely forthcoming in the attention and affection departments where I was concerned. As a result, I'd concluded that I was not deserving of them. Later in life, I came to realize the self-sabotaging programs I'd integrated within my system based on this belief. When loving, gifting energies presented themselves to me, I was not only unwilling to allow myself to accept them, I was utterly unable to. It was impossible for me to receive so much as a compliment. As a for instance, someone admires your home, your car or the way that you look. Versus cordially accepting the sentiment, do you discount, justify or deflect? *"Oh, but it's a mess"* or *"Yeah, but it won't be paid off for years"* or *"Oh, this is a new outfit, but I really need to lose a couple of pounds"*. Perhaps you can identify?

Have you found yourself to be primarily more of a giver than a receiver, whether it's in the personal or professional realms of your life (perhaps both)? Do you ever wonder what drives this compulsion within you and what it would take or be like to receive that which you gift more consistently? If this resonates with you on any level, I ask you: *Do you gift this type of consideration to yourself? Are you a priority on your own list? Are you even <u>On</u> your list?* If your response to any of these questions is *'No'*, or perhaps a reticent *'Not really'*, lest I remind you of The Golden Rule/Ethic of Reciprocity? *One should treat others as one would like others to treat oneself.* While this is true, the polar is equally true and absolutely essential where self-love is concerned. *Treat yourself as you wish to be treated by others.* After all, generosity begins at home.

The word *Reciprocity* triggered a memory for me here. Years ago, one of my Sisters worked for a large insurance company in Boston. I was young at the time and did not yet have an appreciation for the workings of Corporate America. However, I recall her coming home at the end of what I perceived as very long, unfulfilling days, recounting her experiences at work. It was clear that she was overworked and undervalued. Most importantly, she was unhappy in her role. Ironically, the name of the department she worked in at this company was the Reciprocity Department. *Digression,* but you see my thought process here. Being an unfulfilled slave to another's grind is a reminder of what *not* to do. Needless to say, my Sister moved on. While this particular example pertains to the business world, the essence of its message applies to every aspect of our lives.

As Raphael Cushnir tells us, the cause of harmful patterns in our lives is unfelt emotion. I realized that rather than identifying, acknowledging and processing some of the deficits and accompanying emotions I'd experienced as a child, I'd adopted a pattern of re-creating them in my adult life. My parents took good care of me and raised me well. I know they loved me, yet I also realize that they simply weren't capable of giving me the type of love that I desired. I came to understand that in order for me to receive, it was first necessary to provide for myself, regardless of my upbringing or past.

In *Love For No Reason*, Marci reminds us that genuine care for others can easily turn into over-care when you don't pay attention to your own well-being simultaneously. Healthy giving makes you feel good, but unhealthy giving depletes you. Over-giving can lead to the neglect of your own needs, leading to exhaustion, frustration and resentment which results in emptiness. Compromise, compassion and generosity are admirable. However, when they evolve into a chronic pattern of self-depletion, it's a red flag. Habitually putting yourself last is actually confirming and solidifying a program of unworthiness. This is something that has plagued me ever since I can remember, and I know the symptoms well.

Interestingly, another book I'd purchased a while back on the recommendation of a dear friend but had not yet read also found its way back onto my radar: Cheryl Richardson's *The Art of Extreme Self Care.* Cheryl tells us that over-giving is a sign of deprivation; and that deprivation is the unconscious desire to receive that which you are giving. I came to understand my over-giving as a symptom of muted self-love. This was a huge *Aha* for me in that it was the root of many of the self-sabotaging and codependent patterns in my life.

I began asking myself some questions, which I learned from Anita Moorjani:

- *Whose life am I living?*
- *Who am I trying to please?*
- *Who am I trying to be?*
- *Did I create this out of being me or out of trying to meet everyone else's expectations – or what I thought was expected of me?*

Anita Moorjani, Dying to Be Me, Copyright 2012, Hay House, Inc., Carlsbad, CA

These questions revealed the beliefs I'd adopted and programs I'd been running which created the deficits in my life. Love is not something to be earned. It is a gift to be nurtured, savored and shared.

To avoid falling into this pattern, be mindful around your giving. Take care that it doesn't stress, weaken or drain you. Ensure that your needs are equally provided for and that your gifting comes from a place of love. When you gift from fullness, in a healthy way, it enlivens your own heart.

"It's not how much you give but how much love you put into the giving." - Mother Teresa

Self-care is a misunderstood art which is largely under practiced within our culture. Self-care is not selfish, nor is it intended to be regarded as a reward - something you do after all else is done…*If* there's bandwidth. It is an intrinsic part of living. In many ways, we're conditioned to look outside of ourselves and apply Band-Aids® to the surface without realizing that everything we need already exists within. Self-care is a critical missing link to our energy and vitality which enables us to actualize our objectives and experience life fully with ease.

Implementing the strategies in *The Art of Extreme Self Care* helped me to identify many of my self-sabotaging patterns and put me on the fast track to nurturing my overall well-being. I highly recommend Cheryl's book and doing so for yourself.

~ Nurturing those you love begins with taking care of yourself. ~

One thing I've found to be invaluably beneficial is compiling an agenda each week. Notice I call it an agenda, not a schedule. Agenda seems to have a more esthetic resonance for me. Typically, the only calendar I pay heed to is the one in the kitchen for appointments, birthdays, etc. Although I've utilized some of the methods I mentioned in Chapter Six relative to procrastination and the To-Do's in my life, I'd forgone any real structure during the final phases of editing this book. There were a number of things I'd set on the back burner for some time which were haunting me in various degrees - exercising consistently for one. I spent so much time at the computer that there were days when I felt my muscles had atrophied. During this phase came the coldest, snowiest Northeast winter we'd had in some time, so getting outside for a walk was out of the question. Still, I had no excuse. There was a treadmill just down the hall. As far as exercise goes though, treadmills bore me. Besides, it was in an unheated room and...*yada-yada, poo-poo.* There were days and evenings where I'd be so absorbed in what I was doing that the hours simply evaporated. I found myself getting no exercise and very little sleep. Although I loved what I was doing, I was thoroughly drained.

I'd been longing for an elliptical machine for some time, and a dear friend gifted hers to me. It was positioned in a comfortable spot where my stereo and DVD player were available for inspiration. I was thrilled. I used it regularly when it first arrived; but, alas, I fell off that wagon too. Each time I'd pass through that room, I'd think *'Hmm, I should jump on that for a few minutes'*...as I continued on to *other things.* My little Saboteur was at it *Again.* With the painful muscle condition I was dealing with, along with some other stressful issues looming within my life at the time, the best gift I could have given myself was exercise, yoga and more meditation time, yet on the back burner they sat. Still I forged on…while the layers of should and dust on those back burners deepened.

Once again – a nudge from the Universe prompted me to attend a webinar with John Eggen regarding the best ways to publish and market your expertise as an independent professional. This man is a wealth of information, experience and expertise; and I was absolutely inspired by everything he had to share. Without hesitation, I signed up for a free mentoring session with John and was invited to enroll in his publishing and marketing program. It was a most beneficial curriculum - not only where my book and business were concerned, but my life in general at the time.

In addition to learning how to traverse the optimal avenues for my endeavors, I learned more efficient ways by which to utilize my time overall. This added inspiration brought a new spark into my life. When I began the program, there were a number of modules to complete which included listening to audio files, reading transcripts and completing assignments. They were relative to setting goals, outlining action items and scheduling time-frames and deliverables. Knowing what my goals were, yet having so much on my plate, I just wanted to push the fast-forward button and set about completing my tasks. The last thing I wanted to do was take the time to write it all out and put a schedule together; yet doing so was part of the program. Once I completed those items and compiled a weekly agenda, however, everything changed.

It was amazing how much I was able to accomplish - efficiently and with ease. While I allotted time within my agenda for things such as completing the last few pieces of material for my book, renovating my web site, etc., I also included items such as exercise, more meditation and quality time with my Son. I printed my agenda and taped it to the wall over my desk in front of my computer. I set a timer for various task intervals and timely transitions from one agenda item to another. It was a complete value-adding contribution to my life - One whose R.O.I. (Return On Investment) will continue as I move forward. I highly recommend incorporating John Eggen's material and expert guidance to anyone seeking to become an author and/or bring their business, as well as their life to a higher level of fulfillment and success.

~ Every gesture, large or small, as an investment in your well-being is a contribution to love.

In the *Harry Potter* books and movies, there's an entity known as *Erised,* a mirror that shows the deepest desires of one's heart. The name Erised is the word Desire spelled backwards, as if reflected in a mirror.

Inscribed across the top of the mirror's frame is the text:
'Erised stra ehru oyt ube cafru oyt on wohsi'.

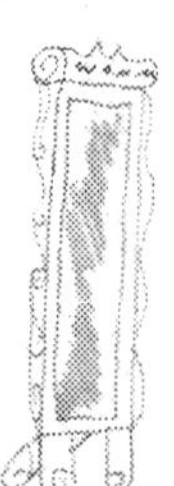

Reversing the inscription and rearranging the spaces produces:
'I show not your face but your heart's desire'.

According to Dumbledore, one of the characters in the series, the happiest person on earth would be able to use the *Mirror of Erised* like a normal mirror. That is, they would look into it and see their self exactly as they are. Dumbledore goes on to say that *The Mirror* shows neither truth nor knowledge; and since each person is unique, only they can see it from their perspective.

Don Miguel Ruiz tells us that truth simply is, and that the mind is a reflection of the truth of the lies we choose to believe. There is no mind behind the mirror, only judgment of a mind which has chosen to believe in lies. Truth simply is, and a mirror is merely a reflection of what exists.

Most shortcomings (health, wealth, happiness, etc.) in our lives can be traced to an underlying deficit of self-love to one degree or another. Louise Hay emphasizes the importance of learning to love one's self as a prerequisite to attracting joy, abundance, wellness and meaningful experiences in our lives. In her book, *You Can Heal Your Life*, she recommends the practice of mirror work and utilizing affirmations to arrive at a place of allowance, worthiness and self-love, suggesting that we say *"I love you"* when looking in the mirror.

Initially, you may feel rather uncomfortable performing such an exercise. It can lead you to discount yourself by calling attention to any judgments you may have about yourself. Nonetheless, I recommend giving it a try; and I'd like to offer some suggestions to assist you. We'll discuss the use of affirmations in detail during the next chapter; however, if you're in any way running at a deficit for self-love, an affirmation of this caliber can sometimes make you feel worse rather than better. You may feel as though you're lying to yourself because some affirmations can highlight where you *aren't* and just how far away you are from where you'd like to be. If saying *"I love you"* to yourself makes you even the slightest bit uncomfortable in any way, it could enhance or solidify *not* loving yourself to some degree. Therefore, I suggest choosing gently persuasive affirmations which provide a sense of relief, comfort and believability ~ ones that will produce a reachable vibration. Focus on something you *do* love, and build from there. For example: *I love myself enough to try this exercise" ~ "Love is available to me, and I love that I can choose it for myself."* Affirmations such as these can provide a graceful, gradual pace for moving toward a healthy, confident and enduring comfort level with authentic self-love.

That being said, when you choose to focus only on the exercise and practice it on a regular basis, magic begins to happen. Self-criticism begins to subside; you start to care more for and about yourself; and your relationships begin to shift in positive ways. I whole-heartedly recommend implementing this practice. Once you've chosen a comfortable affirmation, practice this exercise 3 times a day for two weeks. Stand in front of a mirror, look yourself in the eyes and say your affirmation, preferably out loud. You can do this at any time; but for the next two weeks, a minimum of three times per day - especially if such a practice is new to you. You may want to journal about the affect this has on you over the course of the two weeks. The intention is for it to become an intrinsic practice as a gift and celebration of love for yourself.

I'd like to note that Self Esteem and Self Love are not synonymous. Self Esteem is a term used in psychology to reflect a person's overall emotional evaluation of one's own worth. It's a judgment of and attitude toward the self regarding the confidence in one's own abilities and therefore, worth. As a judgment, esteem involves comparability and some degree of skewed perception. Self-love, on the other hand, is a clear, healthy regard for one's own well-being and happiness – one which does not depend on outer circumstances or judgment. Where there is self-love, there is self-esteem.

"It is our choices that show what we truly are, far more than our abilities." -Dumbledore (Harry Potter Chamber of Secrets)

The key to embracing self-love is *knowing* that you are loved, simply because you *are*; and the beauty is living within that mindset.

Louise Hay has devoted her life to cultivating love in our lives. She provides an enlightening audio of her live presentation of *How to Love Yourself - Cherishing the Incredible Miracle That You Are* which I highly recommend gifting yourself with. (*See Resources*)

*"Love yourself as if your life depended on it…
because it does." -Anita Moorjani*

When you hold your well-being as a priority, you embody self-love. From a place of self-love, all else flows with ease. That being said, let's talk about relationships.

Our encounters with others can be likened to Quantum Entanglements which are regarded as our interaction with everything in existence. It's been said that once we interact with someone or something, our energy becomes entangled with theirs; and the effects of the entanglement become part of our energetic existence; i.e. memories, core beliefs – those that work for and those that work against us. The nature and status of our entanglements are altered by our choices as we evolve.

It's essential to understand that your relationships with others are reflective of the relationship you have with yourself. You can view others as choice accomplices on your journey. While the same applies to all associations, we'll focus foremost on our primary partner/significant other relationship.

What is it that you seek in a primary partner relationship - companionship, kindness, gifting and receiving – being with someone who's supportive and in total allowance of you being your authentic self with no judgment? I once heard someone say that these descriptions reflect the qualities of gratitude more so than love; and that love, with enough judgment attached to it, can turn to hate. Yet the same is not true of gratitude. With this in mind, I'd like you to consider the gratitude you would embody within your ideal partner relationship and what that would entail. Even if you're currently in a relationship (perhaps with your ideal partner), take a few moments to compose a description of your ideal partnership. Include everything that comes to mind – anything from what your partner may look like to the contribution they would be (are) to your life, things you'd have in common, the gifting and receiving between you, etc. How would you *be* within this relationship?

Attributes of my Partner and our Relationship	**Gifts/Receipts Between us**	**States of Being ~ Gratitude ~**

The intention of this exercise is to come to an awareness of the ideal partner relationship for you. We'll talk more about this in a bit; but first, let's look at some of the dynamics and realities of primary partner relationships.

Many people grow and evolve in their relationships with beautiful compatibility and symmetry, yet many do not. Have you ever been in a relationship and at some point found that you were losing or had lost yourself therein to some degree? Many aspects of our lives shift and change in relation to being single or within a relationship. Some expand our lives in desirable ways; yet they can constrict and overshadow them undesirably in others.

After many years of allowing my life to happen *To* me, I decided to take the reins. I began to revisit and reclaim parts of me that had become disconnected over the years. I wanted real – substance, meaning – not just companionship or day-to-day dynamics. I spent less time in front of the television and eventually gave it up almost entirely. It's one of the Programmers I voted off my island. Don't get me wrong - I still love to cuddle up on the couch and watch a good movie or interesting documentary, especially on a rainy summer's eve or snowy winter's night, but it's now more of a menu selection than an unconscious routine. I began doing more of the things that I loved: listening to music, dancing, reading expansive and inspirational material, taking walks and spending time with real, like-minded people and cherished friends. I vowed never to lose myself within any association, whether it be a job, a friendship or a lover.

Many of us disconnect parts of ourselves within relationships. For example, you enjoy music and dancing, yet begin spending more time with your partner (who doesn't enjoy music and dancing) to show them that you really care. This is one of the ways we tend to disconnect pieces of ourselves over time. We're often attracted to the aspects of others which we'd like to foster in ourselves. However, in lieu of adopting in ourselves that which we admired in our partner - which often attracted us to them in the first place, we prosecute them for it when we cannot. I have personally experienced this phenomenon. As a result, I found myself conflicted and overwhelmed - handing the keys over to *Cody*. While compromise has its place, forsaking any part of yourself (aside from any parts that you may wish to shed for healthy reasons) for a relationship does not work in the long run; and we wonder why relationships fall apart and the divorce rate is higher than 50%. A beneficial relationship is one where you don't have to abandon any part of you in order to be in a relationship with someone else. It's a place where everyone and everything you are in a relationship with can become greater as a result of the relationship.

I'd like you to take a few moments here - without any judgment, guilt, blame or shame for any party, to acknowledge some of the things which you may have disconnected from over time, either knowingly or unknowingly, in favor of a relationship. While there may be things that you don't really miss, it's the ones for which you harbor a desire to reclaim that you're seeking to uncover here.

- Name three things that you loved to do that you don't anymore relative to your primary partner relationship.
- Name three people that you used to connect with that you don't anymore relative to your primary partner relationship.

3 Things You Loved to Do	3 People You Lost Connection With

Once you've completed your list, ask yourself:

- What would doing these things and/or reconnecting with these people change/contribute to my life?
- Would reintroducing them create contention or contribution to the relationship with my partner?
- What would my life be like if I choose/do not choose to reclaim these?

Everything this is and brings up and anything that stands in the way of my creating and living my preferred reality, whether known or unknown consciously or unconsciously where this is concerned, I choose to release and transmute its energy to a higher vibrational frequency across all timelines and energetic fields under grace with ease. And so it is.

Now let's talk a bit about marriage and divorce. Divorce typically refers to the legal process involved in disengaging from a licensed marriage contract. This is the paperwork aspect. The disengagement aspect, however, involves many facets. Where this process is concerned, I prefer the term uncoupling, as it applies to disengaging from any relationship.

I know that my parents loved each other. I also know that they each had their individual issues as well as those within their marriage. Many of my own issues stemmed from witnessing theirs and growing up in the environment that I did. Divorce in those days was almost unheard of, especially compared to current statistics. Perhaps it is best that things have changed a bit.

I was in my second marriage to the Father of my Son during the early phase of my Soul searching and shifting. While I was enjoying the expansion and partaking more in the activities I'd gradually abandoned over the years, I came to realize that other than in relation to my Son, this man played almost no role in my life - we had almost nothing in common. I had uncoupled long ago. We simply coexisted.

His contributions were commendable and an aspect for which I'm eternally grateful. I came to realize, however, that while they were demonstrations of a good man and father, he was not the partner I preferred in my life. I knew that remaining in the marriage would mean forsaking myself, as well as everyone concerned. I would also be remiss in providing my Son with a healthy representation of a fulfilling, joyful partnership. It was time to make a shift.

For some time after the divorce, my Son's Father and I continued to share the same home for temporary financial reasons. Although doing so was not unheard of during the economic climate of that time, it is not something I recommend – especially for an extended period. Not only is it uncomfortable for the parents, it can create unnecessary confusion and contention - particularly where those uninformed regarding the details of the situation are concerned. Although my choices were made with lucidity and I was vigilant in nurturing clarity with my Son regarding those choices, I bore the weight of judgment relative to external appearances around the situation based on the ignorant conclusions of others. Although this weighed heavily on me at times, while allowing others to do the same, ultimately it was up to me to make the best choices for myself.

I offer compassion and counsel to uncoupling parents. Regardless of living arrangements, finances, etc., it is essential to provide children with a clear understanding of the situation and to set their anticipations regarding the relationship of the parents to each other as well as to them going forward. I was consistent in expressing to my Son that just because Daddy and I were no longer married, it did not mean that we did not love him; and although we would eventually be living separately, we would always be his Mum and Dad, loving him and caring for him as we always had and always will. I began fostering this awareness early on; and as time went by, I grew more grateful that I had.

I'm not familiar with the laws of other states; however, in certain counties within Massachusetts, it's mandatory for divorcing parents to participate in a court-approved parent education program. The issues discussed within this program brought awareness to some red flags to avoid; for example, speaking negatively about the other parent to or in the presence of the child. The experience was also confirmation that I'd chosen the best approach where the long-term big picture was concerned. Keeping in mind that children tend to absorb their parents disposition on both ends of the spectrum, it is vital that their emotional well-being be held paramount and handled with the utmost sensitivity at all times - especially in these situations.

Rosalind Sedacca reminds us that we have the power to minimize the negative impact that uncoupling can have on children. She sums it by posing the following question: *When your children are grown, will they thank you for the way you handled your uncoupling or will they be filled with anger, shame and resentment because of the mistakes you made that you will later regret?* Rosalind is a Certified Corporate Trainer and is recognized as *The Voice of Child-Centered Divorce,* a network she founded which provides valuable resources for parents facing, moving through and transitioning after uncoupling. She is a Divorce and Parenting Coach and the author of the E-Book, *How Do I Tell the Kids about the Divorce? A Create-a-Storybook Guide to Preparing Your Children - With Love!* which I highly recommend.

I also chose a civil, gradual approach in order to foster a compassionate uncoupling for all concerned. In doing so, I came to appreciate countless unforeseen blessings within the process, particularly the transitional living arrangement. Due to other situations in my life at that time, I appreciated precious wisdom relative not only to survival, but most importantly to respect, forgiveness and unconditional love. As frustrating as it all was at the time, by following my heart and trusting the process, I received much to be grateful for overall. It is true that what may seem like the worst can often turn out to be for the better in the process of unfolding.

In her book, *Thank You For Leaving Me,* Farhana Dhalla offers an honest and raw look at how to recover and rebirth yourself after the end of a relationship. While the process of uncoupling can often expose the unruliest of our shadow side, it can also facilitate the revelation of our magnificence. Farhana says the truth is that we don't really know who we are until we are faced with the crumbling of who we are not. And then, the most exquisite realization comes that changes everything: that nothing is ever done *To* you; rather, Everything is done *For* you. Her book is a guide to finding your way to truth, peace and gratitude, enriching your life and relationships with those who matter most to you.

It's essential to know yourself, as well as your partner, in all aspects as honestly and realistically as possible and with regard for each other's bandwidth for flexibility prior to committing to these types of relationship indentures. Recall from the beginning of this chapter our discussion on the euphoria of falling and being in love. During the early phases of any relationship, many of our day-to-day attributes, especially the less than desirable ones, can be subdued; and if they are demonstrated, their impact may be somewhat diminished when viewed through rose colored glasses. As Richard Brodie once said, *"Marriage is the world's best (and frequently most expensive) personal growth workshop."* You wouldn't enter into a binding business contract without first acquiring a clear representation of the specifications. Why then, would you do so in your personal life?

What brings us to create, allow ourselves to be drawn into and linger within relationships which may not be in our best interests? While we've touched on some of the possible underlying modus operandi relative to doing so, we've yet to discuss abandonment, or fear of it. Fear of abandonment or being alone directly relates to our survival instinct. Abandonment encompasses neglect, rejection and desertion. It can be brought on by any experience – disrespect, disregard, the end of a relationship, death, etc. - from childhood onward. It's a feeling of isolation, lack of connectedness and fear. These types of experiences always leave a wound. Fear of abandonment or being alone is often an obscure element behind our tolerance for less than desirable relationships.

During a conversation with a friend around this subject, I came to realize that I had my own abandonment issues. In exploring this, I began to see their role in many of the patterns in my relationships - which was enlightening to say the least. In researching this, I discovered the material of a Susan Anderson, Psychotherapist and Abandonment Expert. She describes abandonment as a cumulative wound, a crucial loss of connectedness - a loss of love itself. In her book, *The Journey From Abandonment to Healing,* Susan describes *S.W.I.R.L.*, an acronym summarizing the five phases of abandonment grief and recovery: *S*hattering, *W*ithdrawal, *I*nternalizing, *R*age, and *L*ifting. She illustrates that as we process abandonment, we swirl through these stages - going back and forth between phases until we emerge on the other side.

As I digested Susan's material, I recognized a cumulative wound as a common aspect within my less than desirable relationships, both personal and professional. Albeit frightening and sad, it was a welcome *Aha* for me. It can be rather comforting to identify such an element - not so much in a compartmentalization sort of way, but more in the light of an expansion of awareness.

Compartmentalization is described as an unconscious psychological defense mechanism used to avoid cognitive dissonance - the mental discomfort and anxiety caused by having conflicting values, emotions and beliefs. Being able to identify this with a practical approach to healing and overcoming the effects it was having on my life was like finding another oasis in my desert of disorientation.

Although fear of being alone relates to our survival instinct, it can also relate to an avoidance or dislike of the self in some ways. Focusing on others and occupying ourselves with our relationships with them tends to place our own issues on the back burner. That being said, if you've found within yourself patterns of self-sabotage by attracting people who are unavailable to you in the ways you prefer, it's possible that abandonment, or fear of it, is lurking within the mix. While abandonment issues generally stem from being or feeling abandoned by another, creating or fostering abandonment-prone relationships is an expression of self-abandonment. Considering this was a brilliant *Aha* for me, and something to be mindful of as you move forward.

In my mind, sometimes it is healthier to be alone than in a relationship which only serves to impair vs. enhance your life. Identifying these issues and choosing accordingly strengthens the foundation for a loving relationship with yourself which is the catalyst for cultivating healthy relationships with others.

SWIRLING is recognizable and common. Although some phases, as with any healing crisis, may be perceived as unpleasant and undesirable, they're a natural and healthy part of the overall process. Susan says that the goal of abandonment recovery is to benefit by the experience rather than be diminished by it. I'd initially intended to provide an explorative exercise for this portion of the chapter. However, I found Susan's material so comprehensive, that referral shall suffice. She offers a wealth of information and resources on her site.

As we know, our choices and actions are filtered by our software. Therefore, it's essential to be mindful of what your programs and filters are, consciously bearing them in mind when considering your options. There are many reasons why you may *think* that the possibilities are limited. However, this is only true when you're basing them on narrow perspective. As an educated consumer, you wouldn't shop only one store or make your selection from the options provided by only one manufacturer. Why then would you approach any aspect of your life in such an abstract or constricted manner? In the banquet of life, the possibilities are vast. Recall Anita Moorjani's Flashlight Exercise and ask: *What else is possible?*

While they may be more amplified in some than others, the people in our lives are mirror versions of the various aspects within ourselves. They reflect our strengths as well as our weaknesses. The dearest are those who embody the aspects which provoke and provide the greatest lessons of our evolution - some as reminders of what *not* to do and others as inspiration for aspiring to our objectives. They are all contributions to our evolution and support system. I liken them to angels, each exemplifying a particular characteristic or strength, similar to archetypes. When we call upon an angel by name, we're actually invoking the capacity of their strength within our self. While we may vote some off the island, the key companions for our journey are a matter of choice. Generally speaking, my assertion regarding partner relationships is quite simply this: You're either together or you're not - regardless of marital status, living arrangements, finances or anything else. We flourish by partnering with like-minded people. With this in mind, I suggest choosing your company wisely.

Healthy relationships are like bank accounts wherein you can only withdraw from an existing balance, accumulated from mutual deposits. Bear in mind though that when it comes to self-love, you always have cosmic overdraft protection in the Bank of Networthiness.

Networthiness (Not *to be confused with Net Worth*) is defined as the result of an operational assessment of I/T (Information Technology) to verify compliance with security, interoperability, supportability, sustainability, usability regulations, guidelines and policies. *That's a mouthful*, yet it all applies here. This term is also used in reference to military defense protocol, yet the same considerations are relative to self-love, boundaries and relationships. The United States Air force certification system utilizes a Certificate of Networthiness, or CON, which I equate to a Doctrine. When navigating relationships, you'll want to ensure that yours is in order.

Taking the message of these works of wisdom to heart, I resolved to get off the hamster wheel and balance myself. At first, it was like surfing a seesaw. I'd tip from one extreme to the other, opening up, closing down and at times, falling off altogether. During the journey to find my center, I did eventually come into more balance - another possibility I'd not fully known before. With well-being a priority, I surmised there were too many cooks in my kitchen. I fired my Network and Database Administrators and began to design my own recipe for the creation of my life.

This process included a review of my likes, dislikes, beliefs, objectives and intentions which evolved into a tangible list of my boundaries, non-negotiables, intentions and affirmations. I call it *'My Doctrine'*. I highly recommend creating one for yourself. In doing so, be sure to phrase it in the present tense: *I Am* - no I will's; and sign your name to it. Your doctrine can include anything from universal items such as compassion, generosity and gratitude to particulars of your personal preference. A doctrine is a living will of sorts, and evolutionary edits can be incorporated as you move through your life. This is mine:

~ My Doctrine ~

Core Beliefs: Love, Worthiness, Safety and Wholeness
Non-negotiable Essentials:
Respect, Honesty, Trust and Understanding
The Three C's of Mindfulness:
Consciousness, Communication and Contribution

- *I wake in the morning rejuvenated and grateful, asking "What energy, space and consciousness can I be today that will be a contribution to me and all whom I encounter?"*
- *I consistently provide healthy nourishment and exercise to my body, mind and Spirit.*
- *My energy and time are disbursed efficiently and effectively as a contribution to myself and others.*
- *I treat myself and others with respect, compassion, kindness and love.*
- *I insist of myself to uphold my boundaries and hold myself accountable for all of my choices, words and actions.*
- *I opt only for beneficial relationships. Everyone and everything is a donation, not a detriment to my life.*
- *I direct myself to be mindful and present – No judgment, No drama, No regret.*
- *I live in question, awe, gratitude and love.*
- *I listen to and follow my heart in all endeavors.*
- *I go to sleep at a reasonable hour marinating only in gratitude, peace and love.*

- *I affirm consistently that all of life happens 'For' me and that I experience it through ease, joy, grace and gratitude.*

-Maureen Marie Damery

I must say that coming to an enduring embodiment of self-love has been an arduous process for me, and it is ongoing. That being said, equally as challenging was authentically putting this message into words here. While I'd been applying what I'd learned in varying degrees on various levels, I realized that doing so had not yet become an intrinsic manner of being for me. Having slipped off the wagon countless times in the past, the hardest fall came during the compilation of this chapter – which I'd been recoiling around throughout the writing of this manuscript.

Reading the books, taking the classes and acquiring the CEU's is one thing. However, unless or until the content is integrated and employed, its wisdom is nothing more than a proposition. Fortunately, one of the gems of life is that, although our license may occasionally be suspended, our learner's permit never expires – nor does our option for change. Evolution is a process ~ one which I came to fully appreciate through experiencing this phenomenon during the final stages of editing this book.

Several years into a relationship, some highly undesirable discoveries came to light. Albeit in the interests of love, I allowed myself to be drawn into a vortex of dark polarity. Through rose-colored glasses, I surrendered the keys to *Cody* by allowing a man with significant issues back into my heart and my home ~ believing that through my love, I was saving him.

My GPS encountered a GPF. Unable to see the forest for the trees, driven by the culmination and complexity of all of my convoluted programming, creations of rebellion and fairytale dreams, which had all converged and come to the surface, my Spirit uncoupled from my Soul, and I was utterly offline. I'd abandoned ship and was adrift in a swamp of divergent chaos during a dark night of epic proportions. It was the perfect storm.

What I did not realize was that this man did not want deliverance. I could not rescue him as a mermaid would; but I also could not abandon someone in desperate need of help. I took it upon myself to heal him, and I was unable to detach from the outcome. As an empath, I feel the pain of others. Yet this was so closely personal, that the pain paralyzed the healer within me.

While I could hear the voice of reason, I was crippled to heeding her call. Skimming just under the radar of her lighthouse beam, I spiraled down the rabbit hole. In the height of the swirling current, I came to light on a rock near its base. Utterly depleted and overwhelmed with fear, I found myself wondering how, with all of the wisdom I'd accumulated, could I have landed in a place so far from self love?

My Soul and The Universe had their directives; and no matter how hard or often I tried to delude and distract myself, this was not going to change until I fully embraced and embodied authentic self-love.

"Nothing ever goes away until it has taught us what we need to know." ~ Pema Chödrön

It took a very long time for me to realize and understand that both the burden of healing and the cost of the medicine would come from my spiritual purse, not his. It was sink or swim ~ time to walk the walk; and the only way to find my legs was through the mercy of tough love. As I swam to shore, I knew that walk required the acceptance of what was not mine to change, the courage to change what was and the wisdom to distinguish between them.

I had encountered the ultimate Jekyll and Hyde; and the only means of healing and expansion through this quantum entanglement was to view it as a Sacred Contract from a 'happened *For* me' perspective. Among the hurt, disappointment and fear came the soul-searching quest of a lifetime – A journey to unconditional love through allowance, understanding and forgiveness. While it did not end happily or miraculously for him, the miracle was in my realization that I had been loving someone else my entire life ~ to the exclusion and punishment of my own Soul. So many of us, especially women, allow ourselves to be caught in cycles of self-abandonment and abuse, unable to exit the endless loop and end the pattern. Well, guess what? The F--k stops here!

During the spiritual spin cycle of the healing crisis in the wake of that storm, I retreated into the solace of seclusion for self-reflection and healing…and subsequently, the long procrastinated final draft of this book. It was primitively painful, yet profoundly proactive. I knew that if this book ~ and most importantly, my life and all that led up to and contributed to it ~ was to hold any meaning or value, reverse engineering was in order. My self-love software, which was clearly Beta (*a test version of a program*), would require a complete rewrite in the source code of my soul. Without these upgrades, my operating system would be nothing more than virus-laden crippleware.

Through recontextualization, a healthy shift in perspective was birthed. By detaching the labels of 'Villain' and 'Victim', the poisons of judgment and wrongness began to dissipate. I could see clearly the gifts bestowed upon a heart broken wide open. Within a chrysalis of compassion through the grace of gratitude, my phoenix arose. As the title of Goldie Hawn's book evokes, *A Lotus Grows in the Mud.*

It is, indeed, what we choose to appreciate from our experiences which matters most.

"Love After Love"
~ Derek Walcott

The time will come
when, with elation
you will greet yourself
arriving at your own door,
in your own mirror
and each will smile at the other's welcome,
and say, sit here. Eat.

You will love again the stranger who was your self.
Give wine. Give bread. Give back your heart to itself,
to the stranger who has loved you all your life, whom you ignored
for another, who knows you by heart.

Take down the love letters from the bookshelf,
the photographs, the desperate notes,
peel your own image from the mirror.
Sit. Feast on your life.

~

Let's consider some of the ways that more mindfulness, contribution and joy can be brought to all concerned.

With a healthy CON/Doctrine in place, you can determine the relative rate of exchange within your relationships. Have a look at your price tag. Perhaps you've valued yourself inappropriately. If so, it may be time to adjust your terms of engagement; and negotiations may be in order. While some of this terminology may conjure the essence of money, let's be mindful that while compromise may come into play, money ought not be an ultimate determining factor where your choices in this realm are concerned. ~ Recall the money exercise from Chapter Five.

Henry Winkler once said that *"Assumptions are the termites of relationships."* This statement speaks volumes. With that in mind, prior to taking your intentions to the drawing board with your partner, it's essential to be clear regarding your expectations ~ I prefer to use the term preferences. The word *Expect* conjures requirements and demands; whereas the word *Prefer* conjures favor and choice and imparts appeal, invitation and opportunity. Where reciprocity is concerned, expressing an appeal as a preference is a more subtle approach and a far gentler bargaining tool for negotiation. You cannot force another to be or do anything beyond their will as a result of a complaint, from demand or out of guilt...You really wouldn't want to receive or gift with that sort of weight attached anyway.

"Even after all this time, the sun never says to the earth, 'You owe me',
Look what happens with a love like that.
It lights the whole sky." ~Hafiz

With balance in mind and win-win as the objective, mindful negotiation is key. Criticizing and complaining will calculate into catastrophe. Complimentary computing, however, is conducive to conciliation. When approaching such a consultation, bringing gratitude for what's already contributed prior to expressing your preferences fosters an atmosphere for gracious negotiation.

When I was growing up, it became apparent to me that the television was far more appealing to my Mother than anything I'd attempted to bring to her attention. Most efforts to interact with her were deflected in being told to wait for the next commercial or until her show was over… and there was always another in the queue. As a result, I'd concluded that the television was more important than anything I may have to bring to the table. I realized some years later that television was an addiction, an escape for her. I also understood that although that addiction belonged to my Mother, I'd carried my conclusion into adulthood.

The television was often not only a distraction but an intrusion to me. In more than one relationship, it was on constantly, and at a very high volume no less - irrespective of the viewers' attention to the broadcast or subconscious need for background noise. When the preference for any discussion or attention arose, I found it difficult to welcome the television into the mix…especially nowadays with the options of pause, rewind and record. Although division of focus may be a perceived skill or virtue by some, I find it distracting and difficult to interact with one whose eyes and/or ears are diverted.

While this particular scenario may not be the most definitive, perhaps even miniscule to some, it touches on essential elements which apply to all relationships – consideration, respect and attention. Naturally, there's a time and place for everything. However, when the charge of this issue triggered an underlying wound, it was time to address it. I'm certain that you can relate this principle to some triggers of your own.

It's always best to conduct any exchange outside of the heat of the moment, employing NVC. Non-violent communication is a process which focuses on three aspects of communication: Self-empathy (deep and compassionate awareness of one's own inner experience), Empathy (listening to another with deep compassion), and Honest Self-expression (expressing oneself authentically in a way that's likely to inspire compassion in others).

World renowned expert, Dr. Marshall B. Rosenberg, PhD, explains that NVC is based on the principles of a natural state of compassion when no violence (anger) is present in the heart. NVC begins by assuming that we are all compassionate by nature and that violent strategies are culturally learned. It also assumes that we all share the same basic human needs, and that each of our actions are a strategy to meet one or more of these needs. There are four components to the NVC model: Observations, Feelings, Needs and Requests. Utilizing these components enables you to clearly express how you are without blaming and criticizing when addressing an issue of your concern. It also enables you to empathically receive how you are without hearing blame or criticism when you are on the receiving end of such an address. A free document outlining these components and how they may be utilized is available for download (*See Resources*).

Prior to initiating a conversation, it's essential to be clear on what your wishes and concessions may be. Asking yourself some open-ended questions provides clarity and assists you in communicating clearly. While these questions can also take the other person into consideration, they are primarily for you:

- What's right about me where this is concerned?
- What do I prefer?
- What is my suggesstion for ensuring that my needs are met?
- What is possible here?

When undertaking this type of communication, compassionate navigation and reasonable negotiation is essential. A *Doctrine* provides lucidity; and while it outlines your rules of engagement, it's best to maintain a level of flexibility concerning reciprocity because we all expresses ourselves, gift and receive in our own unique ways. Ultimately, clarity and consent are the keys. You want to be precise when expressing your preferences to ensure that the other party involved is clear on what is being requested of them. Three key questions can provide clarity where this is concerned:

- What do I prefer from the situation?
- What do they prefer from the situation?
- Are we both on the same page?

Also, the sentiment *'Help me to understand'* provides an invitation for both parties to contribute and can often fill in the blanks for any questions that either may have.

While you can explain your preference to another, you cannot understand it for them. With this in mind, asking the person what it looks like to them provides clarity for all concerned. For instance, after sharing your preferences and perhaps making some suggestions where gifting and receiving are concerned, ask them *'How do you see this working out?'* Otherwise, they may just tell you what they *think* you want to hear. Don't get stuck in give-and-take exchanges, lest you'll get lost in conflict without dealing with what's really going on in the relationship. Words only go so far. It is the actions which tell the story. Compromise occasionally, settle never. Settling is the seed of disappointment which breeds distress. Without clarity and consent, you will find out very quickly that things will not work out.

Actions speak louder than words; therefore, you must be prepared to deal and deliver. For instance, let's say that you tell your child not to do something, yet they proceed nonetheless. You then deal: *'If you do that again, Consequence X'*. When they push that envelope, you must deliver *Consequence X*. Otherwise, your word carries no weight and your deal is nothing more than a sandcastle awaiting the tide. The same applies to any situation. For example, you're dealing with someone who is chronically late or a habitual no-show. Deal: *"If you're not here by 7:00, I will go with my original plan."* At 7:01 if they have not arrived, the ball is in your court; and you must be prepared to deliver. Perhaps next time, they'll either arrive as agreed or call within a reasonable amount of time to notify and renegotiate. Moving forward, you may choose to refrain from making plans with them altogether.

I've also found myself in scenarios where I have an intention for my evening, yet allowed it to be interceded by the impetuous intrusions and agendas of others. Occasionally changing your mind or going with the flow is desirable. Be mindful, however, that when doing so becomes a chronic pattern, resulting in regret and resentment, you are depreciating yourself.

There are times when issues and relationships can be navigated with ease, yet there are others where you may find yourself in *Relationship Deadlock*. Wiki defines deadlock as a situation in which two or more competing actions are waiting for the other to complete and thus, neither ever does. The examples are from computer science and technology relative to operating systems and transactional databases, but the same is true within human relationships. While you may believe that you're taking steps to improve a relationship, you may be secretly wishing the other person to be different, which doesn't work.

David Noor is a Licensed Mental Health Counselor Associate with a successful background in I/T. His specialty is improving mental health and work/life balance for software professionals and their families. In his article, *How to End Your Relationship Deadlock Today,* David describes four phases by which to process deadlock:

- Reality Check: You cannot change another. If you think that you can or believe that you have, it likely won't last very long.
- Hope & Plan: *Love hopes all things.* Falling or being in love with the *potential* of another places you into false hope. As a result, you begin tolerating and negotiating which does not

help either party. There's a fine line (if any at all) between tolerating and enabling which can, and often does, lead to codependency issues.

Planning does not mean giving up hope. It means planning for today's reality, while leaving room for change. This is simple algebra: I need to hold some part of this equation Constant (*their behavior*) in order to solve for X (*the choices I make*). This can be the hardest step of the process emotionally because there's often a sense of loss and grief when you stop trying to make the other person behave in a certain way. This emotion should not be underestimated or ignored because it's a real loss of the idealized (*potential*) person. In this type of relationship, it's beneficial to enlist the assistance of someone who's not entrenched in the relationship to help you identify and process these emotions. Once you've made your observations and acknowledged your intentions, you can hope for possibility and change, yet you must plan for it staying the same.

- Communicate: You understand that you cannot change another, and you're hoping for the best while planning based on a specific timeframe. Now it's time to Deal & Deliver. Once you have dealt, it is essential that you deliver consistently for a sustained period of time. Your communication should not be utilized as *manipulation* in its derogatory sense ~ Recall from Chapter Six that manipulation is using possibility to get the most beneficial outcome for all concerned. Provide a clear sharing of your intentions and the presentation of your choices, your deal.
- Re-Evaluation: Once you've delivered for a sustained period, it's time to evaluate the current state of affairs. Perhaps things have changed significantly, and you'd like to make a new plan based on the current data; or you may decide

> that, although they remain the same, you want something different. Either way, it's acceptable to re-solve your equation, leaving the door open to possibility. Be mindful, however that living from hope, settling into frustrating, unfulfilling patterns and relationships indefinitely is not only abandoning yourself, it's a recipe for disaster.

It's one thing to be on different pages, yet quite another when you can't agree on the same book. Look at the relationship and consider what needs to change in order for you to be happy. If it requires either of you to change who you inherently are, it's likely best to go your own ways. It's a tough call, but leopards can't change their spots; and you both deserve to be happy.

In situations like these, it's beneficial to step back and evaluate the circumstances without judgment. Judgment puts us into conclusion and takes us out of possibility which halts our ability to be generative. Consult the elements within your Doctrine. Use the *Soul Logic* method we discussed in Chapter Seven to recontextualize. This valuable tool can provide you with a broader perspective and assist you in arriving at the most favorable choice for the highest and best of all concerned.

During a global online seminar discussing his *Three Secrets to Ending the Struggle and Making Your Life Work,* Neale Donald Walsch presented a scenario where recontextualization was applied in regard to an abusive relationship. The message within this particular situation can be applied in a broad sense to any scenario. Neale suggested that in lieu of perceiving the parties involved as Villain and Victim, the relationship be viewed from what I refer to as a *Sacred Contract perspective* wherein the mutual agenda of the Souls are mutually held and experienced. The following is in paraphrase of the dialog which was spoken to the person viewed as the Villain by the person perceiving themselves as the Victim:

> These behaviors that you are demonstrating are not new to this particular experience of you and I. I get that this is your understanding of the only way to be and survive in the world. I'm not going to make you wrong for your behaviors because I understand them. I get that you are deeply mired in the illusions of life that drive your experience. I get that; and so I don't even have to forgive you for the abuse that you have placed in the existence of our experience. However, I will no longer receive and accept that level of abuse from you. I will love myself enough to remove myself from the space of that abuse, and I will love you enough to tell you that demonstrating yourself in this particular way is not the highest and most glorious aspect of who you are.

By approaching this type of situation in this context, the Victim can view what has transpired as occurring in their life so that they might announce and declare, express and fulfill, become and demonstrate who they really are ~ Part of who they really are being not only a person who forgives others when they have forgotten who they really are, but also one who loves the self. They may now choose to demonstrate their love of self, inspiring others to do the same. Neale says that in perceiving and living this way, we give ourselves the strength and courage to remove ourselves from these types of situations. In doing so, we often discover that, in the long-term big picture, the worst thing that could have happened can turn out to be the best to have happened.

Having this awareness removes the toxicity of anger, resentment, righteousness and frustration. When these are removed, their poison dissipates. When we eliminate that, we're more available not only to the consciousness of our roles in each other's lives, but more clarity and kindness. You may then look at your Villain, as well as yourself, with compassion which is the greatest healer of all. Doing so provides access to more ease and love within your life. Being in the experience of life, having the consciousness that *there are no mistakes, only choices and opportunities,* provides full access to your power. You can then be your true self, using this wisdom as a tool of choice for your highest potential in the creation of your life.

When you care deeply for someone, particularly a partner (or a potential one), who carries a belief system contrary to your own or conducts their life in a manner which is unacceptable to you and affects yours undesirably, you have a choice to make. Your initial expressions may come from anger, blame, fear, frustration, disappointment or hurt and judgment. Judgment puts you into conclusion, taking you out of possibility and your capacity to be generative. At some point, you may embrace allowance and gain perspective and clarity by removing judgment. Doing so does not mean that you condone or accept that which you are not aligned with. It simply means that you are not making the other person wrong; but at the same time, you are choosing not to engage. You must consider whether you're able to accept this person as they are and determine the depth of the role you will allow them to play in your life.

When you find yourself at the precipice of choice and change, it's essential to embrace compassion and unconditional love for all concerned. In the case of a child, while your energy and focus may have been devoted to nurturing their roots, the time comes when you must allow them their wings. In the case of a partner, it may be time to change the dynamics of the relationship or perhaps move on from it altogether.

People come into your life for a reason, a season or a lifetime. -The Title of a Poem by an Unknown Author

A partner is intended as a contribution to your life. Allowance and forgiveness frees those concerned from the bondage of incompatibility. You can agree to disagree. This allows both parties to be present vs. stuck in the past or an endless loop. Choosing to do so may not be simple or easy, but it is a choice nonetheless. There are times when the most loving choice you can make is to take varying paths. Taking those paths does not mean that you stop loving each other. It simply means that your love transforms as your relationship changes. Moving on from a relationship, especially one of depth and/or long-term, is never without reservation or consequence. However, doing so with clarity and compassion as an act of unconditional love endows the strength to implement the necessary adjustments and move forward with more ease.

Licensed psychotherapist and best-selling author, Katherine Woodward Thomas, MA, MFT coined the term 'Conscious Uncoupling'. In her book, *Conscious Uncoupling: 5 Steps to Living Happily Even After,* she provides a process to assist couples in consciously completing their relationship with an honorable ending, releasing the trauma of the breakup and reclaiming their power to reinvent their lives. Katherine offers a free online course entitled *How to Heal the 3 Breakup Mistakes That Cause Suffering, Steal Joy and Prevent Future Love* which I highly recommend.

No one can impose upon you that which you are not willing to carry. We all experience disrespect, disappointment and hurt. When this happens, there's no question that we're bruised and wounded. We traverse the stages and degrees of grief and healing throughout the experiences of our life. The key is the manner by which we choose to utilize the wisdom gifted within these experiences. We can become our story, carrying its baggage around the same cul-de-sac or we can choose an alternate path, turn the page and begin a new chapter in our lives. Keep in mind that what you're not changing, you're choosing. When you are willing to make a change, the Universe will provide all that's required to ensure success. You will know that you have made the best choice when you begin to feel lighter more of the time.

Navigating ourselves can seem complex at times, even more so within our relationships. Yet, traversing the aspects of our lives need not be as overwhelming as it may seem. When I was able to recontextualize around significant relationships in my life, I was able to ask what was true from a Soul level. Doing so changed a lot of things for me. Through compassion, forgiveness and unconditional love, I was able to see the mutual agenda of the Souls mutually held and experienced which enabled me to make mindful, authentic choices for myself. I wondered how it would be if the others involved understood the manner by which I came to my place of choice and transition where they were concerned - that I give and ask for compassion, forgiveness and unconditional love every day; and what may be possible if they chose to do the same.

Like attracts like; and as we shift within ourselves, so shifts that which we attract into our lives. In order to attract the type of partner that you prefer, you must first embody the qualities that you wish for in your ideal partner. Katherine Woodward Thomas, MA, MFT has written an empowering book on this element as well. Her teachings focus first and foremost on achieving liberation from your own limiting and negative beliefs so that you might experience happy, healthy relationships that support you to fully flourish and thrive in your life. Her book, *Calling in "The One": 7 Weeks to Attract the Love of Your Life,* is based on the Law of Attraction, which is the concept that we can only attract what we're ready to receive. Katherine also provides an on-line course of the same name to assist not only in calling in the most exceptional love of your life but also the most exceptional *You*.

It's important to understand that you are the co-creator of your life. When you choose to embrace this perspective, and your personal power within it, life unfolds with ease in the most amazing ways.

"The measure of love is to love without measure."
~Original Author Undetermined

~ Love is...Everything ~

For more information, please visit Resources.

Musings...

"When I let go of what I am, I become what I might be." -Lou Tzu

Chapter 11

The Secret Sauce ~ Creating From the Inside Out

In this chapter, you'll cultivate your personal recipe for living in the magic of life.

Now that you've opened that pretty box with your name on it and reviewed your *Owner's Manual*, you'll compose your 'Hello World' software for the game of life in the *Source Code of Your Soul.*

'Hello World' is used as the new developer's induction into programming. When run, it simply displays *"Hello World"* on the screen, allowing the programmer to test their installation and proper operation.

As mentioned earlier, we've designed information technologies in our own likeness. With that in mind, there's one more set of techie correlations to consider, as they will be of great value in the process of actualizing our objectives. While we've discussed viral infections and such, there's also the matter of bandwidth. In computer networks, the term bandwidth is used to describe the data transfer rate - the amount of data that can be carried from one point to another in a given time period (usually a second) - like radio, television or cell phone signals. For our purposes here, it's likened to the connection with your higher self and the capacities for living at your fullest potential. I'm sure you've either experienced or heard tell of slow internet connections or general system sluggishness. When you're fractured, frustrated or overwhelmed, your bandwidth is extremely taxed. You become disconnected, and you can feel stuck ~ a condition I refer to as *inertia*. To remedy such impediments, once the possibility of a virus is eliminated, efficiency must be attended to. A slow internet connection can be rectified by upgrading your service. A sluggish system, however, must be cleared out, updated or perhaps reformatted entirely. To this end, let's have a look at the three types of memory in your system:

ROM (Read-Only Memory) is the hardwired instructions for basic functions like turning on ('Booting Up') the operating system (OS) and activating hardware such as printers, etc. The OS is stored on the hard disk. This is your unconscious. When the computer is started, the OS is copied from the hard disk into RAM.

RAM (Random Access Memory) is where your OS, programs and any data that you're currently working with are active. The data in RAM only stays there as long as your computer is running. When you turn it off, this data is either saved on ROM or lost. This is your subconscious.

VM (Virtual Memory) is your conscious mind. It's a feature of the OS that enables a process (program or application) to use a memory space that's larger than the actual amount of available RAM by temporarily relegating some of the contents from RAM to a disk - like putting things on the back burner whilst focusing on other things ~ suppressing, procrastinating, etc.

Your unconscious mind (ROM) is your long-term storage where all of your memories, beliefs and programs were installed and stored since birth. Your subconscious (RAM) is your short-term storage which holds the current software you're running - your patterns, habits, recurring thoughts and feelings. Your subconscious is in constant communication with your unconscious. Your conscious mind is the Virtual Memory, the mode of communication between you and the outside world ~ your Virtual Machine.

The hard drive is like a disk, divided into sectors of memory. As you work with your system, over time the addition and deletion of files may not be done very efficiently. For example, a few small files may be stored in various sectors on your disk. When they're deleted, they leave these sectors empty. After some time, your disk may look like a piece of Swiss cheese - the holes being the empty sectors where these files were deleted from. This is called fragmentation. When you add a new file to your system, it may be stored in pieces, filling these empty sectors. When you attempt to work with this file, your system must coordinate the activity among these sectors. I liken this process to our *Monkey Mind* - a Buddhist term describing the manner in which our mind flits from one thought to another as a monkey jumps from tree to tree. When you're fragmented, you're unable to focus or function efficiently, much less at full potential. Your computer doesn't enjoy being fragmented any more than you do. This is why defragmentation, ('defrag') is so important. Recall from Chapter Six that Defrag is an operating system utility that reorganizes fragments of data on a computer's hard drive to maximize disk space and performance.

When you're feeling the symptoms of fragmentation, it's time to evaluate your system and the quality of the software you're running. When there's too much on your plate, it's time to prioritize in terms of nutritional value. Sometimes, less is more. Addressing fractures and toxic emotions as we discussed is a tremendous investment in your system which will yield precious returns. Releasing what does not serve you will expand your bandwidth. The most effective ways to defrag and ensure optimal functionality is to incorporate a consistent practice of self-care, meditation and mindfulness.

Meditation, which we'll discuss comprehensively in a bit, can be likened to a System Restore, a Windows® utility that allows a user to restore their computer to a specific former state (known as a restore point), undoing any objectionable changes made since that point.

Meditation aids in returning your Mind/Body to a healthier state prior to the infiltration of undesirable external influences - beliefs which do not serve your best interests and the programs consisting of them.

Science tells us that the shape of certain cells in our body actually become more elliptical when they're influenced by negative thoughts, feelings and emotions, which is the first step toward dis-ease. Your brain waves actually slow down during meditation, allowing behavioral patterns, belief systems and points of view that you've been running to be accessed and realigned, enabling you to return your Mind/Body to balance. This impacts your cells, allowing them to return to their more spherical shape, facilitating more ease in the body.

While the subconscious rules 95% of your life, the conscious 5% is what starts the subconscious onto a particular track. The subconscious is like a dumb terminal (DT) – a device consisting only of a monitor, keyboard and a connection to an intelligent computer - the conscious mind. DT's have no aptitude, meaning that they can't do any data processing. They depend entirely on the computer they're connected to for data storage, retrieval, computations, etc. DT's are used by airlines, banks, etc. for inputting data to and recalling it from the connected computer.

In I/T, RAS is an acronym for Reliability, Availability & Serviceability. It's essential that these attributes be considered when designing, manufacturing, purchasing and using computers and software. RAS is also used to describe Remote Access Services, a term originally coined by Microsoft referring to their NT (New Technology a.k.a. Networking Technology) which allows services to be accessed over a network. When you connect to the internet and download something, you're likely connecting to a RAS server. Internet Protocol (IP) is the method by which data is sent from one computer to another on the Internet. Each computer (known as a host) has an IP address that uniquely identifies it. Your Soul is your IP, and all of your experiences have led you to your current address or state ~ the present.

For our purposes, however, we'll focus on our Reticular Activating System (RAS) which is the portal through which information enters the brain. As we discussed in Chapter Two, your RAS is what filters incoming information. It determines what gets access to your brain and affects what you pay attention to. It takes instructions from your conscious and passes them along to your subconscious. RAS also responds to novelty which is why you'll notice anything new and different.

You can deliberately program your RAS by choosing which messages you send from your conscious mind utilizing discernment, visualization and affirmation. And here's the key: RAS cannot distinguish between *real* events and *synthetic* reality. Basically, it tends to believe whatever message you give it. What is required for change is becoming conscious of your unconscious self, creating a specific picture of your objective in your conscious mind and aligning your beliefs, thoughts, feelings and actions with that objective. The RAS will then pass this information on to your subconscious whose compulsion, as we discussed in Chapter Four, is to actualize that objective. It does so by bringing to your attention information relevant to your intention (books, people, opportunities) which you may otherwise cast aside as 'background noise'. However, if your beliefs are not congruent with your objectives, your RAS will obscure if not block pertinent information from getting through to your subconscious. ~Recall the lottery winner phenomenon from Chapter Five.

> *"If you think* (Believe) *you can do a thing or you think you cannot do a thing, you're right." ~Henry Ford*

As you know, over ninety percent of your thoughts which stem from your beliefs and produce your feelings and emotions aren't intrinsically yours; yet they're the engineering components of your software. With over 95% of your life being run by your subconscious programs, your objective is to use the physics of life to get it purposefully working for you with that 5% at an IP that's congruent with your objectives.

Now let's discuss beliefs, visualizations and affirmations. Beliefs are simply thoughts that you keep thinking. Thoughts are just thoughts, and they don't have any power - unless you give it to them. Beliefs can be regarded as myths – traditional stories or widely held ideas (*memes*) – to which, subscription is a matter of personal choice. As Seth suggests: *"It helps to think of your beliefs as furniture that can be rearranged, changed, discarded or replaced"* - a concept that we'll explore deeper in just a bit. Visions are templates for your objectives; and affirmations are building blocks for them. They anchor your beliefs and support the foundation for the actualization of your objectives. Utilizing these tools with the LOA (Law of Attraction) enables you to employ RAS to your advantage.

Michael Bernard Beckwith provided clarity and enlightenment around visualizing during one of his Agape *Law In Reverse Conversations* in 2012. He says that while visualization is good, it's an entry level use of the law. Visualization professes that if you can see it, you can achieve it. While it demonstrates to you that there *is* a law and that manifestation is a result of utilizing the law, visualization can be a form of limitation because you can only visualize based on the past – something that's already happened, been done or seen.

Vision***ing***, however, is creating something that does not yet exist *for you* and asking the Universe to show you what's next. It's a higher frequency where there's good waiting for you that you may not yet be able to see. Visualization can tend to limit what the Universe brings you. Visioning helps you break through your paradigms. When you believe it, you will see it. When you envision your preferences and present them to the Universe, include the words *'or better'*. Phrasing it this way says that X is what I'm available to, yet I know there's something more ~ *Bring it on*!

When you're recalling a memory, you're feeling what you felt when it was occurring (real). When you're visioning the future, you're feeling what's anticipated (synthetic). Your RAS cannot distinguish between the two. The same is true of your subconscious because as far as it is concerned, whatever you're feeling is what presently exists. Therefore, you can use this to your advantage. Everything you'd prefer already exists within the field of possibility. Actualizing it is simply a combination of knowing (*believing*) that it is yours, taking the appropriate actions to escort it into your reality and being open to receive it.

Denis Waitley, Ph.D. refers to this process as a dress rehearsal for the Mind/Body. The author of several international best-selling books and one of the most sought after speaker/consultants in the world, he has studied this process for more than 40 years in his work with Olympians and Astronauts. When athletes run an upcoming race in their mind, the same neurons in the brain and muscles in the body fire as if they're physically experiencing the event. In addition to the physical stimuli, visioning builds mental readiness and emotional confidence. This technique is referred to as 'Feelization'; a term which has earned its place in the Merriam-Webster dictionary. Waitley asserts:*"The mind can't distinguish between something that is imagined and something that really has happened. So why not preplay the preferred result and shape it in your memory?"*

Your heart feels before your mind is aware of it. There's a tremendous difference between looking forward and looking through. Visioning provides your subconscious with images, and affirmations afford verbal confirmation of them. However, it is essential to infuse your senses with the tangible attributes of your objectives - to breathe the power of emotion into them, imbue them with life and feel them in your heart.

In Louise Hay's film, *You Can Heal Your Life - The Movie*, Gregg Braden tells us that the feelings in your heart change your heart's electromagnetic field which then changes the field of the world around your body. We, and everything around us, are made up of atoms. When you change the field that the atom is in, it changes the atom itself. Changing the atoms alters your physical reality.

Louise Hay and Friends, You Can Heal Your Life - The Movie, Copyright 2007 by Hay House, Inc., Carlsbad, CA

Bruce Lipton, Ph.D. has done extensive research on this phenomenon which he expands upon within his book, *The Biology of Belief - Unleashing the Power of Consciousness, Matter & Miracles,* mentioned earlier.

With all of this in mind, if your objective is to be PersonX, doing X and having X, then step in to *Being* PersonX - feeling the way PersonX feels. See the world from inside of you *as* PersonX. If PersonX drives a particular car, they know what it feels like. If you had this car, you would know what it feels like. To impart these feelings within your senses, go to the dealership and drive your car. Experience the sensations - the feel of the cloth and/or aroma of the leather seats. Incidentally, scent goes straight to the brain's emotional area - *new car smell* ☺ Adjust everything to your preference – the seat, mirrors, temperature, etc. Put on your favorite radio station or bring your favorite CD. Feel the road under your tires, and become one with your car. Drive to your favorite place. Drive it home, and take a photo of your car parked there - with you in the driver's seat. Commit the entire experience to memory. This affirms that you're experiencing your objective as it presently exists which will anchor it into your subconscious and imbue the feelings into your heart.

> *"Think from the end. We must use imagination masterfully, not as an onlooker thinking 'of' the end, but as a partaker thinking from the end."* - Neville Goddard, Author of *The Power of Awareness*

The expression *"I'll believe it when I see it"* is actually a reversed polarity version of the manner by which this process actually works. If you subscribe to this belief, you've likely been spinning your wheels in an endless loop believing everything that you see and being programmed by it. How's *that* been working for ya? How about exiting that loop and trying something different? The expression *"I'll see it when I believe it"* is more in line with the Natural Laws of the Universe and flow of the forces of creation. That which you see on the outside is a reflection of that which exists within; and everything begins as a thought. When a thought is imbued with feeling, it becomes a belief. When inspired action is taken with intention toward that belief, it's an exquisite recipe for actualization.

One of my intentions is to assist young folks in fostering this consciousness. In the latter stages of writing this book, the LOA provided an opportunity to do so. My Son is in the Boy Scouts of America®, and they were discussing Religion and Spirituality in relation to one of their badge requirements. Taking inspired action, I volunteered to speak to them on the topic of Spirituality and meditation. Doing so prompted me to envision and create a presentation. Experiencing it put me into the role, affording feelization and preparedness for future opportunities. The Scouts®' motto is *"Be Prepared"*. In the words of Seneca, *"Luck is when preparedness meets opportunity."* This is the LOA in action. There is no mystery or secret to this process. Any aspect of elusivity is simply that which you've created within the shadows of your beliefs.

Affirmations are verbal fertilizer for your internal garden. As do the produce on a farm, affirmations must be sensitively selected and carefully cultivated. Raising your vibration with positive thoughts and affirmations without first adjusting your beliefs and clearing your blocks is like watering the leaves not the roots of that which you intend to grow. The results of doing so are often temporary because your limiting beliefs and the programs composed of them are still running in the background. You can't expect a healthy salad to be the outcome of arbitrarily tossing seeds into an overgrown toxic field. As a farmer tills the soil, it is essential to clear what may impede your affirmations from taking root and flourishing. You can have all the intention, knowledge and best tools in the Universe available to you; but if your conscious thoughts and subconscious beliefs are misaligned, you'll reap only frustration, no fireworks. Before you begin planting affirmations, you'll want to do the belief work first.

"Whatever the mind of man can conceive and believe, it can achieve." -Napoleon Hill

-Your Beliefs Are the Source Code of Your Software.

Beliefs are the operating system on which our programs are installed to run the creations of our realities; and yet, we're often unaware of them and the power they yield. Limiting beliefs are simply miscoded subconscious hindrances which can be deleted, upgraded or overwritten.

The circumstances in our lives are not what limit us. It is the constriction of negative beliefs and the expectations surrounding them which create our conditions and hinder our capacity for being generative. Quite often, our beliefs and/or the depths of their reach operate beneath our awareness, as they are hidden within our shadow side. Our shadows are the negative as well as the positive parts of ourselves that we have hidden, repressed or denied - yet our shadow side is where the gold lies. Deepak Chopra, Marianne Williamson and Debbie Ford provide an enlightening and empowering look at this aspect of ourselves in their book, *The Shadow Effect – Illuminating The Hidden Power of Your True Self*, which I highly recommend exploring.

Negative beliefs limit the possibilities that we entertain as being available to us. This is why we often experience the same disappointments and recurring themes throughout our lives. Sometimes, and quite often unknowingly, we may hold on to limiting beliefs either because we're unaware of them or because it may seem easier than facing and adjusting them. It may feel safer to simply carry on as is because of a false sense of security through familiarity. Change or anything new can be frightening to our reptilian brain, hence our fear of the unknown as we discussed during Chapter Six. Remember, though, that the unknown is the field of possibility.

The first step in clearing limiting beliefs is becoming aware of them. You can uncover them by looking for any undesirable patterns and/or recurring themes in your life and considering the limiting beliefs that may lie behind them. For instance: You never get the promotion or job you desire or you attract partners who are not ideal for you. Perhaps in the shadows of your subconscious you hold a belief of not being worthy or good enough to actualize your true preferences.

Truth is described as anything that is accepted as true – the key word there being 'accepted'. Your beliefs are anything that you have accepted as true. When exploring your beliefs, I suggest employing the question: *Who does this belong to?* as we tend to subscribe to what is handed down to us often without discerning for ourselves – especially during our key developmental years when most of our beliefs take root. Autonomy regarding beliefs is not typically the focus as is the teaching and absorption of them through protocol and osmosis. Beliefs, even those which are deeply rooted within our subconscious, can be reverse engineered – first by identifying them, then by questioning them: *Is this true for me?* and overwriting them when they are not.

Among its many benefits, EFT/Tapping (as we discussed in Chapter Six) is a fabulous tool for cultivating your Soul. Tapping beliefs contributes to nurturing your subconscious while building new neural pathways for success. Perhaps you have limiting beliefs around success itself. You may believe it's not safe to be successful because you'd be vulnerable or hurt in some ways – financially, emotionally, etc. Success may mean having more responsibility and less free time or perhaps expose you to judgement - all of which are merely points of view that are only true if they are also your beliefs. You can tap on these concerns to neutralize them, lower your resistance and raise your vibration. For example: *I'm afraid of success - No wonder I've been blocking it. I'm just trying to stay safe. I understand it now. Even though I'm afraid of success, I choose to accept who I am and that I'm doing the best that I can. I can choose to let go and release this fear. I forgive myself for sabotaging my success and choose to relax around this issue. I deeply accept and love myself. I feel better already."*

As with clearing the negative, the first step in activating positive beliefs is becoming aware of them. While acknowledging and processing the negative is effective, the most efficient overall approach is to activate and cultivate positive beliefs. While there are many ~ kindness, compassion, forgiveness, gratitude ~ to mention but a few, there are four core beliefs which exist within the essence of our authentic self ~ love, worthiness, safety and wholeness. Intrinsically, children, especially age seven and under, have no concept of not being lovable, worthy, safe or whole. Unfortunately, these core beliefs can become compromised by limitation within the mires of conditioning and assimilation. However, by cultivating and affirming these core beliefs, limitation dissipates and personal power expands.

Your external reality is a reflection of your inner state and core beliefs. If your external experiences are not a positive reflection of these generative beliefs, it is an indication that they have been compromised in some way. As an example, you attract partners into your life that are not ideal for you. This is an indication that perhaps your self-love and worthiness beliefs may be compromised. When this happens, we can tend to re-act and focus our energy on the external. However, when you have a negative experience, especially if you recognize it as a recurring pattern, you can choose to view it from a Sacred Contract / Happened *'For'* Me perspective and look for the gifts ~ the lessons within the situation; i.e. an opportunity to embrace and nurture self love. By doing so, you take responsibility for yourself which will provide you with an awareness of how to heal your beliefs and make mindful choices going forward. This process can unfold through grace within meditation. When you cultivate these core inner beliefs, your external experiences acclimate in tandem. This is the magic wherein your Soul becomes the author of your life whereby your Spirit writes the script.

"You are what you believe yourself to be." ~ Paulo Coelbo

Now let's discuss words and their employment as affirmations. Words are powerful entities. They construct our thoughts which create our beliefs and feelings and thus, our realities. Many dictionary definitions and social nuances of various words have changed over the years from their original energetic descriptions and historical connotations, with revisions and additions being made as we evolve. Words are living organisms in that they are dynamic; and we can all relate to their transformative nature.

The same word may have multiple meanings depending on the language environment, context and inflection with which they're expressed. The meaning and/or interpretation of words can change from one conversation to another and multiple times within the same conversation. In the absence of the emotional or expressional nuances behind the chosen terminology, a conversation in textual form can have an entirely different connotation and interpretation when conducted verbally.

Words have vibrations and energy; and as living organisms, they embody the capacity of transformation and the power of creation. Affirmations are auto suggestions, personal statements communicating and confirming your beliefs and intentions to your subconscious. They produce sponsoring thoughts which promote sponsoring feelings ~ a powerful combination for programming as it gets your mind and body working together toward your preferred objectives.

Émile Coué de la Châtaigneraie was a French psychologist and pharmacist *(~a rather interesting combination)* who introduced a method of psychotherapy and self-improvement based on optimistic autosuggestion, referred to as *The Coué Method* or *Couéism*. His book, *Self-Mastery Through Conscious Auto Suggestion*, was published in England in 1920 and in the United States in 1922. Although Coué's teachings were more popular in Europe than the U.S. during his lifetime, many Americans who adopted his ideas and methods, such as Norman Vincent Peale, Robert H. Schuller and W. Clement Stone, became famous in their own right by spreading the message of his words.

It is essential to choose our words wisely because as we know, the RAS and subconscious will accept all data on blind faith.

"Our subconscious minds have no sense of humor,
play no jokes and cannot tell the difference
between reality and an imagined thought or image." ~Robert Collier

When embarking on the implementation of affirmations, there are several words which carry low vibrational energy to be mindful of as their usage will undermine your intentions:

Why screams circular logic. It's typically used to defend or justify a conclusion or point of view, bringing the logic around to the beginning of the circle (looping).

Try eludes to an 'attempt'. It also implies that you may not succeed.

But negates whatever you've just said or intended. Add a 't', and let that be the *end* of it!

Can't closes the door to possibility.

Never implants limitation; Period.

> *"Never say never because limits, like fears, are often just an illusion." ~Michael Jordan*

Should imparts judgment and reprimand. Therefore, I suggest you refrain from Shoulding on yourself and *Must*erbating.

Need implies lack. Remember, like attracts like. If you're in lack, you'll attract lack.

Want also implies lack. '*Need*' I say more?

Desire implies longing and yearning which basically translate to lack, need and want.

I suggest that when you find yourself inadvertently using the words need, want or desire, replace them with prefer or like. To prefer is to favor or choose. Like is to enjoy or love ~ similar…*or better* ☺. Using these words expresses your intentions and the feelings derived from actualizing them. For example: *"I would like very much* -fill in the blank- - and allow yourself to feel the feelings of –fill in the blank-.

The words you choose are for your brain and subconscious to produce feelings of a higher vibration. The Universe doesn't hear the words you speak. It senses the vibration that you feel. So it's best to choose high-vibrational words. This process encompasses the Law of Entrainment, bringing your mind and body into vibrational coherence with your objectives. Entrainment is described as the synchronization of rhythmic cycles on their interaction with each other. This phenomenon was discovered by Dutch mathematician and scientist, Christiaan Huygens in the mid 1660's when he set up a room full of pendulum clocks and found that when he returned to the room a day or two later, the sway of the pendulums in all of the clocks had synchronized. A common demonstration of this phenomenon is the manner by which women's menstrual cycles will synchronize when they live closely with one another.

It is essential to be the vibrational frequency of your objectives in order to bring them forth from their vibrational holding space within the realm of possibility because as we know, like attracts like.

As we discussed in Chapter Ten, when using affirmations, it's essential that gradient moderation be employed - especially in the beginning. This tool will not work by lying to yourself. If you try to, your RAS and subconscious will toss your affirmations to the wind. As a for instance: If you're in a less than abundant financial state and you use an affirmation such as *I am wealthy*, they'll point to the stack of unpaid bills and retort *"Liar, liar, pants on fire"* as they turn their back on you, snickering beneath their breath. You wouldn't just walk up to a pair of German Shepherd guard dogs and reach out to pat them. Well, *I* wouldn't. It would be advisable to first test their temperament, offering kind words and perhaps a snack to secure their esteem. Lest we forget that these are the guardians of your current beliefs and programming. Start slowly and progress gently...*Goood Doggies*☺

When you look at things with disdain (i.e. a stack of unpaid bills), you add to the energy of them. Identify the things you don't appreciate, yet look for things to appreciate around them. For instance: Even if an unpaid balance is due to the utility company, embrace gratitude for the electricity that is present in your home. This is another great place to use EFT/Tapping. For example: *Even though there are bills to be paid, I appreciate that I'm acknowledging and working on it. I accept and love myself anyway.* Begin with subtle shifts and settle into them gradually.

Implementing these processes in a gentle stride with steady, enduring increments is the optimal approach. Experiencing all of Disney World® cannot be done in a day. You can't go from zero to 100 instantly because you currently have no reference point for 100. If you try to, your system will tune out, and your auto pilot will return to running its default programs. It's similar to working out or weight lifting. When you begin, you may not be comfortable using 100 pounds, but you may be with 10 or 20. The same is true with these processes. Once you're comfortable at plateau X, raise the bar. You can begin with broad, expansive affirmations such as:

"Every day in every way I'm getting better and better." Émile Coué

Affirmations are stated in the present tense. While it may be a stretch to use an affirmation such as *I am healthy, wealthy and happy.* A generic version such as *Health, Wealth and Happiness* provides your subconscious the awareness that they are available and that you can choose them ~ affording a reachable vibration for the present. This subtle approach will quell resistance and open space for new neural pathways. As your comfort level rises, you can shift to more specific affirmations.

When you find yourself thinking or saying anything that's not in alignment with your objectives, *re*-frame it in a way that *is.* Erase the footprint from the old and create space for the new. Employ the *S-T-O-P* technique we touched on in Chapter Six. *Word Policing* (yourself and others) is a constructive manner by which to affirm and solidify only your preferences and intentions. The key is to be mindful of your language, and that of those around you, as it is a potent programming tool. A friend of mine often interjects the comment, *"Good Times"* into a conversation – particularly when the subject matter involves a less than joyful issue. A simple statement, yet one that can completely change the energy.

The act of hand writing your affirmations can expand their effectiveness. Neural activity in the brain is greatly enhanced during handwriting, resulting in stronger and longer-lasting integration of the material. There's just something about handwriting that makes it real. Not that any of you folks had this experience, but I recall during my grade school years being charged with writing 100 times "*I will not*...whatever it was that I did." I may not enjoy admitting it, but perhaps those authority figures had something there.

A bit of advice: Refrain from putting any pressure on yourself where affirmations are concerned. Simply allow yourself to know that they are possible, and they'll have a gradual, natural and positive effect on your belief system. One of my favorites from Louise Hay is: *"My garden of affirmations is bearing fruit."*

Your beliefs become your thoughts.
Your thoughts become your words.
Your words become your actions.
Your actions become your habits.
Your habits become your values.
Your values become your destiny.
-Mahatma Gandhi

Now let's talk about focus and meditation.

The human brain/mind is an amazing entity with astounding capacities. It can store enormous amounts of data, glean and disburse millions of bytes of information at astonishing speeds and analyze and resolve the most complex of conundrums. While we humans credit ourselves with the capability of multi-tasking, the truth is that our mind's capacity for true focus is singular. You can have the washer & dryer running while preparing dinner, listening to music or an audio book and minding the time on the clock. However, at any given moment, you can truly focus on only one of them at a time.

Our active lives are such that we're constantly divided and distracted which is the main cause of stress, a major contributing factor to dis-ease. Hans Selye popularized the word 'stress' in describing the body's response to certain stimuli, saying that small amounts of stress are created when we're forced to refocus our attention. Over 60 years ago, it was considered stressful to refocus more than 10 times in one hour. The average television show triggers us to refocus every 3-6 seconds, approximately 10-20 focus changes per minute or 6-1200 per hour…Even more incentive to minimize the time spent in the company of the almighty box – or at least be selective regarding content choice. On average, how many focus changes (a.k.a. dis-tractions) do you experience in an hour?

Division and distraction inevitably hinder our ability to be present throughout much of our day. Eckhart Tolle, author of the best-selling book, *The Power of Now: A Guide to Spiritual Enlightenment,* tells us that all negativity is caused by an accumulation of psychological time and denial of the present. Guilt, regret, resentment, grievances, sadness, bitterness, and all forms of non-forgiveness are caused by too much past, and not enough presence. Unease, anxiety, tension, stress, worry and all forms of fear are caused by too much future, and not enough presence. The most important relationship in your life is your relationship with the now ~ the present moment. Keep in mind that when you are not fully present, you are operating from your programming. The manner by which you choose to be in the present moment effects not only your now, but also your future and every aspect of your living.

As we saw in Chapter Three, when we attempt to multitask, cognitive dissonance is the result. Holding wealth and poverty thoughts at the same time cancel each other out, resulting in confusion, uncertainty and frustration. However, our dominant thought wins; and what's more, a mere 5***1*** percent is all that's required to attain that trophy. So let's focus on our objectives and begin building on that 51 percent.

Feeling stress is a signal that we're coming from a place of fear or doing things which are not aligned with who we truly are. Part of the reason we struggle through life is because we tend to re-act without observing. Reaction depletes our energy while observation conserves it. Being mindful and present enhances our capacity for observance wherein we can make more considerate, optimal choices that are in line with our well-being. Meditation, among its many benefits, contributes more presence and mindfulness to your life. It takes you from activity and overwhelm into stillness and focus, giving your body and mind a deep level of rest and healing while expanding your awareness.

Meditation takes you beyond the mind's noisy chatter and limitation into an entirely different place - the silence of a mind that's not imprisoned by the past or the future, bringing you home to the peace of present moment awareness. The benefits of meditation are boundless – reduction of stress and anxiety, lowered blood pressure, strengthened immune system, enhanced sleep patterns and reduced fatigue to name but a few. Through meditation, old habits and patterns of thinking, feeling and behaving begin to fall away of their own accord. A growing body of studies is finding that when people meditate regularly, they influence the activity of their genes - helping to turn on the good genes and turn off the bad ones.

During my exploration of meditation, the LOA provided an invitation to attend the *Neuro Summit* on Lisa Garr's *Aware Show.* Among the many experts interviewed was Neuroscientist, Dr. Andrew Newberg. His research focuses on the development of neurotransmitter tracers for the evaluation of neurological and psychiatric disorders as well as neurotheology and religiosity. I learned a great deal from the information he shared.

Certain chemicals are released in the brain and body during meditation. Dopamine is one of the major neurotransmitters related to the reward system of the brain. It's what makes you feel good. The high experienced by people using cocaine is a result of an excess of dopamine in the brain. Gaba is the neurotransmitter system affected by Benzodiazepine. Common Benzodiazepines include Diazepam (Valium), Lorazepam (Ativan), Alprazolam (Xanax) and Clonazepam (Klonopin) to name but a few. When people meditate, there's an increase of these chemicals in the brain. Regular meditation can produce these effects naturally, eliminating the need for medication and possible adverse side effects which come along with them. Our objective is to replace Medi***C***ation with Medi***T***ation wherever possible.

Studies have shown that long-term meditators have thicker brains, particularly the frontal lobe. Those who meditate consistently have more function and activity in the frontal lobe - assisting with focus, regulating emotions, etc. Consistent meditation is likened to working out in that exercising strengthens your muscles. Over time, regular meditation enhances and fortifies your entire system.

What is meditation, and what is it not?

From early childhood, the focus of our education is on the external world. Rarely are we taught or encouraged to look within, to know ourselves and the true nature of our being. In many ways, we are strangers to ourselves – focusing more on our external relationships and getting to know others.

Although it's often misconceived as such, meditation is not mysterious, illusive or a practice reserved only for sages, gurus and the like. Meditation is a dynamic, introspective process, as is relaxation or prayer. From an esoteric perspective, some meditation is done as part of a Spiritual or Religious tradition. The nature of Spirituality and Theology are objective and diverse in that they relate to the manner by which we perceive reality and how we think of ourselves in relation to that reality.

Meditation is the practice of taking time away from the chatter of outside influences to be still. It is a technique of resting the mind, becoming familiar with and knowing ourselves, reconnecting with our Soul. One misconception is that your mind should be void of thought during meditation. As we know, our mind is a very active entity. At times, it can be overactive – the *Monkey Mind.* Our thoughts can place our focus into the past or the future, inhibiting our ability to ground ourselves in the present. We don't really know what thoughts are or where they come from. We simply know that we have them. Having thoughts is an intrinsic function of your brain/mind, and attempts to not have them are futile. We're not responsible for the thoughts that come to us, only for what we do with them. Thoughts are just thoughts. You can be mindful of them, but you don't have to believe them or live within the stories they're telling. As Jack Kornfield phrases it, "*You can allow them to be good servants vs. a bad master.*"

Louise Hay suggests likening thoughts to soft clouds gently floating across the sky on a summer's day – particularly during meditation.

The intention during meditation is to allow your mind to detach from its usual preoccupations and experience the space between thoughts – often referred to as '*The Gap*'. In his book, *Getting in the Gap*, Dr. Wayne W. Dyer discusses this Soul-nourishing meditation technique and provides a powerful, accompanying audio CD to assist in this practice. By allowing your mind to enter this Gap, it is able to return to its own source. Deepak Chopra refers to this space as '*a window, the corridor to the infinite field of pure potentiality – the womb of creation*'. This is a place where we can experience what is referred to as 'The Observer Effect'. In science, this term refers to changes the act of observation makes on a phenomenon.

A beautiful demonstration of this is Masaru Emoto's findings when experimenting with the molecular structure of water. He found that directing positive words, music, pure prayer and gratitude toward water resulted in the formation of beautiful crystals in the water. Directing the opposing negative expressions to the water resulted in disfigured crystals. In his New York Times best-selling book, *The Hidden Messages in Water,* Masaru speaks of the influence that affirmative thoughts, feelings and words have on water molecules and how they can also positively impact many aspects of our existence.

During meditation, consciously becoming aware of your unconscious thoughts, feelings, habits and behaviors is 'The Observer Effect'. When you can observe yourself and make preferred changes, you are no longer programm*ed*; you become the programm*er,* the creator. Through meditation, your mind can be escorted down the corridor to the field of pure potentiality where the manifestations of your objectives are birthed. When intention is brought to this space, it orchestrates its own fulfillment. In his best-selling book, *The Power of Intention*, Dr. Wayne W. Dyer discusses intention as a force of creation in nature. His book is a fabulous guide to applying this principle in the co-creation of our lives, one which I highly recommend exploring.

During the *Oprah & Deepak 21 Day Meditation Experience*™ in 2014, the focus of which was *The Energy of Attraction: Manifesting Your Best Life*, Deepak Chopra imparted an extensive amount of profound wisdom in a comforting, comprehensive manner. The key message was that through Spiritual manifestation, all material needs are met intrinsically. Within a Soul body connected to Spirit and its objective in coming here, your preferences and their actualizations manifest from your true self through consciousness. Having a sense of ease, fulfillment and joy - which is your Soul's objective - is the concept of living in the energy and consciousness of your intentions *while* their actualizations are being manifested.

Deepak Chopra once shared that *"ancient sages and seers declare that we ought focus first and foremost on our highest needs which include love, truth, creative power, compassion for ourselves and others, tending with care to the natural world and waking up to who we really are. Your true self is not available to your limited personal self, your ego; but once you consciously connect with cosmic* (inconceivably vast) *intelligence, your desires will be fulfilled at exactly the ideal time and place. This is one of the great secrets of the world's wisdom traditions. With expanded awareness and the absence of constraint from past conditioning, traumas and painful memories, you automatically see more possibilities. You rise above the level of the problem to the level of the solution."* You can look at life, not as a series of problems to be solved, but a series of gifts and opportunities through which to evolve.

Deepak went on to discuss the mechanics of manifestation, sharing that the Spiritual tradition of India known as Yoga describes three elements that must come together for manifestation.

Unbounded Awareness (*Samadhi*)

Unbounded awareness is the ability to go deep into the mind, into silence to the core of your existence. It is found in the gap mentioned earlier; and it is the reservoir of possibilities. One may call Samadhi the matrix of manifestation. Deepak says that *"When you experience Samadhi, it may seem as though nothing is happening because you're so used to bounded awareness which is filled with thoughts, feelings, sensations and images constantly flowing through your mind. It may be silent, but it isn't empty and far from blank."* The key is to realize that unbounded awareness is real.

Focus (*Dharana*)
"Creative power increases the more one-pointed your focus is. When you're sitting in the silent depth of the mind, focus comes easily. The magic is the coming together of two things that seem like opposites: Unbounded Awareness and Focused Awareness. They're really not contradictory. The power that creates a laser beam is generated by the total unbounded field of light, yet the laser beam is the sharpest, most focused light in existence. Harnessing the energy of attraction requires being unbounded and focused at the same time. This is what occurs during meditation."

Flexible Consciousness (*Dhyana)*
"This element is detachment, allowing yourself to receive with an open mind the results that the Universe sends you. Achieving flexibility is dependent on not expecting or judging. Receiving is a state of openness. When you're flexible in this way, you don't get stuck at any level of the mind (bounded awareness). *This takes practice."*

Once you have mastered all three elements of manifestation, you can truly create at will in support of your highest aspirations.

How do I approach meditation?

Initial attempts may lead you to wonder…*Am I doing it right* or *Am I there yet?* It was like that for me at first. Rest assured, *You can't do it wrong.* That being said, allow yourself to have no expectations regarding your meditations, i.e. encountering angelic beings and the like. Although you may, meditation is about allowing your true inner core, your unbounded awareness, to have a voice and listening to it. Meditation is about aligning your body, mind and Soul; and each experience is unique to every individual. Regardless of the technique(s) you choose, the benefits of meditation will lend themselves naturally; and you will experience these benefits during the rest of your day and life as a result of consistent practice.

Not every method of meditation is ideal for everyone because we all process slightly differently. There are a plethora of techniques available; the multiplicity of which can be likened to that of healing modalities in that the one(s) you choose are dependent upon your personal objectives and intentions at any given time. Through experimentation, the key is to find one(s) that resonate with your overall perspective and approach to life – something that you can easily connect with will provide the greatest benefits.

After listening to Lisa's interview with Dr. Newberg, I immediately purchased the package he was offering. One of the gems included therein was a document entitled "*Finding the Right Meditation Practice*" which outlines his research over the years and elaborates on some basic meditation methods. Dr. Newberg has also written and co-authored numerous best-selling books on this and related topics. Links to his work are provided in the *Resources.*

I began by using guided meditations. I found then to be most beneficial - especially in the beginning; and I occasionally use them as part of my meditation practice. Overall, however, I have found that engaging a Mantra works best for me. Many people confuse Mantras with affirmations, mottos or slogans. The word Mantra comes from two Sanskrit words: *Manas*, meaning *mind*, and *trai*, meaning *to free from*. In a literal sense, it means *to free from the mind.* [Note that this does not infer being void of thought. It simply entails not being governed by them.] Mantra is a Sanskrit term describing *vehicle of the mind* – one which takes you to the more peaceful, creative levels of the mind. A Mantra is a word, sound or vibration used to aid concentration during meditation.

"Quiet the mind, and the Soul will speak." -Ma Jaya Sati Bhagavati

During meditation, you don't resist thoughts, feelings or physical sensations as they arise. You simply allow them while focusing your attention on silently repeating your Mantra. Developing this non-resistance cultivates a state of consciousness that can move and remain centered at the same time (focus/*Dharana*). You also cultivate adaptability by not holding on to a Mantra if it starts to fade away or change. Within this space, you allow yourself to experience pure, unbounded awareness. Learning to live from this pure consciousness is known in Sanskrit at *Siti.* It is here that encountering your Soul occurs effortlessly. By connecting with your Soul through expanded awareness, your objectives are manifested and actualized for your highest and best – better than you could imagine.

There are thousands of Mantras. Many have particular meanings and can be used during purposeful meditations to project a certain vibration in relation to a specific intention. To begin, however, I suggest using Om.

Om (or 'aum') is a primordial sound vibration, the most elemental sound of creation. Om actually has four sounds: Ahh, Ohh, Mmm with the fourth being silence - the vibration which is beyond verbal pronunciation. The three syllables are not distinct or separate, but a continuous motion of body, breath and awareness. Om represents everything – Beginning, middle and end (Past, present and future) and is said to be the seed and frequency of creation.

"If you want to find the secrets of the universe, think in terms of energy, frequency and vibration." -Nikola Tesla

The following is an overview of a mantra meditation as Deepak guided us during the *Oprah & Deepak 21 Day Meditation Experience*™. Optimally, you'll want to choose a quiet time and place where you won't be interrupted. It's helpful to have a muted timer such a soft bell to notify you when twenty minutes (or your personal choice of duration) has elapsed.

"Make yourself comfortable and close your eyes. Become aware of your breath, and just breathe slowly and deeply. With each breath, allow yourself to become more deeply relaxed. Then, gently introduce the Mantra, "Om". Repeat it silently to yourself. With each repetition, see yourself opening to your natural state of unlimited possibility. Feel your body, mind and Spirit open and receive just a little more. Whenever you find yourself distracted by thoughts, noises or physical sensations, simply return your attention to silently repeating your Mantra. As you say your Mantra in meditation, there will be gaps where the Mantra has faded away. It's quite incredible from the viewpoint of the active mind that these seemingly insignificant blips of silence contain the true power of the mind. After experiencing silent, pure awareness in the gap, with practice, your mind will have this ability all the time; and every thought will have full creative power."

The *Primordial Sound Meditation*, rooted in the Vedic tradition of India, is the meditation practice which is taught at the *Chopra Center*. The object of attention is a Mantra that is repeated silently to yourself. When you learn the Chopra Center's Primordial Sound Meditation, you receive a personal Mantra. Calculated following Vedic mathematic formulas, this Mantra is the vibration that the universe was creating at the time and place of your birth. Unlike guided meditations or those which utilize certain mantras for a particular objective, the intention of the *Primordial Sound Meditation* and Mantra is simply to guide you inward.

Meditation is one of the best ways to connect to your true self in pure consciousness. It gives you a direct experience of your Soul; and in the process, loosens the grip of limitation and dissolves the impurities which are preventing its Spirit from shining forth in your life. You always have access to this inner stillness and calm. At any time, you can bring yourself to this place of inner peace which exists just beneath the echelon of thoughts, feelings and emotions and the distractions of everyday life.

One technique I've found to be tremendously refreshing and empowering is a mini meditation which you can use anywhere at any time within your day in just a few seconds utilizing your breath as your focus. It's a wonderful ISR (Interrupt Service Routine), especially during highly stressful situations. If possible, you can close your eyes if you choose while you take in a long, slow, deep belly breath. As you breathe in through your nose, focus on the air entering your body through your nostrils and follow it down your throat, through your heart center and into your abdomen. Observe the breath moving in the opposite direction as you slowly exhale. You can do this once or several times depending on your preferences. This brief exercise will not only relax your entire mind/body, it will center and ground you in the present moment with ease.

Consistent meditation enables your mind to reach a higher level of consciousness, affording an unyielding sense of well-being and balance, supportive of engaging in life's activities with clarity and ease. Meditation is about connecting with this inner peace and unbounded awareness and integrating it within every aspect of your life.

Making time for meditation in the morning is optimal as the effects linger throughout your day. A second afternoon or early evening meditation enhances the benefits. Activating and nurturing your Mind/Body connection in a state of gratitude creates new brain cells and neural pathways which translate to every cell in your body to the level of your genes. This process begins with your first meditation. Over time, more and more of this expansion will remain with you, enabling you to embody its ease and peace as a natural state within your life. Deepak once shared that the most important experience of his life has been learning to meditate as it's been the key to his creativity, well-being and happiness.

Meditation fosters a lifestyle of mindfulness. Mindfulness is not *thinking*. It is the practice of having a perpetual awareness of your thoughts, feelings and sensations without having any judgment where they are concerned. It is choosing to be fully present in every moment. The term Mindfulness has become a buzzword due to Western psychology being impressed by the significant research documenting its effectiveness. It isn't a new phenomenon, however; it originates from Buddhist meditation practices. Dr. Elisha Goldstein, author of *The Now Effect: How This Moment Can Change the Rest of Your Life* (mentioned in Chapter Six), offers a comprehensive 28-day program entitled *"Basics of Mindfulness Meditation"* which guides you on a progressive lifestyle into living mindfully.

Although it may be regarded as a technique for meditation, mindfulness isn't merely a tool, it is a lifestyle choice. In the words of Jon Kabat-Zinn, *"The real meditation is how you live your life."*

~ Fostering Early and Enduring Mindfulness With Our Children ~

From the age of zero to seven+, we're absorbing everything around us and developing patterns within. By the time we begin school, we're bombarded with programming – being molded with *Do/Be this and Don't do/be that's.* We begin to conform and adjust to assimilate and *fit in*, tending to forsake our natural autonomy and some of the internal wisdom and capacities we're born with.

When I spoke with the Scouts® about Spirituality and meditation, I was pleasantly surprised at how receptive they were. It was clear that these guys already knew this stuff on some level. One of the boys asked if I could teach his Dad what we'd discussed. I suggested that he begin by being the change he preferred to see and sharing that energy with his Father. *-There are times when the child becomes the parent.*

It is my assertion that the capacities we've discussed herein are somewhat lacking, perhaps missing altogether, from many of our societies, particularly within our school systems. While the 3R's (Reading, Writing and Arithmetic) are important, it's essential that we teach kids how to learn and evolve - empower them to discover what motivates them, excites them and brings meaning to their life. During my presentation to the Scouts®, I shared that my interpretation of Spirituality is that which brings meaning to your life; and that meaning doesn't lie in external things, it lies within.

During my explorations, I discovered *MindUP*™, a research-based program for educators and children created by Goldie Hawn and The Hawn Foundation in collaboration with neuroscientists, cognitive psychologists and educators. *MindUP*™ has been rigorously researched and accredited by CASEL (Collaborative for Academic, Social, and Emotional Learning). It equips children, educators and parents with vital social and emotional literacy skills. Rooted in neuroscience, the program teaches self-regulatory behavioral control while offering engagement strategies for learning and living. *MindUP*™ has proven to reduce stress, strengthen concentration and increase academic performance, helping children and educators thrive within a community of learners.

In a Huffington Post blog, "*MindUP: How Goldie Hawn Is Out to Change the Landscape of Childhood Learning*", Dr. Lloyd I. Sederer, Medical Director of N.Y. State Office of Mental Health, says that *"Hawn's conviction to develop MindUP™ grew out of the strong science base for SEL (Social and Emotional Learning). SEL programs improve academic achievement as measured by standardized tests and grades, as well as address conduct problems -- disruptive behaviors, aggression, bullying and delinquency. Studies show reductions in emotional distress - depression, anxiety, stress and decreased alcohol and drug use. School attendance improved, and kids liked school more in programs using SEL."*

MindUP™ is not a curriculum add-on; it is interwoven within the students' lessons and integrated into the culture of the classroom. It fosters a learning environment where a child's ability to academically succeed and personally thrive is maximized, contributing to their overall sense of self and well-being. The program was developed as a joint effort with Scholastic®, one of the oldest publishers of educational materials in the United States. It consists of fifteen lessons depicted for three age groups: K-2, 3-5 and 6-8. The core practice of *MindUP™* consists of a simple, ten minute centering exercise done three times each day. One Sixth-Grade Student had this to say about MindUP™: *"Being mindful calms me down when I'm angry. It helps me not get in a big fight because I don't want to hurt my friends. It also helps me focus on my work."*

During a TEDMED presentation in 2009 with Goldie Hawn, Dr. Daniel J. Siegel discussed the neuroscience behind the beauty of *MindUP™*. He asserts that our present educational system may be imprisoning the brains of our children by focusing primarily on the 3 R's (Reading, Writing and Arithmetic) while overlooking an equally essential 3 R's - Reflection, Relationships and Resilience which is what the *MindUP*™ program provides. He says that by incorporating reflection as a skill, we can develop a capacity known as Mindsight - a term he coined to describe our human ability to perceive the mind of the self and others. He discusses this capacity in detail within one of his many best-selling books, *Mindsight: The New Science of Personal Transformation.*

Dr. Siegel says that mindsight can be ignored or it can be taught by offering a basic reflective skill which has the capacity to take a wandering attention and return it again and again to its target. This can be accomplished through a simple exercise of observing the breath, a practice within every major wisdom tradition in the world, ancient and modern. Unfortunately, we don't do this in schools because we call it 'Religion'. It's actually a brain hygiene practice which develops an integrated brain from which vital capacities emerge – Such as the abilities to:

- Regulate your body - keep your heart, lungs, intestines, etc. working well.
- Tune in to yourself and others
- Balance your emotions so that life has meaning and energy, but not so much that it's revved up and chaotic, and not too little that it's rigid and depleted.
- Extinguish fear after being traumatized.
- Pause before you act so that you're flexible.
- Have insight into yourself – being connected to the past, present and the future.
- Have empathy and compassion for others as well as morality.
- The ability to be in touch with Intuition.

How many of these would you like to develop? How many would you like our children to? Practices and programs such as these provide children with balance and the capacity to regulate energy and information flow within themselves and others. Imagine what life would be like with this practice incorporated within our education systems. What would change if kids were gifted with skills that allow them to conduct their lives with more confidence and ease? What would be possible if every child knew that they have a choice in every moment?

Although what we say can become a child's inner voice, what we do has an equal, if not greater, impact. It is essential that we begin with ourselves because kids learn by example. What would life be like with these practices incorporated within our home and work environments and applied within our daily interactions throughout our lives? By integrating these practices, they instinctively translate to our children and everyone around us, rippling to future generations.

We all have the capacity to create our lives and our future, regardless of the situations we're born into and the environments within which we evolve. Practices such as those we've discussed herein provide an invitation to a greater awareness of what is possible for us all. Through shared awareness, we can all be more of a contribution to each other and the changes, ease and joy we wish to see and experience in our world.

"What I hear I forget.
What I see, I remember.
What I do, I understand."
~ Confucius

For more information, please visit Resources.

Musings...

"Life isn't about finding yourself. It's about creating yourself." - George Bernard Shaw

Chapter 12

Moving Forward With Mindful Ease

In this chapter, you'll embark on the first day of the *Best* of your life - which, optimally, can be every day.

When we reflect on the creation of our lives, we often lament: *If I'd known then what I know now…* yet doing so need not carry an essence of remorse. Every experience in your life has contributed to whom and where you presently are. In the words of Dr. Maya Angelou, *"We delight in the beauty of the butterfly, but rarely admit the changes it has gone through to achieve that beauty."*

Maya Angelou used with permission by Caged Bird Legacy, LLC www.MayaAngelou.com

I'd like to share something that I wrote quite some time ago during an automatic writing session which recently found its way back to my attention:

Dearest Maureen,

Please stop torturing yourself with dissatisfaction around your creations. Doing so does not serve you. These creations were birthed from your needs and desires at the time. Do not languish near failure, disappointment or sorrow - they do not contribute to you. There is no room for sadness in one so filled with love. You always have a choice, and you can create new energies with your wisdom and clarity. You must love yourself before you will allow yourself to be loved. Give, but give to yourself as you do to others, and you will appreciate all of your aspirations tenfold. Be at ease with the process, as it is yours to direct. Allow your vibration to expand and soar. Trust and nurture yourself; believe in yourself, and love yourself. Be empowered by your own strength and beauty. Follow your heart with ease in joy. All is well.

In his book, *I Can See Clearly Now*, Dr. Wayne W. Dyer shares his experiences, referring to them as 'quantum-moment recollections'. In his own words: *"I wasn't aware of all of the future implications that these early experiences were to offer me. Now, from a position of being able to see much more clearly, I know that every single encounter, every challenge and every situation are all spectacular threads in the tapestry that represents and defines my life; and I am deeply grateful for all of it."*

Dr. Wayne W. Dyer, I Can See Clearly Now, Copyright 2014 by Dr. Wayne W. Dyer, Hay House, Inc., Carlsbad, CA

What might be possible by embodying this perspective, not only in reflecting upon your past, but in your present moments and as you move forward in the creation of your life?

By looking at your experiences and appreciating them through a 'happened *For* me' perspective, what gifts can you see that perhaps may have eluded you previously? Kris Carr offered an inspiring post that I'd like to share. Consider how you might re-parent yourself by completing the remainder of this sentence: *If I could give my younger self some nurturing advice, I would tell her/him…* Consider your insights in relation to the various aspects of your life; i.e. Relationships, Career, Activities, Interests, etc. Kris suggests writing a note to your inner child:

> What would you tell him or her? Does she need some kind words to help her get through a tough

time? Maybe he's hanging onto self-doubt or shame and could use your unconditional love to finally release what's holding him back. Or perhaps she's got a big dream and needs your encouragement to take a leap of faith. Whatever it is, show your support for your inner whippersnapper.

If I could give my younger self some nurturing advice, I would tell her/him ...

~No one has to see this note, so don't edit your words. ~

____

____

____

____

Kris refers to this practice as 'a love note from your true self'; adding that the more often you do it (and listen to your own advice) the easier it will be to embrace who you are right now.

~ ***What is possible now and as I more forward in my life?***

You don't just live once, you live every moment of every day; and the best way to appreciate your past is by living fully in the present. What if there were no past – only the present and future? If you were being you - *All* of you, who might that be? What would be possible if every day you woke up and asked: *If I were truly being all of me, living today from the total joy of being alive, what would I choose* ~ and conducted your day according to those choices?

"Yesterday I was clever, so I wanted to change the world. Today I am wise, so I am changing myself." ~Rumi

When downsizing targeted my last job in the corporate world (post Microsoft), ordinarily I'd have been panicked without having something else lined up to step into. However, I recall having a sense that I'd received a gift in that I had, in some way, been set free. I'd been longing for some time and space to simply just *Be* - a period where there was no schedule to adhere to, no projects to be absorbed by and a few hours each day where I was not responsible for anyone or anything else but *Me.* When this gift arrived, I accepted without trepidation.

For me, it was almost impossible not to jump into other endeavors or projects to utilize my energy - particularly at that time of the year when the weather was conducive to my little Cleanaholic's spring cleaning itch. I decided to have a psychic astrology reading with Nancy Foley - an amazingly wise, gifted and generous woman - to get a sense of perspective. One of the things Nancy suggested during the session was to take some time for reflection; and that if necessary, literally sit on my hands to avoid squandering this precious time with mundane tasks. I opted to heed her advice. It was a glorious time of self-discovery and reconnection. The most spiritual time I'd experienced in my life to that point. It was during this time that the insights from my Dark Nights and Healing Crises began to come together with clarity, meaning and purpose.

In considering the financial aspects of my sabbatical, I realized that I was hesitant about returning to the corporate arena - concerned that the expansion I'd cultivated may somehow evaporate within the mires of doing so. During a conversation with my Reiki Master Teacher, Katie Ramaci of *Women of Wisdom,* I expressed this concern as well as my calling to open my own healing practice. This wise woman explained that not everyone with healing gifts is meant to hang out a shingle, as it is essential that they be sprinkled amongst all facets of the world. Her ultimate words of wisdom were *'Wherever you go, take it with you'.* Katie's message was profound.

I realized that my concerns were nothing more than fears – points of view based on old beliefs and past experiences. I also realized that true freedom and living an inspired life is a state of mind and a lifestyle choice, regardless of lineal aspects or details. Everything is an inside job. That being said, albeit with financial reservation, I did not return to the corporate world at that time; and I knew that if I chose to do so in the future, it would be different…because *I* would be different. It was during this time that my healing practice and the contents of this book began to take form.

We are who and where we presently are in our lives by way of our thoughts, feelings and choices - choices which are based on our beliefs. When our beliefs are pure and boundless, so too are our choices and lives.

Everything within *Source Code* is familiar. I say with certainty that you have not read anything here that you don't already know as truth on some level. It's entirely possible that if you'd encountered these bits of wisdom previously - *and you likely did in one form or another*, you simply weren't open to receiving or embracing them at the time. You were likely unaware that you even *had* programs, much less the personal power corrupted by them. As Confucius said, "*It is not the problem that you don't know; it's the problem that you don't know what you don't know*" which begets the question: What will you do with what you *now* know?

With this in mind, avoid allowing what you've conceived from your *Owner's Manual* to slip into sleep mode. Nobel Laureate, Eric R. Kandel, found that learning just one bit of new information doubles the number of synaptic connections in the brain. He also found, however, that if this new information was not applied and integrated within hours or days, these connections would subsequently wither. Embody this wisdom and mindfully utilize it within every aspect of your life. *Wherever you go, take it with you.*

There will always be *Stuff.* The gems of living an inspired life at your full potential are mined from the manner by which you interact with *Stuff,* and it's all a matter of perspective and choice. In speaking with a friend around the topics discussed herein, I shared that I've been saturating myself with this material for years now. To this, he replied *"I've got a long way to go".* I've thought the same on many occasions. While I'm more conscious than ever before, I continue to evolve; yet I'm able to do so more mindfully with greater ease; and I have experienced the joy that doing so brings.

Question everything, and keep an open mind as the possibilities in life truly are infinite. Nourish yourself with consistent self-care and meditation. Develop a habit of checking in. Schedule periodic meetings with yourself. If necessary, write them on your calendar just as you would any other appointment. Doing so is a great way of nurturing your connection with your Soul, honoring and celebrating *You* and your life. I've provided a *Personal Check-In* template that you can use as a guide for this practice in the back of this book.

During the *Oprah & Deepak 21 Day Meditation Experience*™ in early 2015, the focus of which was *Manifesting True Success,* Deepak Chopra shared that *"No matter how much you have disconnected from your true self, it exists; and it cannot be harmed. Your true self is giving you unconditional support and love. Knowing your true self is the greatest achievement you can attain. It is the success beyond all success; and nothing is more precious."*

"A successful life is one that is loved by the person living it." -Sandy C Newbigging

There are those who believe that life occurs through the random chaos of happenstance. While ambiguous perceptions exist, it is my belief that life is orchestrated according to our co-creative capacities and the choices we make of our free will. Everything happens *For* a reason - That reason being the provision of opportunities from which to make our selections. Each of us perceives life through the lens of our own objectives. We can only make assumptions regarding the perceptions of others ~ making the best choices for ourselves while they do the same. It is my assertion that our feelings and emotions are the only things that are truly *real*; and the realities we create from them contain more magic than anything else. We are all participants in the eloquent dance of life, playing our chosen roles in each other's game of Kismet. While the personal wisdom you acquire is your own, those around you benefit from your choices based on that wisdom by way of the ripple effect. What might be possible by choosing to be the one to cast the first pebble of change into the pond?

Nancy Foley once said:*"Love is the dividend that comes from our investment in others."* She also said: *"A writer's words live on long after they are gone; for once expressed, they take on a life of their own in the Universe."* It is my sincere wish that *Source Code of Your Soul* inspire and empower you to create and live a fulfilling life of ease and joy.

Dr. Wayne W. Dyer once said *"Don't die with your music still in you."* It is these words which birthed my inspiration to write this book. Thank you for listening to mine.

Follow the song of your heart ~ embrace its gentle whispers,
for they are composed in the Source Code of
Your Soul. ~Maureen Marie Damery

For more information, please visit Resources.

Musings...

"The only person you are destined to become is the person you decide to be."

-Ralph Waldo Emerson

Let me see the truth of who I am - No matter how beautiful it is.

Chapter 13

The Author of My Life

My Soul is the author of my life;
and my Spirit writes the script of my reality.

Resources

I'd like to express my sincere gratitude and appreciation for the material provided by the following which has contributed not only to my own clarity, but to this book as well as the world.

Wikipedia
The Free Encyclopedia. This compendium of wisdom, and its numerous contributors, is an invaluable contribution to the world!
http://www.wikipedia.org/

Thesaurus.com
The most innovative and comprehensive digital source for everything related to words.
http://www.thesaurus.com

Margaret Rouse
Tech Target
A knowledge exploration and self-education tool about information technology.
http://whatis.techtarget.com/

Merriam Webster online Dictionary
http://www.merriam-webster.com/

FOREWORD

Jack Canfield
Co-creator, #1 New York Times best selling series Chicken Soup for the Soul®
Author, *The Success Principles*
http://jackcanfield.com/

Chicken Soup Book Series:
http://www.chickensoup.com/books

PREFACE

Holistic Health Care Facts and Statistics
http://www.disabled-world.com/medical/alternative/holistic/care-statistics.php

Statistics on Complementary and Alternative Medicine
National Health Interview Survey
http://nccam.nih.gov/news/camstats/NHIS.htm

2014 Schedule of NCHS Statistical Products and Reports
http://www.cdc.gov/nchs/pressroom/calendar/2014_schedule.htm

CHAPTER 1:

Dr. Karl R. Wolfe
True Silence: The True Self is Revealed in the Stopping of the Mind
http://karlrwolfe.com/

"Consciousness is the programming language of the universe."
Quote taken from the video ***"The Matrix of Illusion"***
Article: http://noetic.org/discussions/open/305/
Video: http://www.youtube.com/watch?v=CRkDicwjRQs&feature=related

CHAPTER 2:

Leadership Brain for Dummies
Marilee B. Sprenger
http://www.amazon.com/s/?ie=UTF8&keywords=leadership+brain+for+dummies&tag=googhydr20&index=aps&hvadid=24019153991&hvpos=1t1&hvexid=&hvnetw=g&hvrand42325

99390375726579&hvpone=&hvptwo=&hvqmt=b&hvdev=c&ref=pd_sl_5hc51w4gpb_b

Marilee Sprenger
http://www.marileesprenger.com/

Baroness Susan Greenfield CBE
British scientist, writer, broadcaster and member of the House of Lords, specializing in the physiology of the brain
http://www.susangreenfield.com/

Susan Greenfield's Psychology Today Blog
https://www.psychologytoday.com/experts/susan-greenfield-phd

Dr. Wayne W. Dyer
http://www.drwaynedyer.com/

The Cookie Thief
Valerie Cox
From: ***A 3rd Serving of Chicken Soup for the Soul***

Chicken Soup Book Series:
http://www.chickensoup.com/books

CHAPTER 3:

The Selfish Gene
Richard Dawkins
http://www.amazon.com/Selfish-Gene-30th-Anniversary-ebook/dp/B000SEHIG2/ref=sr_1_1?s=books&ie=UTF8&qid=1404164662&sr=1-1&keywords=the+selfish+gene

Virus of the Mind: The New Science of the Meme
Richard Brodie

http://www.hayhouse.com/catalogsearch/advanced/result/?author=richard+brodie

Getting Past OK - The Self-Help Book for People Who Don't Need Help
Richard Brodie
http://www.hayhouse.com/getting-past-ok

Richard Brodie
http://www.memecentral.com/rbrodie.htm

The Biology of Belief - Unleashing the Power of Consciousness, Matter & Miracles
Bruce Lipton, Ph.D.
http://www.hayhouse.com/the-biology-of-belief-1

Bruce Lipton, Ph.D.
https://www.brucelipton.com/

Do People Only Use 10 Percent of Their Brains?
Scientific American
http://www.scientificamerican.com/article/do-people-only-use-10-percent-of-their-brains/

Dr. Wayne W. Dyer
http://www.drwaynedyer.com/

CHAPTER 4

Keys to Success: The 17 Principles of Personal Achievement (Think and Grow Rich)
The 12 Great Riches of Life: The Keys to Success
Napoleon Hill

http://www.amazon.com/s/ref=nb_sb_noss?url=search-alias%3Daps&field-keywords=Napoleon%20Hill%E2%80%99s%2012%20Great%20Riches%20of%20Life%20

The Napoleon Hill Foundation
http://www.naphill.org/

The Kybalion**: **A Study of The Hermetic Philosophy of Ancient Egypt and Greece
The Three Initiates
http://www.amazon.com/dp/1603864784

The Universal Spiritual Laws
Joanne of Sacred Scribes
http://psychicjoanne.hubpages.com/hub/UNIVERSAL-SPIRITUAL-LAWS

Dr. Joseph Murphy
http://www.dr-joseph-murphy.com/

Anne Lamott Books
http://www.amazon.com/s/ref=nb_sb_ss_i_1_10?url=search-alias%3Dstripbooks&field-keywords=anne+lamott+books&sprefix=anne+lamot%2Cstripbooks%2C183

Life Visioning: A Transformative Process for Activating Your Unique Gifts and Highest Potential
Michael Bernard Beckwith
http://www.amazon.com/Life-Visioning-Transformative-Activating-Potential/dp/1622030508/ref=sr_1_1?s=books&ie=UTF8&qid=1442522811&sr=1-1&keywords=life+visioning+michael+bernard+beckwith

Michael Bernard Beckwith
Agape International Spiritual Center
http://www.agapelive.com

Michael Bernard Beckwith
Books and Courses
http://www.hayhouse.com/catalogsearch/advanced/result/?author=Michael+Beckwith

Anita Moorjani
http://anitamoorjani.com/

Dying to be Me
Anita Moorjani
http://www.hayhouse.com/dying-to-be-me-paperback

CHAPTER 5

The Pursuit...or the Practice of Happiness
Chip Conley
http://lettersofhappiness.org/letters/39

Authentic Happiness: Using the New Positive Psychology to Realize Your Potential for Lasting Fulfillment
Martin E. P. Seligman, Ph.D.
http://www.amazon.com/Authentic-Happiness-Psychology-Potential-Fulfillment/dp/0743222989

Dr. Martin Seligman
For more information:
http://www.authentichappiness.sas.upenn.edu/Default.aspx

Positive Psychology Center
http://www.positivepsychology.org/

Sacred Contracts: Awakening Your Divine Potential
Caroline Myss
http://www.amazon.com/Sacred-Contracts-Awakening-Divine-Potential/dp/0609810111

Archetypes - Who Are You?
Caroline Myss
http://www.hayhouse.com/archetypes

Caroline Myss
http://www.myss.com/

Determining Your Archetypes
http://www.myss.com/library/contracts/determine.asp

Gallery of Archetypes
http://www.myss.com/library/contracts/three_archs.asp

Caroline's Blog
http://www.myss.com/blog/

Happy For No Reason - 7 Steps to Being Happy from the Inside Out
Marci Shimoff
http://www.happyfornoreason.com/Home.asp

Centerpointe Research Institute
Bill Harris
http://www.centerpointe.com/v2/

The Passion Test
http://thepassiontest.com/

The Passion Test – The Effortless Path to Discovering Your Life Purpose
Janet Attwood and Chris Attwood

http://www.amazon.com/s/ref=nb_sb_ss_i_2_17?url=search-alias%3Dstripbooks&field-keywords=the+passion+test.+by+janet+and+chris+attwood&sprefix=the+passion+test+%2Caps%2C179

CHAPTER 6

Susan Jenkins
Shamanic Healer
http://www.shamanichealingwork.com

A Return to Love: Reflections on the Principles of "A Course in Miracles"
Marianne Williamson
http://www.amazon.com/s/ref=nb_sb_noss_2?url=search-alias%3Daps&field-keywords=return+to+love

Marianne Williamson
http://marianne.com/

The Tapping Solution: A Revolutionary System for Stress-Free Living
Nick Ortner
http://www.hayhouse.com/catalogsearch/advanced/result/?author=nick+ortner

The Tapping Solution
Nick and Jessica Ortner
http://www.thetappingsolution.com/

What Is Tapping And How Can I Start Using It?
The Tapping Solution
http://www.thetappingsolution.com/what-is-eft-tapping/

The Genie in Your Genes: Epigenetic Medicine and the New Biology of Intention
Dawson Church, Ph.D.

http://www.amazon.com/s/ref=nb_sb_ss_i_1_23?url=search-alias%3Dstripbooks&field-keywords=the%20genie%20in%20your%20genes%20by%20dawson%20church&sprefix=The+Genie+in+Your+Genes%2Cstripbooks%2C259

Lisa Garr
The Aware Show
https://theawareshow.com/

Acupressure & Acupressure Points & Meridians
Acupressure.com
http://www.acupressure.com/articles/acupuncture_and_acupressure_points.htm

The Procrastination Equation: How to Stop Putting Things Off and Start Getting Stuff Done
Piers Steel, Ph.D.
http://www.amazon.com/The-Procrastination-Equation-Putting-Getting/dp/B005CDTQ1O

Dr. Steel's Procrastination Survey:
http://procrastinus.com/the-procrastinus-survey/

Poem: Autobiography in Five Short Chapters
There's a Hole in My Sidewalk: The Romance of Self-Discovery
Portia Nelson
http://www.amazon.com/Theres-Hole-My-Sidewalk-Self-Discovery/dp/0941831876

The Bucket List - Kopi Luwak 2
https://www.youtube.com/watch?v=VVJqwCdzZnw

American Society of Addiction Medicine (ASAM)
http://www.asam.org/for-the-public/definition-of-addiction

You Can Heal Your Life
Louise Hay
http://www.hayhouse.com/catalogsearch/advanced/result/?q=You+can+heal+your+life

Louise Hay
http://www.louisehay.com/

Excuses Begone! How to Change Lifelong, Self-Defeating Thinking Habits
Dr. Wayne W. Dyer
http://www.hayhouse.com/excuses-begone-1

Ram Daas
https://www.ramdass.org/
Ram Daas Books and CD's
http://www.amazon.com/Ram-Dass/e/B001HCS3GS/ref=dp_byline_cont_book_1

Psilocybin Project
http://www.isites.harvard.edu/icb/icb.do?keyword=k3007&panel=icb.pagecontent44003:r$1?name=historicprofs.html&pageid=icb.page19708&pageContentId=icb.pagecontent44003&view=view.do&viewParam_name=learyandalpert.html

The Language of Letting Go
Melody Beattie
http://www.amazon.com/Language-Letting-Go-Hazelden-Meditation/dp/0894866370/ref=sr_1_1?s=books&ie=UTF8&qid=1387388029&sr=1-1&keywords=letting+go+melody+beattie

The Codependency Quiz
http://www.codependencyquiz.com/

The Codependency Project
http://www.codependencyproject.com/

Paul Elmore, M.A., M.S., LPCi
http://www.paulelmore.com/

Codependent No More: How to Stop Controlling Others and Start Caring for Yourself
Melody Beattie
http://www.amazon.com/Codependent-No-More-Controlling-Yourself/dp/0894864025

Joseph Vitale
Zero Limits - The Secret Hawaiian System for Wealth, Health, Peace and More
http://www.amazon.com/Zero-Limits-Secret-Hawaiian-System/dp/0470402563

The Now Effect: How a Mindful Moment Can Change the Rest of Your Life
Elisha Goldstein Ph.D.
http://www.amazon.com/The-Now-Effect-Mindful-Moment/dp/1451623895

STOP: A Short Mindfulness Practice *(Video Demonstration)*
Elisha Goldstein, Ph.D.
http://www.youtube.com/watch?v=PhwQvEGmF_I

Elisha Goldstein, Ph.D.
http://elishagoldstein.com/

Mindful.Org
Taking time for what matters
http://www.mindful.org/

About MAC 50 and Project MAC
MIT Computer Science and Artificial Intelligence Laboratory (CSAIL)
http://mac50.csail.mit.edu/about

Right Recovery For You – Empowering You to Move Beyond any Addictive or Compulsive Behavior
Marilyn M. Bradford, MSSW, MED
http://www.amazon.com/Right-Recovery-You-Marilyn-Bradford/dp/1939261473/ref=sr_1_1?s=books&ie=UTF8&qid=1454604042&sr=1-1&keywords=right+recovery+for+you

The 5 Stages of Grief: Sobriety Edition
Beth Leipholtz
http://www.huffingtonpost.com/beth-leipholtz/the-5-stages-of-grief-sob_b_6182050.html

On Grief and Grieving: Finding the Meaning of Grief Through the Five Stages of Loss
Elisabeth Kübler-Ross, David Kessler
http://www.amazon.com/Grief-Grieving-Finding-Meaning-Through/dp/1476775559/ref=sr_1_1?s=books&ie=UTF8&qid=1454604223&sr=1-1&keywords=ON+GRIEF+AND+GRIEVING

Frenemies: How They Threaten Recovery And What To Do About Them – Part 1
http://www.addictiontreatmentmagazine.com/recovery/recovery-tips/frenemies-how-they-threaten-recovery-and-what-to-do-about-them-part-1/

CHAPTER 7

HeartMath Institute®
Expanding Heart Connections
http://www.heartmath.org/

The Glitch In Your Brain
Raphael Cushnir
http://www.cushnir.com/emotional-connection/the-glitch-in-your-brain

Raphael Cushnir
http://www.Cushnir.com

Dawn Clark
The Essential Upgrade, Repairing Core Fractures and Clearing Toxic Emotions.
http://www.dawnclark.net

The Forbidden Text
Dawn Clark
http://www.amazon.com/The-Forbidden-Text-Transformational-Thriller/dp/1608322807

Eram Saeed
From Heartache To Joy
http://fromheartachetojoy.com

Neale Donald Walsch
http://www.nealedonaldwalsch.com/

The SouLogic Process (Recontextualization)
Neale Donald Walsch
http://www.nealedonaldwalsch.com/doc/soulogicprocess

Demonstration of the Soul Logic Process from ***Conversations With God***
Neale Donald Walsch
http://www.youtube.com/watch?v=NcfuyNjiGV8

Conversations With God - Giving People Back to Themselves
Neale Donald Walsch
http://www.cwg.org/

The Only Thing That **Matters**
Neale Donald Walsch
https://www.amazon.com/Only-Thing-Matters-Conversations-Humanity/dp/1480516244

Unapologetically You: Reflections on Life and the Human Experience
Dr. Steve Maraboli
http://www.amazon.com/Unapologetically-You-Reflections-Human-Experience/dp/0979575087

Forgiveness: 21 Days to Forgive Everyone for Everything
Iyanla Vanzant
http://www.amazon.com/Forgiveness-Days-Forgive-Everyone-Everything/dp/1401943616

The Amy Biehl Foundation Trust
http://www.amybiehl.org/

The Art of Forgiveness, Lovingkindness, and Peace
Jack Kornfield
http://www.amazon.com/The-Art-Forgiveness-Lovingkindness-Peace/dp/0553381199

Jack Kornfield
http://www.jackkornfield.com/

The Abraham-Hicks Emotional Guidance Scale
http://www.discoveringpeace.com/the-abraham-hicks-emotional-guidance-scale.html

Ask and It Is Given: Learning to Manifest Your Desires
Esther Hicks and Jerry Hicks
http://www.hayhouse.com/ask-and-it-is-given-paperback

Esther, Jerry and Abraham Hicks - The Teachings of Abraham
http://www.abraham-hicks.com

CHAPTER 8

Dark Night of the Soul
John of the Cross
http://www.amazon.com/Dark-Night-Soul-John-Cross/dp/1573229741

You Can Heal Your Life
Louise Hay
http://www.hayhouse.com/catalogsearch/advanced/result/?q=you+can+heal+your+life

'The List':
Heal Your Body A-Z: The Mental Causes for Physical Illness and the Way to Overcome Them
Louise L. Hay
http://www.hayhouse.com/catalogsearch/advanced/result/?q=heal+your+body+a-z

Louise Hay
http://www.louisehay.com/

Fake Knee Surgery as Good as Real Procedure, Study Finds
Joseph Walker
http://www.wsj.com/articles/SB10001424052702304244904579278442014913458

You Are the Placebo: Making Your Mind Matter
Dr. Joe Dispenza

http://www.amazon.com/You-Are-Placebo-Making-Matter/dp/1401944582

Dr. Joe Dispenza's Website, 'Change from the Inside Out':
http://www.drjoedispenza.com/

A Course in Miracles
http://www.acim.org/

Morry Zelcovitch
http://www.themorrymethod.com/

"What is a healing crisis; and when is a healing crisis not a healing crisis?"
Self Care with Pamela Miles
http://reikiinmedicine.org/clinical-practice/healing-crisis-what-is-it/

CHAPTER 9

Dying to be Me
Anita Moorjani
http://www.hayhouse.com/dying-to-be-me-paperback
http://anitamoorjani.com/

Anita Moorjani
http://www.anitamoorjani.com/

Psychosynthesis: A Manual of Principles and Techniques
Roberto Assagioli, M.D.
http://www.amazon.com/Psychosynthesis-A-Manual-Principles-Techniques/dp/B0007DLD8I

The Disidentification Process
Ali Harrison
A Podcast which walks you through the exercise

http://www.aliharrison.com/psychosynthesis/Podcast/Podcast.html

The Eureka Factor: Aha Moments, Creative Insight, and the Brain
John Kounios, Mark Beeman
http://www.amazon.com/The-Eureka-Factor-Moments-Creative/dp/1400068541

The Art of Insight: How to Have More Aha! Moments
Charles Kiefer and Malcolm Constable
https://www.bkconnection.com/books/title/the-art-of-insight

The Aha! Moment - The Cognitive Neuroscience of Insight
John Kounios and Mark Beeman
Drexel University and Northwestern University
http://groups.psych.northwestern.edu/mbeeman/documents/CurrentDirxns_Kounios-Beeman_2009.pdf

CHAPTER 10

Louise L. Hay
http://www.louisehay.com/

Dr. Wayne W. Dyer
http://www.drwaynedyer.com/

The Secret
Rhonda Byrne
http://www.amazon.com/Secret-Rhonda-Byrne/dp/1582701709/ref=sr_1_1?s=books&ie=UTF8&qid=1425422491&sr=1-1&keywords=the+secret+rhonda+byrne

The Secret DVD
Rhonda Byrne
http://thesecret.tv/

Anita Moorjani
http://anitamoorjani.com/

Love For No Reason: 7 Steps to Creating a Life of Unconditional Love
Marci Shimoff
http://www.thelovebook.com/Landing

Dr. J. Andrew Armour
Neurocardiology ~ Anatomical and Functional Principles
J. Andrew Armour, M.D., Ph.D
http://store.heartmath.com/item/enro/heartmath-neurocardiology

HeartMath Institute®
http://www.heartmath.org/

***Science of the* Heart**
HeartMath®
http://www.heartmath.org/research/science-of-the-heart/introduction.html

Professor Karl Pribram
http://www.karlpribram.com/

The Quick Coherence® Technique for Adults
HeartMath® Institute
https://www.heartmath.org/resources/heartmath-tools/quick-coherence-technique-for-adults/

The Quick Coherence Technique® for Ages 12-18
HeartMath® Institute
https://www.heartmath.org/resources/heartmath-tools/quick-coherence-technique-for-ages-12-18/

You Can Heal Your Life, The Movie
Louise L. Hay
http://www.hayhouse.com/you-can-heal-your-life-the-movie-landing

Christiane Northrup, MD
http://www.drnorthrup.com/
Dr. Northrup is a visionary pioneer and the world's leading authority in the field of women's health and wellness. She is also a New York Times best selling Author of several books.
http://www.hayhouse.com/catalogsearch/advanced/result/?author=Christiane+Northrup

Karen Paolino-Correia
Heaven on Earth, A Spiritual Oasis for the Soul
http://www.createheaven.com/

What Would Love Do? A 40–Day Journey to Transform Your Fears Into Miracles of Love
Karen Paolino-Correia
http://www.amazon.com/What-Would-Love-Karen-Paolino/dp/1467500569/ref=sr_1_1?s=books&ie=UTF8&qid=1425781103&sr=1-1&keywords=what+would+love+do

A 40 Day Affair with Your Self-A Journey of Self Love and Owning your Divine Magnificence
Karen Paolino-Correia
http://www.createheaven.com/index.php/angels/heavenonearth/spiritual_workshops/

The Art of Extreme Self-Care
Transform Your Life One Month at a Time
Cheryl Richardson
http://www.hayhouse.com/the-art-of-extreme-self-care-2

Raphael Cushnir
http://www.cushnir.com/?cbg_tz=300

John Eggen
The Leading Mentors Publishing and Marketing Program
Mission Marketing – A division of The Mission Marketing Mentors, Inc.
http://missionmarketingmentors.com

Harry Potter Series
J. K. Rowling
http://www.harrypotterhogwartscollection.com/
http://www.jkrowling.com/

Harry Potter Books and Movies
J.K. Rowling
http://www.amazon.com/s/ref=nb_sb_ss_c_0_12?url=search-alias%3Daps&field-keywords=harry%20potter&sprefix=harry+potter%2Cstripbooks%2C265

Mirror of Erised
Harry Potter
http://harrypotter.wikia.com/

Don Miguel Ruiz
http://www.miguelruiz.com/

You Can Heal Your Life
Louise Hay
http://www.hayhouse.com/you-can-heal-your-life

Love Yourself, Heal Your Life Workbook (Insight Guide)
Louise Hay
http://www.hayhouse.com/love-yourself-heal-your-life-workbook

How to Love Yourself (Audio)
Cherishing the Incredible Miracle That You Are
Louise Hay
http://www.hayhouse.com/how-to-love-yourself-1

You Can Create An Exceptional Life
Louise Hay and Cheryl Richardson
http://www.hayhouse.com/catalogsearch/advanced/result/?name=You+can+create+an+exceptional+life

Divorceless Relationships
Gary M. Douglas
http://www.amazon.com/Divorceless-Relationships-Gary-M-Douglas/dp/193926104X/ref=sr_1_1?s=books&ie=UTF8&qid=1454604699&sr=1-1&keywords=divorceless+relationships

Rosalind Sedacca
Child-Centered Divorce
A support network for parents
http://www.childcentereddivorce.com/

How Do I Tell the Kids about the Divorce? A Create-a-Storybook Guide to Preparing Your Children -- with Love!
Rosalind Sedacca
http://www.childcentereddivorce.com/rosalind-sedaccas-books/

Thank You For Leaving Me
Farhana Dhalla
http://www.amazon.com/dp/0980975123

Farhana Dhalla
Speaker – Author - Guide
http://www.farhanadhalla.com/

The Journey From Abandonment to Healing
Susan Anderson
http://www.abandonment.net/journey-from-abandonment-to-healing-susan-anderson

Dr. Susan Anderson
http://www.abandonment.net

Black Swan
Susan Anderson
http://www.abandonment.net/black-swan-book

Love After Love, Derek Walcott
The Poetry of Derek Walcott, 1948-2013
https://www.amazon.com/Poetry-Derek-Walcott-1948-2013/dp/0374125619?ie=UTF8&*Version*=1&*entries*=0

Dr. Marshall B. Rosenberg, Ph.D.
Center for Nonviolent Communication
http://www.cnvc.org/

Speak Peace in a World of Conflict: What You Say Next Will Change Your World
Marshall B. Rosenberg
http://www.amazon.com/s/ref=nb_sb_noss_2?url=search-alias%3Dstripbooks&field-keywords=Speak+Peace+in+a+World+of+Conflict+&rh=n%3A283155%2Ck%3ASpeak+Peace+in+a+World+of+Conflict+

Dr. Rosenberg's books:
http://www.amazon.com/s/ref=dp_byline_sr_book_1?ie=UTF8&field-author=Marshall+B.+Rosenberg+PhD&search-alias=books&text=Marshall+B.+Rosenberg+PhD&sort=relevancerank

How to End Your Relationship Deadlock Today
David Noor, MA, LMHCA
Counselo PLLC - Redmond, WA
http://www.counselo.com/how-to-end-your-relationship-deadlock-today

Three Secrets to Ending the Struggle and Making Your Life Work
Neale Donald Walsch
http://www.elevatedexistence.com/blog/2012/10/01/neale-donald-walsh-shares-3-secrets-to-ending-struggle/

Neale Donald Walsch
http://nealedonaldwalsch.com/

Conscious Uncoupling: 5 Steps to Living Happily Even After
Katherine Woodward Thomas
http://www.amazon.com/Conscious-Uncoupling-Steps-Living-Happilyebook/dp/B00RKWAGUU/ref=sr_1_2?s=books&ie=UTF8&qid=1425335279&sr=1-2&keywords=conscious+uncoupling+katherine+woodward+thomas

How to Heal the 3 Breakup Mistakes That Cause Suffering, Steal Joy and Prevent Future Love
Katherine Woodward Thomas, MA, MFT
http://evolvingwisdom.com/consciousuncoupling/free-online-class/b/

Calling in "The One": 7 Weeks to Attract the Love of Your Life
Katherine Woodward Thomas
http://www.amazon.com/Calling-The-One-Weeks-Attract/dp/1400049296

Calling In "The One" online course
A 7-Week Program to Identify and Release Hidden Barriers to Love and Become Irresistibly Magnetic to Your Soulmate
Katherine Woodward Thomas
http://evolvingwisdom.com/callingintheone/enroll/e/

CHAPTER 11

The Leadership Brain For Dummies
Marilee B. Sprenger
http://www.amazon.com/s/?ie=UTF8&keywords=leadership+brain+for+dummies&tag=googhydr20&index=aps&hvadid=24019153991&hvpos=1t1&hvexid=&hvnetw=g&hvrand=14556712226387073129&hvpone=&hvptwo=&hvqmt=e&hvdev=c&ref=pd_sl_5hc51w4gpb_e

Marilee Sprenger
http://www.marileesprenger.com/

Denis Waitley, Ph.D.
http://www.waitley.com/

You Can Heal Your Life, The Movie
Louise L. Hay
http://www.hayhouse.com/you-can-heal-your-life-the-movie-landing

Gregg Braden
http://www.greggbraden.com
Books and Audios:
http://www.hayhouse.com/catalogsearch/advanced/result/?author=Gregg+Braden

The Biology of Belief - Unleashing the Power of Consciousness, Matter & Miracles
Bruce Lipton, Ph.D.
http://www.hayhouse.com/the-biology-of-belief-1

Michael Bernard Beckwith
Agape International Spiritual Center
http://www.agapelive.com

The Power of Awareness
Neville Goddard
http://www.amazon.com/The-Power-Awareness-Neville-Goddard/dp/1603865047

The Power of Awareness
http://www.thepowerofawareness.org

Boy Scouts of America®
http://www.scouting.org/

The Shadow Effect - Illuminating the Hidden Power of Your True Self
Deepak Chopra, Marianne Williamson, Debbie Ford
http://www.amazon.com/Shadow-Effect-Illuminating-Hidden-Power/dp/0061962643/ref=sr_1_1?s=books&ie=UTF8&qid=1437412089&sr=1-1&keywords=the+shadow+effect

The Shadow Effect - A Journey from Your Darkest Thought to Your Greatest Dream
http://www.hayhouse.com/the-shadow-effect
This docudrama film guides viewers through eight exercises designed to reveal the shadow effect in their lives and presents opportunities to transcend personal limitations.

The Shadow Effect OnLine Workshop
Debbie Ford
http://www.theshadoweffect.com

Debbie Ford
http://www.debbieford.com

Self-Mastery Through Conscious Auto Suggestion
Émile Coué
http://www.amazon.com/s/ref=nb sb noss?url=search-alias%3Dstripbooks&field-keywords=Self-Mastery+Through+Conscious+Auto+Suggestion

Self-Mastery Through Conscious Autosuggestion
Émile Coué
http://www.amazon.com/Self-Mastery-Through-Conscious Autosuggestion/dp/1420928163

I Can Do It – 2015 Calendar
Louise L. Hay
http://www.hayhouse.com/catalogsearch/advanced/result/?category=7&q=i+can+do+it+calendars

Tera Maxwell
Affluence Coach
http://teramaxwell.com/

Susan Jenkins
Shamanic Healer
http://www.shamanichealingwork.com

The Stress of Life

Hans Selye
http://www.amazon.com/Stress-Life-Hans-Selye/dp/0070562121/ref=sr_1_1?s=books&ie=UTF8&qid=1416110886&sr=1-1&keywords=the+stress+of+life+hans+selye&pebp=1416110906203

A Syndrome Produced by Diverse Nocuous Agents
Hans Selye
http://adaptometry.narod.ru/Selye1stPaper.pdf

The Power of Now: A Guide to Spiritual Enlightenment
Eckhart Tolle
http://www.amazon.com/Power-Now-Guide-Spiritual-Enlightenment/dp/1577314808/ref=sr_1_1?s=books&ie=UTF8&qid=1452536651&sr=1-1&keywords=The+Power+of+Now%3A+A+Guide+to+Spiritual+Enlightenment

Eckhart Tolle
http://www.eckharttolle.com/

Dr. Andrew Newberg
http://www.andrewnewberg.com/

Finding the Right Meditation Practice
Dr. Andrew Newberg
maureendamery.com

Lisa Garr
The Aware Show
https://theawareshow.com/

Jack Kornfield
http://www.jackkornfield.com/

Getting in the Gap
Dr. Wayne W. Dyer
http://www.hayhouse.com/getting-in-the-gap

The Hidden Messages in Water
Masaru Emoto
http://www.amazon.com/Hidden-Messages-Water-Masaru-Emoto/dp/0743289803/ref=sr_1_1?s=books&ie=UTF8&qid=1425678539&sr=1-1&keywords=Water+Knows+the+Answer+masura+emoto

Masaru Emoto
http://www.masaru-emoto.net/english/water-crystal.html

The Power of Intention ~ Learning to Co-create Your World Your Way
Dr. Wayne W. Dyer
http://www.hayhouse.com/the-power-of-intention

Deepak Chopra
The Chopra Center
http://www.chopra.com/

Oprah & Deepak 21-Day Meditation Experience
https://chopracentermeditation.com

Primordial Sound Meditation
The Chopra Center
http://www.chopra.com/search/node/primordial%20sound%20meditation

Guided Meditations
Chopra Center
http://www.chopra.com/ccl/guided-meditations

Oprah Winfrey
http://www.oprah.com

Mutted Timers:

Insight Timer - Meditation Timer
Spotlight Six Software, LLC
http://www.amazon.com/Spotlight-Six-Software-LLC-Insight/dp/B006HL9G10/ref=cm_cr_pr_product_top

Tibet Bowls Sound
Tecworks
http://www.amazon.com/Tecworks-Tibet-Bowls-Sound/dp/B007JXYD4A/ref=pd_sim_mas_4?ie=UTF8&refRID=0SAFKKVY0RXM7Z1M7PEE

On Line Meditation Timer:
http://www.onlinemeditationtimer.com/

Metta Meditation
http://metta.org/

The Now Effect: How a Mindful Moment Can Change the Rest of Your Life
Elisha Goldstein Ph.D.
http://www.amazon.com/The-Now-Effect-Mindful-Moment/dp/1451623895

Basics of Mindfulness Meditation: A 28 Day Program
Elisha Goldstein, Ph.D.
http://elishagoldstein.com/ecourses/basics-of-mindfulness-meditation/

A Mindfulness-Based Stress Reduction Workbook
Bob Stahl and Elisha Goldstein, Ph.D.
http://www.amazon.com/A-Mindfulness-Based-Stress-Reduction-Workbook/dp/1572247088

MindUP™
The Hawn Foundation
http://thehawnfoundation.org/mindup/

CASEL - Collaborative for Academic, Social and Emotional Learning
http://www.casel.org/guide/programs/mindup/

MindUP: How Goldie Hawn Is Out to Change the Landscape of Childhood Learning
Lloyd I. Sederer, MD; Medical director, New York State Office of Mental Health
http://www.huffingtonpost.com/lloyd-i-sederer-md/better-learning-mindfulness_b_859113.html

Scholastic®
http://www.scholastic.com/home/

Goldie Hawn and Dan Siegel at TEDMED 2009
http://thehawnfoundation.org/about-us/

Mindsight: The New Science of Personal Transformation
Daniel J. Siegel, M.D.
http://drdansiegel.com/books/mindsight/

CHAPTER 12

Dr. Maya Angelou
Caged Bird Legacy, LLC
Continuing the work of Maya Angelo
http://mayaangelou.com/

I Can See Clearly Now
Dr. Wayne W. Dyer
http://www.hayhouse.com/catalogsearch/advanced/result/?category=7&q=i+can+see+clearly+now

Kris Carr
Crazy Sexy Wellness Revolution
http://kriscarr.com/

A love note…to your younger self
Kris Carr
http://kriscarr.com/blog-video/younger-self/

Nancy Foley
cienna moon
http://www.ciennamoon.com/

Katie Ramaci
Women of Wisdom
http://www.womenofwisdominc.com/

Eric R. Kandel
Nobel Lecture: The Molecular Biology of Memory Storage: A Dialog between Genes and Synapses
December 8, 2000
http://www.nobelprize.org/nobel_prizes/medicine/laureates/2000/kandel-lecture.html

Deepak Chopra
The Chopra Center
http://www.chopra.com/

Oprah & Deepak 21-Day Meditation Experience
https://chopracentermeditation.com

Oprah Winfrey
http://www.oprah.com

Sandy C. Newbigging
Mind Calm
http://www.mindcalm.com/

Book:
Mind Calm: The Modern-Day Meditation Technique that Proves the Secret to Success is Stillness

CD:
Mind Calm Meditations: Experience the Serenity and Success That Come from Thinking Less

John Karedis
Victors of Circumstance
https://www.linkedin.com/pub/john-karedis/45/525/9bb

Please visit my web site for additional Resources.
maureendamery.com

YOUR OWNER'S MANUAL FOR LIFE
~ Source Code of Your Soul

Creating You and Facilitating Your Life

Contributors

Boston Michael Kirby
Illustrations:
Eye – Heart – U
Mirror of Erised
Om Symbol

Author Photo
Robyn Ivy
http://www.robynivy.com/

Karen Biscoe
For her review and editing ~ particularly her brilliant articulation of a key segment where my ability to transliterate was mired.

Patty Jabotte
For her editing; but most importantly, her validation and beautiful friendship.

About the Author

Maureen was born and raised in Boston, Massachusetts. Her vocations in the corporate world spanned many avenues. The height of her professional career was devoted to Software Engineering at Microsoft Corporation, providing developer support, technical training and writing articles for the Microsoft Knowledge Base. A sample of her technical literature (under her prior married name) can be viewed at http://msdn.microsoft.com/en-us/library/ms811304.aspx

Having immersed herself in the healing arts, Maureen transitioned from computer programming in 2004 and began practicing in the field of integrative complementary medicine. In 2008, she created BarnStone Healing Center, providing private sessions, workshops and inspirational speaking engagements. Maureen is a self-empowerment facilitator whose objective is guiding others to expand their awareness, soften their resistance and re-connect with their own capacities for healing, creating and thriving in a robust, fulfilling life.

Maureen continues to explore, implement and compose literature on the latest developments in the Mind/Body science, holistic field and methodologies of the healing arts. She reminds us that we possess the capacities to actualize our full potential for optimum well-being and realizing our highest aspirations. Her message is living purposefully through meditation and mindfulness.

Maureen is an EIPPY Award-Winning Author and Co-Creator of the Best-Selling *My Big Idea Book.*

maureendamery.com

"Maureen is a very gifted healer whose energy and light are a spiritual joy ride. Her unique and insightful wisdom is imparted with a warm, down to earth sense of humor that is a delight. Her ability to alter a problem's perception is magic. One cannot help but to be uplifted by being in her presence." - Elaine McCall, RN; Pembroke Hospital

CHAPTER 3 EXERCISE:
GETTING TO KNOW YOUR SOFTWARE

"Can you remember who you were before the world told you who you should be?" -*Danielle LaPorte*

Consider the various elements of your life – The people, places and things – and the aspects related to them. Identify those you consider less than desirable – the ones you'd like to change. For example: Your Profession (place of employment, managers, co-workers), Your Home (location, the building), your relationships (partner/spouse, family, friends, neighbors and *You* (body, personality traits, habits), etc. and list these in column one.

Next, consider whether each aspect is a contribution to or deduction from your overall well-being and preferred objectives. This is a Yes or No question. Examine each and consider the volume of the role it plays within your life using a scale of 1-3: 1 being the most relevant, 3 the least and 2 the median. Rate these elements regarding their relevance - How important is it to change them? Note these in column three. This will help to enumerate your priorities.

Then, consider your perceptions and beliefs as well as the potential sources of the programming by which they were created, and list these in column four. Some influences to deliberate upon when compiling your list:

- Culture, Family and Friends, Religion, Education, Advertising, etc.
- Perception of limitation (resources/support)
- Persuasion or pressure, perceived necessity/fear
- Absence of direction, encouragement

In column five, note whether your perceptions surrounding these aspects feel light or heavy. Are they true for you? For example: *"I can't go back to school at my age."* Truth: Can't you?

For each, ask yourself, *Truth: What can I add, subtract or change about this that would generate more possibility, ease, fulfillment and joy in my life?* Note your insights in the last column.

Element Aspects you'd like to change	**Does it compute?** Yes / No	**Relevance:** 1 Most 2 Median 3 Least	**Potential Sources & Programming**	**Light:** *True* **Heavy:** False	**Insights**

"Whatever you are not changing, you are choosing." ~ Laurie Buchanan

With this in mind, for each element in your table above, list one to three action items that you will employ to shift your perceptions, consider and pursue other possibilities. For example, if you prefer a career change, research the aspects of your calling.

Element	Action Items

"Life begins at the end of your comfort zone." -Neale Donald Walsch

CHAPTER 6 EXERCISE 1: UNCOVERING THE ESSENCE BEHIND PROCRASTINATION & SELF SABOTAGE

"I am a work in progress." ~Violet Yates, Lost & Found

I'd like you to identify something that you've been procrastinating. Note this in Column 1.

Acknowledge the resistance surrounding it and ask:

- Why are you here?
- What is it that you want and/or need?
- Are you rebelling against something or someone?
  Perhaps you're rebelling against a *Should*. If so, where did this *Should* come from – Is it yours or someone else's?

Note any insights in Columns 2 and 3.

Next, ask yourself: What do I hate about this? Perhaps that it is stalking you and creating anxiety ~ which causes all sorts of blocks. Make note of your insights in Column 4.

Then ask yourself: What do I love about this? What's the reward? There must be one (or more); otherwise, you wouldn't be allowing it. Make note of your insights in Column 5.

There's always something you actually love about a pattern you *say* that you hate. Whatever brings you to *say* that you hate it is not cognitive (makes no sense) because there's some sort of reward for having the pattern in place that's somehow valuable to you. Otherwise, you wouldn't be allowing it. When you find a Love/Hate program driving your bus, asking *What do I love about this* can get you to the energy of it so that you can begin shifting it.

"Everything that is and brings up, either known or unknown consciously or unconsciously to me where X is concerned, I choose to release it and transmute its energy across all time, space, dimension and reality under grace with ease. And so it is."

Make note of any additional insights in the last column.

I've been procrastinating / resisting:	What does my resistance desire?	What's the Should about? Am I rebelling?	What do I hate about this?	What do I love about this?	Additional Insights

Now let's have a look at any fears which may be instigating the resistance. Ask yourself: *What am I afraid of?* Consider what comes to mind; i.e. *You know what happened to so & so when they… Remember what happened last time? I heard X about X.* Note these in Column 1. Then ask: *Where did this come from? From whom did I learn this? Is it yours or someone else's?* Note your insights in Column 2.

Then ask:

- What's the downside (risks) of procrastinating around this?
- What's the upside (rewards) of procrastinating round this?

Note these in Columns 3 and 4 and any additional insights in the last column.

Fear(s)	Source of Fear(s)	Risks	Rewards	Additional Insights

Awareness of the essence surrounding the issue ignites faith in your capacity to meet, understand and surpass fear and resistance, trusting that you are well regardless of the outcome. Faith refers to a belief which is not based on proof or evidence but on *knowing*. Trust is a belief in truth. Having faith in yourself and trust in the process of life endows tremendous ease. It is from within this space that you can make optimal choices.

"Fear knocked at the door. Faith answered. There was no one there." -Martin Luther King, Jr.

Once you've identified the energy around that which you've been procrastinating, you can make a choice regarding the manner by which to proceed, or not. Perhaps you've decided not to pursue the matter and move on to other things. If it is a must, however, and/or you choose to proceed, once you've arrived at this choice, ask yourself: *What are the next steps; and how can I take them with ease?* Contemplate these and make note of them.

Next Steps	**Taking them with ease…**

"Our deepest fear is not that we're inadequate. It is that we are powerful beyond measure." -Marianne Williamson

TIPS FOR NAVIGATING THROUGH PROCRASTINATION & GETTING THINGS DONE

What are some of the excuses you use to justify your pro status in the crastination game?

- Objection: *"I really don't enjoy doing X".*
  If X is a must, get it done and get it off your plate. Procrastination is an energy drainer.
- Time/Energy: *"I just don't have the time/energy for X".*
  Truth: How much time/energy have you already spent kibitzing over X?
- Competence: *"I'm not sure how to go about X".*
  Find someone who *does* know, and enlist their assistance.
- Fear: "*What if I screw up?*"
  Remember, no mistakes…lessons and opportunities.
- I don't have to do this now; I'll get to it later.
  Ask yourself: *What do I love about putting things off - What's the reward?*
  Perhaps you've adapted ways of working well under pressure and doing so feeds an addiction to adrenaline, *hmm?*

These are the tri-brain negotiation conferences to be mindful of. However, *"The wolf that wins is the one that you feed."* ~from *The Tale of Two Wolves,* a story told by a Cherokee Indian to his Grandson about the battle that goes on within us all. *~See Resources.*

First, decide whether X is really worth doing. If you don't want X badly enough, then it's not worth the effort – which may be why you've been procrastinating to begin with. If you do, however or X is a must, then evaluate the situation, formulate a strategy and begin taking steps to see it through to completion.

To begin, create a bucket list, bug report and agenda. In column one, list your desires, aspirations and intentions. They can be anything from cleaning out a closet to going back to school or taking a trip to an exotic destination. They could also be lifestyle enhancements such as increased attention to self care, practicing meditation and mindfulness, etc.

Consider the distracter factors and self-sabotaging programs in your life, your excuses and the ways you allow them to limit you. Your list can be as short or long, as detailed or general as you prefer. List them in column two.

In column three, consider the strategies, methods and actions you can implement to facilitate the progression of your agenda.

"Do or Do not; there is no Try."
-Yoda (Star Wars V: The Empire Strikes Back)

Desires, Aspirations & Intentions	**Distractions & Excuses -Bugs-**	**Strategies, Methods & Action Items**

Some questions to consider:

- What stupidity am I using to create the distraction, procrastination and sabotage that I'm choosing?
- Who does this belong to?
- What do I hate - more accurately, what do I *love* about this?

- What if I pulled the energy of having or accomplishing X into the now and started creating it and allowing it to manifest right away?
- What will my life be like in 5 minutes, hours, days, weeks or years if I proceed with the expanded consciousness that I now have?

Some tips that can assist you:

- Tell the Lizard (your reptilian brain) to take a back seat, while you take the helm.
- If you're uncertain how to proceed, seek assistance. Asking for and accepting help is an expression of strength and connectedness. There is honor in allowing others the gift of giving and yourself that of receiving.
- Get to it. At the very least, get started. Have you ever found that after accomplishing something you'd been procrastinating, you think *That wasn't so bad or Why didn't I do this sooner?* ~Funny, that.
- To avoid overwhelm, break your project into small, accomplishable tasks. If your objective is to clean out the garage, cut a deal with yourself to open one box or address one section each day or weekend rather than taxing yourself to complete it all at once. Having a portion completed is one step in the right direction that yields a sense of momentum and accomplishment. *Check!*
  ~Take it from *The Cleaning Lady:* Clearing your external environment can be quite therapeutic and is often a catalyst for internal clearing and energetic expansion.
- Outline a goal checklist for yourself. Incorporate Start and Completion Dates with daily, weekly or monthly agendas for scheduled tasks along the way. Designate blocks of time for these tasks and mark them on your calendar. Utilize a timer if that's helpful. Work entirely focused on your task for

a specified amount of time. When that time is up, you can stop and move on to other things. You may find that once you're into it, you're inspired to continue past your allotted time, provided your bandwidth allows. You may even reach your goal ahead of your initial target which lends additional bandwidth and empowerment for pursuing other objectives.

Project / Goal	Start Date	Completion Date

	Monday	Tuesday	Wednesday	Thursday	Friday	Saturday	Sunday
6:00							
6:30							
7:00							
7:30							
8:00							
8:30							
9:00							
…Etc.							

- Set boundaries: If solitude and concentration are in order, choose a quiet location and remove potential distractions - TV, radio, telephone – unless you work better with something in the background. Inform those around you of your intentions and timeframe, requesting that they do not approach you until such time is up – unless, of course, an emergency arises. If necessary, hang a *Do Not Disturb* sign on the door.
- Take regular breaks to rejuvenate and inspire. Get up and walk or sit and rest. Get a change of scenery and/or a snack.
- Build in accountability. Enlist a reliable friend or colleague to check in with you on a regular basis to insure adherence and progression.
- If errands, small tasks and miscellaneous chores are piling up, make a list of them and schedule an odd job day. Make

an effort to complete the least desirable first, or at least sooner rather than later. You'll be able to move through your list with more ease knowing that it's already behind you. Crossing items off your list as you complete them imparts accomplishment and momentum.

- Provide incentive by rewarding yourself for a job well done, and celebrate your accomplishments - a small purchase or perhaps a celebration lunch or dinner with the friend who assisted or kept you accountable.

CHAPTER 6 EXERCISE 2: UNCOVERING BUGS, VIRUSES AND DAEMONS WITHIN YOUR SOFTWARE

"My past has not defined me, destroyed me, deterred me, or defeated me; it has only strengthened me". -Dr. Steve Maraboli

Consider three things that you recognize as entities which you *say* that you hate. These can be any patterns, habits, addictions or afflictions which create any type of dis-ease in your life. List them in Column One. In Column Two, list what you hate about them.

Then ask yourself what you love about them. Consider what you derive from each - What are the rewards? For example, the potency, passion or adrenaline experienced in the midst of rage, the release of stress that accompanies the emission of fury and/or the intimacy and pleasure of making up after a heated argument with your partner - or perhaps the relief (albeit synthetic and temporary) experienced under the influence of a substance. List these in Column Three. In the fourth column, consider the origin of the entity that created it.

Entities (Patterns, Habits, Addictions)	What do I hate about this?	What do I love about this?	What belief(s) or unmet needs contributed to this?

For each, ask yourself:

- What judgments, decisions and conclusions have I made in relation to this?
- What's the meaning that I've given to it?
- What contribution is this entity to my life and living?

For example: *When I drink, I don't have to look at my problems. I can receive calmness from it because I know that it won't yell at me, hit me or judge me.*

What have I made so vital about this that I would give up health and happiness in order to sustain it?

- Who does this belong to?
- What's right about me that I'm not getting?
- What would my life be like in 5 minutes, hours, days, weeks, years if I choose / do not choose to transform this?
- What could I add to my life that would not include doing or using X to receive its rewards?

Everything this is and brings up, whether known or unknown consciously or unconsciously where X is concerned, I choose to release and transmute its energy to a higher vibrational frequency across all timelines and energetic fields under grace with ease. And so it is.

"There is a power inside every human against which no earthly force is of the slightest consequence." -Neville Goddard

CHAPTER 7 EXERCISE: EMBRACING COMPASSION, FORGIVENESS AND FREEDOM

"Forgiveness is the fragrance that the violet sheds on the heel that crushed it." -Mark Twain

In this exercise, you'll consider an experience in your life wherein you've been unable to embrace forgiveness for yourself as well as one wherein you've been unable to realize it for another. For each, the first thing that comes to mind is the best choice. They could be things you consider significant or somewhat miniscule - It's the energy surrounding them that you're addressing. There are two considerations to be mindful of:

- Forgiveness is for *You*. It is a conscious choice – one that only you can make for yourself.
- Should the situation(s) involve someone who no longer plays an active role in your life or perhaps has crossed over, keep in mind that we're all connected energetically, and they can hear you from the other side.

Consider an experience in your life for which you feel that you're unwilling or unable to forgive yourself or feel that you have not been forgiven for - A decision you made, path you took, something you said or did which hurt or violated another in some way. Something for which, regardless of any circumstances surrounding it, you continue to feel remorse. Note this in the first column.

It's important to examine your perceptions and beliefs around the situation. Ask yourself: *What is the meaning that I've given to this?* For example: *Because of X, I am ashamed, embarrassed, unworthy, unloved/unlovable.* List these in the second column. Reflect on the ways in which these perceptions and beliefs affect you - emotionally, physically, financially, socially, etc. - all of the aspects that exist in your life stemming from these experiences – the baggage you carry in relation to them. List these in the third column. In the last column, identify the power you allow them to hold over you. What do you love/hate about them, and how do they serve you – positively or negatively?

I'm unable/ unwilling to forgive myself for:	My beliefs around this are:	My life is affected by this in these ways:	What I love/ hate and how each serves me:

Consider how you would *be* now if the issue(s) had never occurred or if acknowledgement and reconciliation had been willingly consented. Allow yourself to sit with this and ask:

- Truth: Who am I hurting by holding on to this?
- What are the risks / rewards involved in holding on to vs. releasing myself from this?
- Who does this belong to?
- What will my life be like in 5 minutes, hours, days weeks or years if I choose/do not choose forgiveness and release around this?

Risks	Rewards	Insights

Everything this is and brings up, whether known or unknown consciously or unconsciously where this is concerned, and anything that may be standing in the way of my ability to embrace forgiveness around this, I choose to release and transmute its energy to a higher vibrational frequency across all timelines and energetic fields under grace with ease. And so it is.

Consider an experience in your life for which you feel unwilling or unable to forgive another. Something for which you feel that *"I'm sorry"* wasn't or isn't enough and/or that restitution should have been or should be forthcoming. Note this in column one.

Examine your perceptions and beliefs around the situation. Ask yourself: *What is the meaning that I've given to this?* For example: *Because of X, I am hurt, broken, disrespected, unloved/unlovable.* List these in column two. Reflect on the ways in which these perceptions and beliefs affect you - emotionally, physically, financially, socially, etc. List all of the aspects that exist in your life stemming from these experiences – the baggage you carry in relation to them. List these in the third column. In the last column, identify the power you allow them to hold over you. What do you love/hate about them, and how do they serve you – positively or negatively?

I'm unable/ unwilling to forgive ______ for:	**My beliefs around this are:**	**My life is affected by this in these ways:**	**What I love/ hate and how each serves me:**

Consider how you would *be* now if the issue(s) had never occurred or if acknowledgement and reconciliation had been willingly consented. Allow yourself to sit with this and ask:

- Truth: Who am I hurting by holding on to this?
- What are the risks / rewards involved in holding on to vs. releasing myself from this?
- Who does this belong to?
- What will my life be like in 5 minutes, hours, days weeks or years if I choose/do not choose forgiveness and release around this?

Risks	Rewards	Insights

Everything this is and brings up, whether known or unknown consciously or unconsciously where this is concerned, and anything that may be standing in the way of my ability to embrace forgiveness around this I choose to release and transmute its energy to a higher vibrational frequency across all timelines and energetic fields under grace with ease. And so it is.

Remember…

There is wisdom to be mined from every experience, whether windfall or wound. With this in mind, asking: *If X happened / is happening for the highest and best, what might that be?* puts you into a space of question vs. conclusion and leads to gratitude and growth through its wisdom.

It's not our experiences which shape us; it is what we choose to derive from them that does.

Forgiveness is the get well bouquet you gift to yourself.

~ There is grace in compassion, freedom in forgiveness and love in all things ~

CHAPTER 8 EXERCISE: HEALING FROM WITHIN

"All Healing is first a healing of the heart." - Carl Townsend

I'd like to interject a caveat here. Although you may be tempted to select something from a loved one's life in order to assist them, it's important that you do this for yourself. Put your oxygen mask on first. Remember, this is *YOUR Owner's Manual.*

Consider the experiences in your life which have made or are making you ill - physically, spiritually, financially or otherwise. Choose one to work with for this exercise. In relation to this issue, I'd like you to do the following:

- Look up the 'Problem' and review the 'Probable Cause' in Louise Hay's book, *You Can Heal Your Life.*
  Please Note: If you do not currently have access to this book, you can come back to this exercise later. I highly recommend acquiring and incorporating Louise's material into your life. I refer to it often, and it has saved mine as well as the lives of many others in innumerable ways.

  If it makes sense, great. It's possible, however, that you may not initially agree with or be able to see the 'Probable Cause' as a viable component of the issue. If you experience resistance or confusion in that the text may not compute, simply allow yourself to give it the benefit of the doubt for the moment. Remember, your subconscious defense mechanisms and filters will come into play. Any resistance is due in part to the software in your survivalist, reptilian brain encountering what it views as a conflict or intrusion. I will comment that although it was clear when I found this book, the entries pertaining to the dis-eases I experienced may not have entirely registered for me at the time.

- Review the 'New Thought Pattern' for the problem and ask:
  - What message is my Mind/Body brining to my attention with this?
  - Where might this have come from?
  - What are the components involved?
    - What thoughts, feelings and emotions (Resistance, Reaction, Alignment, Agreement –past experiences and patterns, etc.) did I have/am I having that may be contributing to this Problem?
  - Am I willing to acknowledge these components?
  - Am I willing to consider the possibility of this 'Probable Cause' and 'New Thought Pattern' as viable and take action where they are concerned?
  - What will my life be like in 5 minutes, hours, days, weeks or years if I choose/do *not* choose to acknowledge and take action regarding these components?

"Everything this is and brings up, whether known or unknown consciously or unconsciously and anything that may be standing in the way of my healing, I choose to release and transmute its energy to a higher vibrational frequency across all timelines and energetic fields under grace with ease. And so it is.

- Repeat the 'New Thought Pattern' to yourself or write it out (perhaps both) three times.
  Also, include these affirmations from Louise Hay:
  - *I listen to my body's messages with love.*
  - *My body now restores itself to its natural state of vibrant health and wellness.*
  - *I am healed, whole and healthy.*
    Allow yourself to embrace that by acknowledging the issue(s), you are already healed; and allow your body to process the new chemistry.

The crisis is about the issue. The healing is about the acknowledgement, release and adjustment.
Expressing gratitude with a statement such as: *"Thank you for the gifts which I may not yet be able to see or appreciate"* also aids in opening to healing and possibility.

- Whenever you think of the problem, repeat these steps.

Please Note: Any time you suspect that you may have a serious condition, you should seek the assistance of a qualified professional. The tools and methods suggested herein are intended as a supplement to, not a substitute for, medical or psychological diagnosis and treatment.

"Love is the great miracle cure.
Loving ourselves works miracles in our lives." -Louise L. Hay

CHAPTER 9 EXERCISE: YOUR AHA MOMENTS

"A moment's insight is sometimes worth a lifetime's experiences." ~ Oliver Wendell Holmes

Consider the *knowings* you've been acquiring over the course of your life. It may be helpful to refer back to some of your entries in the previous exercises. Collect your gems and ask: *If I knew then what I know now, ~fill in the blank~.* Relate them to the choices you've made and the realities you've created and experienced in your life. Consider the alternate choices you might have made (~ or will now make) by applying your knowing in a more instinctual, intentional manner. Consider the heaviness of any baggage created by not doing so as well as the lightness and rewards of following your heart. For instance:

- Where X was concerned, you 'knew better' (your internal GPS suggested one direction), yet you chose another and thus experienced less than desirable outcomes.
- Where X was concerned, while the external input was pointing in a direction opposing your internal knowing, you chose to follow your instincts and experienced the joys of doing so.

Extrapolate your findings within the table below.

In Relation To:	Knowings	Choices	Baggage	Rewards	Fresh Insights
Education					
Career					
Relationships					
Various Interests: _____________ _____________ _____________					

Ask yourself: *What am I refusing to know, that I truly do know, that if I would allow it would change all of my realities?*

Now, consider the changes you prefer in your life. What baggage would you like to release and/or avoid acquiring as you move forward and what do you intend to create? What options, choices and possibilities exist - regardless of whether or not you were consciously aware of and/or chose to utilize them previously - are you now willing to consider and/or choose to implement? What action items will contribute to the creation of your objectives? Extrapolate these into the table below:

Baggage	Objectives	Options, Choices and Possibilities	Action Items

Everything this is and brings up and anything that stands in the way of my creating and living my preferred reality, either known or unknown consciously or unconsciously to me where X is concerned, I choose to release and transmute its energy to a higher vibrational frequency across all timelines and energetic fields under grace with ease. And so it is.

"It is better to feel your way through life than to think your way through it." -Deepak Chopra

CHAPTER 10 EXERCISE: WHAT'S LOVE GOT TO DO WITH IT?

"Love yourself as if your life depended on it... because it does." -Anita Moorjani

Please choose one person (*other than yourself*) in your life whom you would say that you love. This person could be someone in your present, past or perhaps one who has crossed over. Write their name below.

In Column One, list the top three attributes about this person which compose your love for them. In the second column, list three ways which you express your love for them. Once you've completed your list, please take a moment to reflect on gratitude for the contribution this person is or has been to your life.

____

Attributes of Love	Expressions of Love

Now, I'd like you to choose one person (*other than yourself*) for whom you feel you do not embrace love. Someone you dislike or perhaps even loathe for whatever reason(s). It may be someone you've developed a distaste for or someone who has hurt or violated you in some way- perhaps a combination thereof. Write their name below.

In Column One, list the top three attributes that compose your unfavorable sentiment(s) where they are concerned. Prior to making any entries in Column Two, I'd like you to consider for a moment that this person has come to you as a friend, asking for advice regarding the attributes you listed in Column One - *Regardless of whether they literally ever would or not.* What advice would you offer them regarding these attributes and the manner by which they could bring themselves to a place of increased respect and unconditional love for themselves as well as those around them? List these in Column Two.

Disliked Attributes	Contribution

Bearing quantum entanglements and that we are all mirror versions of each other in mind, ask:

- *What is it within me that attracted this person into my life?*
- *What is the meaning that I've given to this?*
- *What is the message that, through this creation, is attempting to be brought to my attention?*
- *Who does this belong to?*
- *What are the gifts in this that I may not be seeing?*

~ Recall Neale Donald Walsch's *"I am that, I am"* exercise.

As you digest this portion of the exercise, please consider two foundational principles from a Soul level:

- There is only the mutual agenda of the Souls mutually held and experienced.
- No one has control over you unless you allow them to. While you can choose your summations, you can also choose how you will allow them to affect you.

~ Recall our discussion around allowance and acceptance.

Everything this is and brings up, whether known or unknown consciously or unconsciously that is limiting me where X is concerned, I choose to release and transmute its energy to a higher vibrational frequency across all timelines and energetic fields under grace with ease. And so it is.

Once you've completed the aforementioned, please take a moment to reflect on gratitude for the contribution this person is, has been or you may now consider to be to your life as well as you to theirs.

I invite you to do this exercise a second time - for you. We'll approach this portion a bit differently, though; and there's one caveat: Please allow yourself to be completely unconditional with yourself here.

Consider any attributes that you may dislike about yourself and list them in Column One. In Column Two, consider what it is that you dislike about each of them. For example, over giving. While you may consider giving and generosity positive qualities (*and they are*), when they morph into *over* giving, they can become negative ones in that they tend to create resentment which ultimately diminishes the beauty of initial intentions. They also detract from self-love.

Now, consider what it is that you like, or love, about them. As we discussed earlier, what you *think* you hate, you actually love. Ask yourself: *Truth: What's the reward here?* List these in Column Three. Lastly, consider the ways each of these affects you and your life, and write them in Column Four.

Attributes I dislike about me	**What do I hate about this attribute?**	**What do I love About this attribute?**	**This affects me and my life by:**

For each of these attributes, ask:

- *Who does this belong to?* Does it perhaps originate from the judgments and points of view of others to which you've chosen to subscribe?
- *What is the meaning that I've given to this?*
    - *What is the message that, through this creation, is attempting to be brought to my attention?*
    - *What are the gifts in this that I may not be seeing?*

These are the entities your internal Saboteur has been attempting to bring to your attention by creating the issues in your life which are born from them. Keep in mind that your Saboteur is a messenger, alerting you to issues that are sabotaging your best interests. When you find yourself in situations where you may be judging yourself, repeating a less than desirable pattern or selling out, ask: *Truth: If I loved myself, then…*

Once this portion of the exercise is complete, I'd like you to make one final list. Consider what advice you would provide to yourself as your own best friend regarding the attributes you listed. And finally, what loving expressions will you implement to acknowledge your best friend's advice? Having an open rapport with your Saboteur and mindfulness around their messages is a great place to start.

Attribute	Contribution	Loving Expressions

Everything this is and brings up, whether known or unknown consciously or unconsciously that is limiting me where X is concerned, I choose to release and transmute its energy to a higher vibrational frequency across all timelines and energetic fields. And so it is.

Once you've completed this portion, please take a moment to express gratitude to yourself for considering the content of your reflections in these exercises.

In coming to a place of healthy self-love, it is essential to have compassion for yourself - Treat yourself the way that you would a beloved family member or friend. Commend yourself for acknowledging that you may be struggling with Attribute X. As Marci Shimoff suggests: "Love the way that you *are*, not the way that you *think* you *should be*." Incidentally, this is a wonderful place to utilize EFT/Tapping: *"Even though I'm struggling with Attribute X, I choose to accept who I am and love myself anyway. I feel better already."* Be a loving parent to the child inside, and love yourself for taking action in the direction of self-love.

"Your objective is not to seek love,
but merely to seek and find all the barriers within
yourself that you have built against it." -Rumi

Now consider the attributes that you love about yourself. As you consider them, retain clarity for the variance between self-esteem and self-love. Please note that these are things you love about yourself, not what others have said or what you *think* they love or *would/should* love about you. List them in Column One. In the second column, list three ways that you express this love for/to yourself...or that you *will* express to yourself with your expanded awareness.

Attributes I Love About Me	Expressions of My Love for Myself

I invite you to reflect on the attributes which came to mind and the most significant three if you chose more. In considering them, you may realize that you have more or less self-love than you were initially aware of. The key is to have an awareness around them and cultivate an expansion of self-love.

"The measure of love is to love without measure."
-Original Author Unknown

~ Love is...Everything ~

MY PERSONAL CHECK-IN

"We delight in the beauty of the butterfly, but rarely admit the changes it has gone through to achieve that beauty." ~ Dr. Maya Angelou

Maya Angelou used with permission by Caged Bird Legacy, LLC www.MayaAngelou.com

I suggest gifting yourself a diary for your Check-In's so that you have an ongoing reference. The frequency of your Check-Ins is a matter of personal preference; however, to begin, I suggest weekly or monthly. Studies have shown that those who track their progress succeed twice as much and as fast as those who do not.

If you haven't already, I recommend composing your Doctrine and including it as the first entry in your diary. *You can refer to Chapter 10 for a sample.*

~ My Doctrine ~

____

____

____

____

____

~ INSIGHTS FROM THE EXERCISES WITHIN SOURCE CODE ~

-You may want to consider revisiting them from time to time to gain fresh perspective.

____

____

____

____

____

DATE: ___________

- Am I consistently exercising healthy self-care practices?
- Am I upholding my boundaries?
- Am I conducting myself and orchestrating my life in accordance with my Doctrine consistently?
- Are there any adjustments I'd like to make?
- What contribution does my Doctrine provide to my overall perspective and well-being?

____

____

____

____

____

~ MEDITATION ~

For assistance with various meditation techniques, refer back to Chapter 11 and also to Dr. Newberg's document: Finding the Right Meditation Practice

maureendamery.com

- Overall benefits and insights of my meditation practice:

____

____

____

____

____

~ PROGRAMMING ~

Let me see the truth of who I am ~ No matter how beautiful it is.

- What constrictive programs (Habits, Patterns ~ and their underlying Beliefs) have I become aware of?
- What intentions am I setting/action items am I implementing to cultivate and anchor positive shifts where they are concerned?
- What insights has this discovery process gifted me?

~ Core Beliefs: Love, Worthiness, Safety, Wholeness ~

Programs (Habits, Patterns)	**Underlying Beliefs**	**Intentions & Action Items**	**Insights**

- What Archetypes and/or shadow sides have I identified? (Four Universal Archetypes: Child, Victim, Prostitute, Saboteur)

For assistance with archetypes, consult the references listed in *Resources*.

- What message(s) (strengths/weaknesses) do they bring to my attention?
  - What do they need that they may not be getting?
- What do I Love/Hate about them?
- What are the gifts they bestow as contributions to my evolution?

Archetypes/ Shadows	**Their Messages**	**What I Love/ Hate About Them**	**Their Contributions To My Evolution**

Keep in mind that your shadow self is where the gold lies. For assistance with shadow work, consult the references listed in *Resources.*

~ INSIGHTS FROM MIRROR WORK AND AFFIRMATIONS ~

- Reflections on my mirror work and affirmations.
- How's my word policing?

~ May I be happy. May I be safe. May I be peaceful and at ease. ~

____

____

____

____

____

~ EVOLUTON ~

~ Health, Wealth and Happiness ~

At present / Since my last Check-In:

- ○ What has gone / is going well ~ that I am proud of, feeling good and/or excited about?
- ○ What has not gone / is not going as well as I'd prefer?

Brags	Grumbles

~ OBJECTIVES ~

~ Health, Wealth and Happiness ~

What would I like to change?

- What would I like to heal and release?
- What would I like to create and actualize?

Outgoing	Incoming

~ INTENTIONS ~

~ Health, Wealth and Happiness ~

What am I working on?

- Do I see and/or anticipate any challenges (a.k.a. opportunities) as I move forward?
- Do I require assistance in any area(s) where they are concerned? If so, from what source(s) will I seek and accept the gifting and receiving of assistance?

Intentions	Possible Challenges	Contributions

Best Practice: *Choose a role model - someone who is successful in a way that you intend to be. Make note of their practices, express gratitude for them; and mirror and adopt them as your own.*

- ACTION ITEMS -

- Health, Wealth and Happiness -

What actions am I taking / will I take that will contribute to and foster my intentions and their actualizations?

Intentions	Action Items	Insights

- GRATITUDE & CELEBRATION -

- Health, Wealth and Happiness -

What am I grateful for?

- In what ways do I / will I express this gratitude?

Gratefuls	Expressions

~ A LOVE NOTE FROM MY TRUE SELF ~

If I could give myself some nurturing advice, I would tell her/him…

____

____

____

____

____

"You are what you believe yourself to be." -Paulo Coelbo

Namaste!

Printed in the United States
By Bookmasters